Journal of Beat Studies

Volume 2, 2013

PACE UNIVERSITY PRESS • NEW YORK

Copyright © 2013 by
Pace University Press
41 Park Row, Rm. 1510
New York, NY 10038

All rights reserved
Printed in the United States of America

ISSN 2165-8706
ISBN 978-1-935625-14-8 (pbk: alk.ppr.)

Member

Council of Editors of Learned Journals

♾ Paper used in this publication meets the minimum requirements of
American National Standard for Information
Sciences–Permanence of Paper for Printed Library Materials,
ANSI Z39.48–1984

Editors

Ronna C. Johnson — Tufts University
Nancy M. Grace — The College of Wooster

Book Review Editor

Fiona Paton — SUNY-New Paltz

Editorial Board

Ann Charters — University of Connecticut–Storrs
Maria Damon — University of Minnesota–Minneapolis
Terence Diggory — Skidmore College (emeritus)
Tim Gray — CUNY Staten Island
Oliver Harris — Keele University, United Kingdom
Allen Hibbard — Middle Tennessee State University
Tim Hunt — Illinois State University
Cary Nelson — University of Illinois
A. Robert Lee — The University of Murcia, Spain
Jennie Skerl — West Chester University (retired)
David Sterritt — Long Island University
Tony Trigilio — Columbia College-Chicago
John Whalen-Bridge — National University of Singapore, Singapore

Journal of Beat Studies

Volume 2, 2013

	vi	Letter from the Editors
Tony Trigilio	1	"On a Confrontation at a Buddhist Seminary": Naropa, Guru Devotion, and a Poetics of Resistance
John Whalen-Bridge	31	Trungpa, Naropa, and the Outrider Road: An Interview with Anne Waldman
Davis Schneiderman	53	The Miraculous and Mucilaginous Paste Pot: Extra-illustration and Plagiary in the Burroughs Legacy
Rob Johnson	81	Did Beatniks Kill John F. Kennedy?

REVIEWS

Cary Nelson	101	*Jack Kerouac: Collected Poems.* Edited by Mariléne Phipps-Kettlewell.
Terence Diggory	113	*Postliterary America: From Bagel Shop Jazz to Micropoetries* by Maria Damon.
Jennie Skerl	118	*Rub Out the Words: The Letters of William S. Burroughs 1959-1974.* Edited by Bill Morgan.
Fiona Paton	124	*The Voice Is All: The Lonely Victory of Jack Kerouac* by Joyce Johnson.

Nancy M. Grace	**130**	Review of *The Philosophy of the Beats.* Edited by Sharin N. Elkholy, and a survey of the field.
	141	*The Beat Review* Index
	150	Contributors' Notes
	152	Essay Abstracts

Letter from the Editors

We are pleased to present the second issue of the *Journal of Beat Studies*, which includes a special section on Beat writers and Naropa University in Boulder, Colorado. Since its founding in 1974 by Chögyam Trungpa Rinpoche as the Naropa Institute, which included under its auspices the renowned Jack Kerouac School of Disembodied Poetics co-founded by Allen Ginsberg and Anne Waldman that same year, Naropa has played a central role in the nurturing and dissemination of Beat as well as outrider poetics, in addition to serving as a focal point for the presence of Buddhism in the United States.

The history of Beat writers and literature and Naropa is in some respects a contested history, especially that sequence of events that has become known as "The Great Naropa Poetry Wars" of 1975. In 1973 Trungpa Rinpoche inaugurated the Vajradhatu Seminary, an annual three-month retreat for selected advanced students that included intensive meditation practices; during the seventies, Trungpa conducted six seminaries in the northern continental U. S.[1] "The Great Naropa Poetry Wars" erupted at the seminary that was held in fall of 1975, in Snowmass, Colorado, some four hours west of Boulder. Trungpa presided, but neither Ginsberg nor Waldman was present. The poet W.S. Merwin, interested in expanding his Buddhist training, and his then-partner the poet Dana Naone, attended the seminary. On Halloween, a party was given to celebrate the end of the second and the beginning of the intense third and final stage of the seminary. Merwin and Naone attended but did not stay. Summoned by Trungpa, they refused to return, and were confronted in their apartment by other seminary students who, acting for Trungpa, met their resistance by assaulting them and abducting them to the party, where, against their wills, they were stripped naked at Trungpa's order, and humiliated. These facts are not in dispute. This shocking event circulated through published writings in the aftermath and in Buddhist communities, and has reverberated in the record of Beat poetry and poetics.[2]

As this account suggests, Trungpa himself was an extremely provocative and divisive personality. According to the Shambhala website, Vidyadhara Chögyam Trungpa Rinpoche (1939-1987) was the 11th descendent in the line of Trungpa tülkus, important teachers of the Kagyü lineage, one of the four main schools of Tibetan Buddhism. Chögyam Trungpa fled Tibet in 1959, eventually moving to England, where he studied at Oxford University, and then to the United States. In 1970, he established his first North American meditation center, Tail of the Tiger (now called Karmê-Chöling), in Barnet, Vermont. Trungpa's Shambhala teachings, a Tantric practice, are often called "crazy wisdom"; these teachings strive to incorporate rather than eschew desire as the neophyte journeys toward enlightenment. Trungpa was also known as a womanizer and an alcoholic, attended at all times by a personal "vajra guard" of young, muscular Buddhist students in blue blazers (Clark 20). "The Great Naropa Poetry Wars," constituted from word of the assaults on Merwin and Naone at Snowmass in 1975, and from the heated published responses to it, have tainted Trungpa's legacy for some, even in light of the "crazy wisdom" teachings that included the erotic in spiritual strivings and that had strong appeal to Beat-associated writers and their students. For Kenneth Rexroth, "Chogyam Trungpa has unquestionably done more harm to Buddhism in the United States than any man living" (Clark, backcover). For Allen Ginsberg, who declined to indict his teacher Trungpa or to disavow him or his conduct at Snowmass, it was a sore subject to discuss: "I don't want to open up some terrible *yaargh*...about Trungpa," he said in an interview (Clark 58), and reported that "what Trungpa finally said to me about the Merwin thing was, 'This is an opportunity to turn poison into nectar'" (Clark 52). These positions, and many more, on both sides exemplifying the chronic contingencies and ambiguities of the event's fragile contemporaneous records have ever since haunted Naropa and Beat poetry's relation to Buddhism through the lama Trungpa Rinpoche.

John Whalen-Bridge's interview with Anne Waldman explores the origins of the Naropa Institute (later Naropa University), including Waldman's reactions to the "Poetry Wars," her thoughts on Trungpa's approach to Tantric Buddhism, his impact on people such as Joni Mitchell who sought him out for spiritual guidance, the outrider mission of Naropa in the early twenty-first century, and Waldman's thoughts about the future of Buddhisms in the United States. "Trungpa, Naropa, and the Outrider Road: An Interview with Anne Waldman" is an authentic conversation between two individuals highly versed in the history and practice of Buddhism and poetics.

Tony Trigilio's essay, titled "'On a Confrontation at a Buddhist Seminary': Naropa, Guru Devotion, and a Poetics of Resistance," focuses the critical lens to investigate the "Poetry Wars" through the perspective of guru devotion. The essay illuminates the ways in which Naropa's influence on Beat poetics draws from two contradictory categories of understanding: the neo-Romanticist urgency of the unfettered imagination and, in contrast, the obedience and containment required by guru devotion, one of the core doctrinal principles of Vajrayana Buddhism, the mode of Buddhism that Trungpa taught and practiced. The essay historicizes the tension between theory and practice as a way of understanding the complex forces that both enable and vex Beat oppositional writing. Trigilio also discusses a selection of Ginsberg's poems that reflect the Snowmass incident to explore how it dramatizes the gap between Beat oppositional poetics and the spiritual urgency that authorized this same poetics.

This issue also features "The Miraculous and Mucilaginous Paste Pot: Extra-Illustration and Plagiary in the Burroughs Legacy" by Davis Schneiderman. A cross-disciplinary perspective on William S. Burroughs' cutup method, Schneiderman's essay charts the connections between an early user-based textual strategy known as extra-illustration and the cutups practice of William S. Burroughs. Extra-illustration dates from the late eighteenth century through the early twentieth century, and this essay offers the work of John Mansir Wing of the Newberry Library in Chicago as a specific exemplar whose practice aligns with that of Burroughs. The essay is accompanied by images from Burroughs' early cutup work and Wing's.

"Did Beatniks Kill John F. Kennedy?" by Rob Johnson is a cultural and historical discussion of the ways in which the pejorative term "beatnik" became central to the search for John F. Kennedy's assassin and in the 1964 Warren Commission report's now highly suspect conclusion about who killed Kennedy. Johnson's essay draws on passages from the Warren Commission report and extensive research in local Dallas publications. The political aspects of profiling the assassin as a "beatnik" figure are viewed through Texas writer Bud Shrake's 1972 novel *Strange Peaches*, set in Dallas and Fort Worth at the time of the assassination. The dramatic center of Johnson's essay considers The Cellar, a Fort Worth "beatnik" nightclub where, it has been shown, Secret Service agents drank and caroused the night before the day of the assassination. The essay concludes with a review of some Beat writers' reactions to the assassination, including those of William S. Burroughs, Jack Kerouac, Allen Ginsberg, and Gregory Corso.

In this issue, we are joined by Fiona Paton of SUNY New Paltz, who has begun to edit the Review Section.

This issue features reviews of four diverse Beat-focused texts. Joyce Johnson's unauthorized biography, *The Voice is All: The Lonely Victory of Jack Kerouac*, is reviewed by Paton. *Postliterary America: From Bagel Shop Jazz to Micropoetries* by Maria Damon is reviewed by Terence Diggory. Cary Nelson provides a review of The Library of America edition of *Kerouac's Collected Poems*, edited by Mariléne Phipps-Kettlewell. *Rub Out the Words: The Letters of William S. Burroughs 1959-1974*, edited by Bill Morgan, is reviewed by Jennie Skerl. The section concludes with a review by Nancy Grace, a co-editor of this journal, of *The Philosophy of the Beats*, edited by Sharin N. Elkholy. Grace's review entails an extended discussion of the field of Beat studies through the lenses of philosophical and interdisciplinary theory.

Our next issue, slated for Spring 2014, will have a special focus on literary activity in the Cambridge-Boston area in the mid-1950s and the emergence of nascent Beat poetics under fledgling New York School and Black Mountain influences, and even Harvard University. For future issues, we envision a focus on Lawrence Ferlinghetti and City Lights Books, and an inquiry into interactions and interrelations between Beat poets and poetics and L=A=N=G=U=A=G=E arts and artists. We are fortunate to have you, our readers , in these explorations and inquiries.

Onward!

Ronna C. Johnson and Nancy M. Grace

Notes

[1] Tom Clark, 1980. *The Great Naropa Poetry Wars*. Santa Barbara., CA: Cadmus Editions, 17. Print.

[2] As we write this letter, the New York *Times* reports that the renowned Buddhist teacher, Joshu Sasaki, known as the teacher of the poet and songwriter Leonard Cohen, is being investigated by an independent council of Buddhist leaders on charges that he "groped and sexually harassed female students for decades, taking advantage of their loyalty to a famously charismatic roshi, or master." The *Times* recounts that "Sasaki ask[ed] women to show him their breasts, as part of 'answering' a koan...or to demonstrate 'non-attachment.'" A member of the witnessing council interviewed for this article noted that while "people in Japan have some skepticism about priests," in the U.S. many students of Buddhism have a "devotion to the guru or teacher in a way that could repress our common sense and emotional intelligence." Sasaki is 105 years old. See "Zen Groups Distressed by Accusations Against Teacher" by Mark Oppenheimer and Ian Lovett. New York *Times*, 12 February 2013. A13 and A20.

"On a Confrontation at a Buddhist Seminary": Naropa, Guru Devotion, and a Poetics of Resistance

Tony Trigilio

I. "You go against the grain for the benefit of others"

Radical individualism, autonomy, candor, and populism are crucial to Naropa University's experimental tradition and to its influence on Beat Generation literature. Naropa, of course, offered for Beat writers a site of resistance from which experiments in subjectivity and avant-garde writing could be practiced. Yet Naropa's influence on Beat poetics draws from two contradictory categories of understanding: the neo-Romanticist urgency of the unfettered imagination and, in contrast, the obedience and containment required by guru devotion, one of the core doctrinal principles of Vajrayana Buddhism, the mode of Buddhism that was taught and practiced by Naropa's founder, Chögyam Trungpa Rinpoche, whose students included Allen Ginsberg and Anne Waldman, co-founders of the Jack Kerouac School of Disembodied Poetics. Beat writing is, as Waldman has often described Naropa's lineage, an "outrider" practice. "The Outrider," she writes, "rides the edge—parallel to the mainstream, is the shadow to the mainstream, is the consciousness or soul of the mainstream, whether it recognizes its existence or not. It cannot be co-opted, it cannot be bought" ("'Premises'" 185). Waldman sketches a conception of the outrider in her 1994 poem "Oppositional Poetics" that is indebted to Vajrayana Buddhist teachings on altruism: she maintains that oppositional poetics is a "*spiritual poetics*" [emphasis Waldman]; the poet-prophet writes "against the grain for the benefit of others," and the result is poetry that documents "history's revision from a people's point of view" (*Kill or Cure* 109). As the first accredited Buddhist academic institution in the United States, Naropa is a significant institutional site for this spiritualized outrider practice. For nearly four decades, Naropa has provided an institutional location for experimental practice while actively working to avoid the cooptation of such practice by the literary marketplace.

Yet, as this essay will discuss, Beat oppositional poetics associated with Naropa struggled to evade cooptation by the same Vajrayana Buddhist ideals that authorized it. Erica Hunt emphasizes the internal pressures of literary cooptation in her essay "Notes on An Oppositional Poetics" from Charles Bernstein's important anthology, *The Politics of Poetic Form*, arguing that "literature in this culture appears a fragmented professional specialty; oppositional writing tends to be the object of the practices it protests, its social demands illegible in print" (203). Hunt's definition of "oppositional" in her essay encompasses what Naropa's outrider tradition embraces, especially, as she describes it, "dissident cultures," and "'marginalized' cultures cutting across class, race, and gender" (198). Our conventional understanding of Naropa's history suggests, rightly so, that it is an institution where the "fragmented professional specialty" of a university-based creative writing program nevertheless makes oppositional writing legible and, hence, relevant. Still, this essay lingers on a contradiction at the heart of Naropa's influence as a Buddhist institution on Beat writing: the potential for the Vajrayana doctrine of guru devotion to make "illegible," as Hunt might phrase it, the "social demands" of Beat oppositional poetics.

Pointing up a potential contradiction between theory and practice—in this case, between the Beat outrider tradition and the practice of guru devotion—is not new to the study of poetics, of course. I do not frame my argument with this contradiction in order to suggest that poetry demands consistent application of poetics. Indeed, taking a closer look at the relationship between poetry and poetics, quite the opposite is true—contradiction is the norm. From Plato's richly metaphoric exiling of poets for their practice of metaphor, through Wordsworth's defense of common language in elevated diction, through Eliot's embrace of an expansive tradition that, after all, is only Western and male, poetics is a field of study that almost seems predicated on contradiction. Such is the dual necessity of writing one's poetics and maintaining the mystery of poetic composition. My purpose, instead, is to historicize the tension between theory and practice in Naropa's influence on Beat poetics as a way of understanding the complex forces that both enable and vex Beat oppositional writing. I will examine how guru devotion contributed to perhaps the touchstone example of the complicated relationship between the liberatory and spiritual impulses of Beat oppositional practice: the 1975 Snowmass incident, in which Trungpa and his students physically attacked W.S. Merwin and Dana Naone at a Vajrayana Buddhist seminary retreat in Snowmass, Colorado. Looking at representative poems from Ginsberg's later career, with special emphasis on "Elephant in the Meditation Hall," I will explore how Snowmass dramatizes the gap between Beat oppositional poetics and the spiritual urgency that authorized this same poetics. In doing so, I suggest that as we research Beat writing of resistance, we do not neglect a concurrent examination of power relations within Beat communities. My goal is to arrive at a more complete understanding of Beat poetics by examining the collision of guru devotion and the ostensibly antinomian practices of Beat literature and culture.[1]

II. "I shall do exactly as you have said"

In one of the guiding, foundational texts of guru devotion, *Fifty Verses on Guru Devotion,* written by the first-century C.E. Indian philosopher Ashvaghosha, the potential disciple is instructed: "Before entering a formal Guru-disciple relationship, you have complete freedom of choice. But once such a bond has been established, these teachings on Guru-devotion must be followed with total commitment" (n. pag.). As is true of all Vajrayana doctrine, the purpose of guru devotion is to guide the disciple to attain enlightenment for the benefit of all sentient beings. This altruistic aim circumscribes Beat poetry of resistance, too, as Waldman argues in her discussion of the outrider, and in poems such as "Oppositional Poetics," where, as I have noted above, she argues that a poetics of resistance is, at its core, a spiritual poetics. However, as important as the individual prophetic, oppositional voice such as the outrider's is to Beat poetics, it is not an impulse encouraged in the practice of guru devotion—as seen, for instance, in Ashvaghosa's instruction regarding how the disciple should ask for advice from his/her guru: "With palms pressed together at your heart, listen to what he tells you without (letting your mind) wander about. Then (when he has spoken) you should reply, 'I shall do exactly as you have said'" (n. pag.).

Guru devotion is a doctrine vital to Vajrayana Buddhism. Yet the Beat emphasis on the primacy of the individual—and the integrity of the individual utterance, especially speech that goes against the grain—contradicts the culture of obedience and submission required by guru devotion. The doctrine necessitates an all-encompassing relationship, one in which the guru is, as Daniel Capper observes, "responsible for creating the totality of one's experience" (141). As complex as this paradox between submission and individuality might be, especially in modern liberal democracies, the devotee's logic is quite simple. Despite many deaths and rebirths, the disciple has been unable to achieve enlightenment on his/her own. The disciple draws the logical conclusion that s/he cannot do so without the aid of another; the disciple is, then, grateful to have met a lama, by definition an enlightened being, in this lifetime. The lama is the disciple's guide—even lifeline—on the Vajrayana Buddhist spiritual path. From the perspective of the practitioner, the logic of guru devotion is arguably commonsensical. Capper explains this logic in his summary of the conceptual framework that underwrites guru devotion:

> We should all draw the obvious conclusion that we are not going to become liberated on our own. We need help. The only source of this help, the piece that we have been missing, is the spontaneous experience of enlightened "ordinary mind," which can be obtained through the *lama's* blessing and

nowhere else. *Lamas*, as already liberated beings, constantly emanate this blessing energy, yet without devotion, one cannot perceive or integrate the blessing energy. (139)

As Nga-la Rig'dzin Dorje, a lama in the Nyingma School of Vajrayana Buddhism, explains in *Dangerous Friend: The Teacher-Student Relationship in Vajrayana Buddhism,* faith in the enlightened mind of the guru is critical to the disciple's development of wisdom needed to advance on the path to enlightenment.[2] "Without a teacher, you cannot attain enlightenment," he argues. "You have to depend on a teacher. Depending on a teacher means that you have to have this faith—and that this faith itself is the wisdom" (87).

One of the most important questions that arises from the doctrine of guru devotion is whether the practitioner, who has sworn obedient devotion to the lama and has accepted the lama's totalizing influence on his/her life, has enough information to determine whether or not the actions of his/her lama are ethical. Ginsberg acknowledges this danger in his 1979 interview with poet Tom Clark on Snowmass for the magazine *Boulder Monthly*, later reprinted in Clark's *The Great Naropa Poetry Wars*.[3] "Trungpa's image is crazy wisdom," he says, referring to the primal, undomesticated energy of the Tibetan Buddhist lineage of Crazy Wisdom taught by Trungpa. "Traditional crazy wisdom—outrageous behavior, outrageous activity. Total iconoclasm. And there has to be a consensus of lamas to decide the other lamas aren't abusing their scene" (62). Like all Tantric practice, Crazy Wisdom incorporates rather than evades desire—in all of its potential chaos or craziness—as part of an effort to teach its practitioners to find sacred, altruistic experience within the materiality of the world. For North Americans, "Crazy Wisdom" is perhaps a translation that places too much emphasis on "Crazy" and not enough on "Wisdom." As Ginsberg wrote in his notes to an August 29, 1975, lecture by Trungpa, "Wisdom comes before crazy. Shd be Wisdom-Crazy [not Crazy Wisdom]" (Notebooks). Still, as Ginsberg himself acknowledges to Clark, guru devotion carries with it the potential to create a cult-like atmosphere if abused by the lama: "With one bad lama, or one fuck-up—particularly from someone like Trungpa, who's so open—it could really fuck up the whole scene. Just like, you know, Guyana." Ginsberg's reference to the 1978 mass suicide of Jim Jones and 908 of his followers in the Peoples Temple in Jonestown, Guyana, is a recognition of the perils that can occur when a community commits itself in singular devotion to a religious leader in the absence of the protective checks-and-balances of democracy. Jones established a communal religious and political settlement for Peoples Temple in the Guyana jungle, but in the process isolated his followers from their families and all non-Temple life. Peoples Temple was a cult in which Jones' word was unequivocal law.[4]

What further complicates the potential merits and dangers of guru devotion is that it is a necessity for the highest levels of practice in Vajrayana Buddhism. Tantra is a specific level of practice in which, as Mark Finn writes, "nothing is excluded, and the whole tendency of the mind to exclude is challenged" (109). Tantra is an effort to undermine, productively, the mind's discriminatory capacities, rendering untrustworthy the mind's division and classification capabilities; the highest levels of Tantric practice destabilize "the whole tendency of the mind to exclude." Ideally, Tantric practice induces the mind to see its essentialist frame of reference—the self—as a fiction, and in so doing, dissolve the mind's resistance to the nondual teachings on emptiness that are vital to all Buddhisms. However, this decentering of the self can be a terrifying prospect, and the principle of guru devotion is a doctrinal recognition of the dangers of this unstable terrain of subjectivity. Guru devotion is a protective device, insofar as Tantra's subversion of dualistic notions of subjectivity—of all modes of exclusionary thinking—creates what Finn describes as a "lack of conceptual reference points" that potentially "pu[t] sanity and morality up for grabs" (109). The perils of an individual's Tantric practice become manageable, then, and are instructive instead of dangerous, if the guru-disciple relationship is strong enough for the guru to serve as a doctrinal and psychological guide through the chaos that comes with the destabilization of the subject's most critical frame of reference, the belief in a stable, autonomous self.

As an emotional process and a mode of containment, guru devotion resembles the psychoanalytic principle of transference. The disciple projects onto the lama the intimate emotional drives associated with his/her parents. Yet guru devotion significantly expands the childhood emotional dynamics of transference in the analyst-analysand relationship to include the disciple's projection onto the lama of the Buddha himself. The principle of guru devotion is, at its core, rigidly hierarchical: the transference relationship between student and teacher in Vajrayana Buddhism does not produce the attendant de-hierarchizing counter-transference that it would in psychoanalytic practice. Indeed, the guru's resistance to counter—transference is a sign of the guru's ability to guide a disciple. The guru-disciple relationship is not, then, predicated on equality: the lama is perceived as a superior, enlightened being—a projection of the Buddha—whom the student seeks for "the blessing energy," as Capper describes it, of the lama's enlightenment. What the disciple seeks is the blessing energy of, in effect, the lama's infallibility. In contrast, contemporary understanding of counter-transference presumes that the analyst's authority is not infallible; the analyst is capable of, and encouraged to see as inevitable, the same tendency to project primal childhood relationships onto the analysand as the analysand does upon the analyst. This distinction between transference relationships in psychoanalysis and guru devotion is crucial to understanding the guru-student relationship as monologic rather than dialogic. Even as the guru-disciple relationship depends upon the student's transference, it cannot evade rigidly hierarchical Buddhist instruction on the role of the lama that would seem almost tautological: the lama is an enlightened being whose decisions are correct because he is the lama and lamas are enlightened beings.

Thus, the conceptual framework of guru devotion does not seem at first glance to be compatible with the checks and balances of contemporary liberal democracy. Guru devotion exists in an especially uneasy relationship with the ideology of self-reliant individualism that frames intersubjective relationships in the United States. As Ron Garry explains in his translation of Jamgön Kongtrul Lodrö Thayé's nineteenth-century commentary on guru devotion, *The Teacher-Student Relationship*, enlightenment depends on the student first perceiving the lama as a transcendental master:

> To obtain the full blessings of the instruction, the student should view the teacher as Vajradhara, the primordial Buddha, or as Padmasambhava, transmitting the teachings of the lineage that led numerous practitioners to complete awakening. The student should also view this opportunity to receive teachings as rare and precious, and should have uncontrived devotion to the wisdom teacher. (31)

The potential spiritual benefits of viewing the teacher as a god-like being beyond the boundaries of dissent come at great risk, of course, to students who enter into a guru-disciple relationship expecting the civil protections of democracy. As Gregory C. Bogart argues, it is difficult to determine "whether Westerners inheriting a tradition of democracy and individualism can hope to achieve spiritual illumination through non-democratic forms of traditional discipleship demanding obedience and surrender without considerable discomfort" (11). Capper observes, too, that the "merger-like dynamic of the *guru*-disciple relationship" can seem "inherently unhealthy for supposedly independent-minded Americans" (138). Guru devotion may seem "inherently unhealthy" in the United States, yet the non-essentialism of Buddhist practice suggests, of course, that nothing is healthy or unhealthy in itself. That is, if all phenomena are, as Vajrayana Buddhism teaches, marked by the emptiness of nondualist, codependent arising, then the ethos of guru devotion is, like any other intersubjective experience, situational. It would follow, then, that the doctrine of guru devotion could be subject to change, without violating Buddhist teachings, in cultures where absolute surrender of the individual is looked upon with wariness. Bogart asks whether the totalizing tradition of guru-devotion, with the psychic merger it requires between student and teacher, could benefit from relentless self-inquiry on the part of the guru—from de-hierarchizing gestures by gurus in which, most of all, they "show a willingness to scrutinize and, in some cases, correct their own behavior, and relinquish their demand for absolute surrender of the student" (11). Bogart's question is relevant for Western students, who largely come to the guru-disciple relationship with expectations rooted in Western democratic traditions. However, his question is not necessarily compatible with conventional understanding of guru devotion, in which, despite Vajrayana teachings on emptiness, the perception that the lama is enlightened creates the perception that he is infallible.

Dependence on a guru, however, need not mean unquestioning devotion to a guru. In his discussion of *tenpa*, the Tibetan term for guru devotion, Alexander Berzin argues that "guru devotion" is a reductive translation of the word. *Tenpa* is instead, he writes, "a verb that means to come close to someone in one's thoughts and actions, and to rely on that person with confidence" (120). "Devotion," Berzin maintains, is an inadequate translation for the closeness between student and teacher signified by *tenpa*. He emphasizes that *tenpa* "does not imply [. . .] coming close to a charlatan or a scoundrel, or relying neurotically on someone even if the person is competent to help us" (120). In this way, guru devotion could be seen as, simply, the action any student takes to emulate an ethically sound, inspiring teacher in any discipline. However, the line between devotion and mentorship is not always easy to distinguish, as my discussion of Snowmass in Section III of this essay will demonstrate. The relationship between theory and practice in guru devotion can be fraught, and potentially dangerous, if "devotion" is taken literally to mean a subordination of student to a teacher who does not admit dissent.

Capper, Bogart, and Berzin can offer a vocabulary for studying guru devotion and the authority Trungpa exerted at Snowmass. Like any guru-student relationship in Vajrayana Buddhism, devotion to Trungpa potentially effaced the student's subjectivity in favor of the guru's. Despite Trungpa's documented excesses, a guru-disciple relationship with Trungpa promised no inherently true, essentialized outcome: it did not guarantee the realization of enlightenment any more than it guaranteed the kind of trauma associated with the breaches of spiritual authority often associated with unquestioned devotion to a religious leader.[5] The excesses of Crazy Wisdom were not exclusively Trungpa's. His successor, Ösel Tendzin (Thomas Rich), was notorious for sexual promiscuity with his students. Tendzin slept with students even when he knew he was infected with HIV, a scandal that Ginsberg later evokes in the poem "Elephant in the Meditation Hall" (discussed in Section IV of this essay). Tendzin did not tell these students of his HIV status, and in turn he passed on the virus to one of them. While guru devotion, of course, does not assure a perilous outcome for the disciple, the potential dangers of investing transcendental authority in one person, with no theory of power to offer checks and balances, are enormous. That Trungpa represented the counterculture—and, hence, represented a discourse of resistance—could seem to offer protections against the abuse of power. Yet, as seen at Snowmass, physical violence legitimated by potential misinterpretations of guru devotion could happen anywhere in the United States, even in settings otherwise underwritten by the oppositional, countercultural practices of Trungpa and his inner circle.

III. "Rinpoche had sent an order to bring us down 'at any cost'"

The event that triggered the Snowmass scandal took place in 1975, during a Vajrayana seminary retreat supervised by Trungpa in Snowmass, Colorado. Entering the last month of the three-month seminary retreat—on the eve of Trungpa's final month of Vajrayana teachings—Trungpa organized a Halloween party as a cathartic celebration before the group was to undertake this final thirty-day period. At the Halloween party, Trungpa ordered that some of his students be stripped of their clothing in order to experience, physically, the naked vulnerability of mind required to absorb the final month of advanced teachings that awaited them. Trungpa, naked himself at this point, ordered one of his students to bring the poet W. S. Merwin and his companion, Dana Naone, from their quarters to the meditation hall to be stripped. In a July 20, 1977 letter from Merwin to Ed Sanders' Investigative Poetry Group, comprised of students in Sanders' Investigative Poetry course at Naropa who were studying the Snowmass incident as their class project, Merwin wrote that word was passed through the crowd "that Rinpoche had sent an order to bring us down 'at any cost'" (Sanders, *The Party* 84). The description of events provided by Jack Niland, one of those in attendance at the seminary, affirms Merwin's account. Niland recalls Trungpa telling his students that direct action was required to counter what Trungpa described as Merwin's and Naone's "resistance" (Sanders, *The Party* 41). According to Niland, Trungpa said to the students: "I want you to realize that I'm really going to insist that Merwin come down here no matter what, or what it takes" (Sanders, *The Party* 41). When the two refused to be taken to the meditation hall, their telephone lines were disconnected and a group of Trungpa's students crowded into the hallway and the balcony outside their room. Merwin and Naone were trapped in their own living quarters. Merwin fought the students with a broken wine bottle (his assailants later would require hundreds of stitches), but the two were outnumbered. Eventually, they were taken to the meditation hall and their clothes forcibly removed.

In a July 25, 1977 letter to Sanders' Investigative Poetry Group, Naone describes the forcible stripping by Trungpa's paramilitary Vajra Guard as a direct physical attack: "Guards dragged me off and pinned me to the floor. I could see William [Merwin] struggling a few feet away from me. I fought, and called to friends, men and women, whose faces I saw in the crowd—to call the police" (Sanders, *The Party* 91). The only student to try to physically stop the attack, according to Naone, was Bill King, who "broke through to where I was lying at Trungpa's feet, shouting 'Leave her alone' and 'Stop it.' Trungpa rose above me, from his chair, and knocked Bill King down with a punch, swearing at him, and ordering that no one interfere" (Sanders, *The Party* 91). Student Dennis White tried to convince Trungpa to stop, Naone writes, "but Trungpa told him to shut up," and White said nothing else (Sanders, *The Party* 91). The treatment was so severe that Merwin would later characterize it as a "psychic rape" (Sanders, *The Party* 56-57). Yet, in a meeting with Trungpa the next day, Merwin and Naone decided to continue their participation in the retreat, despite their harrowing experience. As they explained it, they had finished two-thirds of the Vajrayana retreat and they decided that the insight of Trungpa's teachings was important enough to finish the final one-third, even under these difficult circumstances. Merwin writes in his July 20, 1977 letter, "We'd come to study the whole course; we'd taken it (as he knew) seriously; we wanted to finish what we'd begun, and not be scared off. The last lap, about to begin, was the famous Tantric teachings" (Sanders, *The Party* 88).

Considering that Merwin and Naone stayed for the duration of the seminary, it would seem that the incident of the night before had been resolved. However, in the letter Merwin cites an important qualification that he and Naone had insisted on: they would not be governed by the discourse and practice of guru devotion while they participated in the remainder of the seminary. He writes, "We said that if we stayed, it would be with no guarantees of obedience, trust, or personal devotion to him [Trungpa]" (Sanders, *The Party* 88). What remained as a residue of the incident—and what would haunt Naropa over the next several years—was that the guiding conceptual framework of the seminary retreat, the doctrinal requirement of devotion to the guru (in this case, devotion to Trungpa, Naropa's founder), created the conditions for the group's attack on Merwin and Naone. The abuse that occurred at Snowmass exposed a gap between the values of guru devotion and the values of participatory democracy. Of his final, private conversation with Trungpa afterward, Merwin wrote to Sanders' students: "I quoted to him [Trungpa] one of his own seminary transcripts, to the effect that the Vajra master [the guru] cannot make a mistake, and I asked him whether, therefore, he couldn't conceivably have made one. He shook his head: no" (Sanders, The Party 88). Submission to Trungpa as guru was not necessarily an eccentric requirement of the seminary retreat, but instead was manifest religious doctrine. "Personally, I think it makes a great difference whether 'surrender' and 'devotion' to another human being is an individual matter, or is made part of the functioning of a group," Merwin writes in this same letter. "I think that's been one of the repeated teachings of political history" (Sanders, *The Party* 87). Snowmass demonstrates, crucially, that without a theory of power to apply to guru devotion, the doctrine potentially stands as a transcendental teaching that exists outside of history—while requiring historically bound individuals nevertheless to submit to it.

As word spread at what had happened about Snowmass, the subsequent exposure of potential abuses of power within Trungpa's religious community threatened Naropa's funding. Merwin writes that "Trungpa—then, at least—was surrounded by people who were scared to death of him, and he seemed to encourage their feelings of dread, as part of their 'surrender' and 'devotion' to him" (Sanders, *The Party* 87). To complicate matters further for the school, Snowmass was not a Naropa event. The seminary retreat was organized under the auspices of Vajradhatu, Trungpa's international network of Buddhist centers. Even though the Snowmass scandal arose from an incident at a seminary retreat not sponsored by Naropa, it came to be associated with the school by dint of Trungpa's role as leader of both Vajradhatu and Naropa. The scandal haunted Naropa into the 1980s, shadowing the institution's growth and raising troubling questions, especially, about its innovative efforts to apply Buddhist theory and practice to the institutional framework of North American higher education. "[T]his may be life or death for the Naropa Institute," Anne Waldman wrote in an April 2, 1979 letter to poet and editor Robert Callahan, who had been circulating a petition asking U.S. writers to boycott the Kerouac School as a result of Snowmass (Clark 52). Waldman's response to Callahan was not hyperbole. Callahan's petition called for a boycott that would last until four demands had been realized: that Naropa issue an official explanation of what actually happened at Snowmass; that Trungpa's students stop intimidating journalists and others who were investigating what happened at Snowmass; that Naropa discontinue its support for the Vajra Guard, Trungpa's private bodyguards; and, as a response to guru devotion, "that institutional efforts be made to prevent the possibility of such an event occurring in the future, and [that] the rights of individuals to dissent according to conscience be at all times respected" (Clark 51).

Ginsberg only complicated the tension between Naropa's ethos of resistance and the obedience required by guru devotion. The poet's *Boulder Monthly* interview with Clark did not help ease a situation in which the wider arts community in the United States had become suspicious that Trungpa's students—and, by extension, Naropa's—saw themselves as, like a cult, above the law. Referring to Naone's urgent cries to notify the police as she and Merwin were being stripped that night in Snowmass, Ginsberg said:

> In the middle of that scene to yell "call the police"—do you realize how *vulgar* that was [emphasis Ginsberg's]? The Wisdom of the East was being unveiled, and she's going, "call the police!" I mean, shit! Fuck that shit! Strip 'em naked, break down the door! Anything—symbolically! I mentioned privacy before—the entrance into Vajrayana is the abandonment of all privacy. And the entry into the Bodhisattva path is totally—you're saying "I no longer have any privacy ever again." (Clark 60)

Ginsberg's remarks on the Vajrayana path are accurate, to an extent; advanced Vajrayana practice indeed calls to question liberal humanist notions such as privacy. What was at stake for Ginsberg was a contradiction that Snowmass exposed in Beat oppositional writing: that Ginsberg, as the most well-known representative of Naropa and as arguably the country's most visible political poet, could bracket off the question of power relations and conclude that the forcible stripping of two individuals by a group of disciples following the orders of their religious leader was merely "the unveil[ing] of the 'Wisdom of the East.'"

Naropa struggled with a similar contradiction, as an experimental academic institution in the contemplative tradition caught between the exigencies of guru devotion and individual freedom. The book on Snowmass that Ed Sanders edited, *The Party: A Chronological Perspective on a Confrontation at a Buddhist Seminary*, which emerged from his 1977 Investigative Poetry class at Naropa, enacts this contradiction between containment and speech. The students in Sanders' class voted that Snowmass would be the class's investigative topic, in effect creating the conditions whereby Naropa would investigate itself. Sanders' description of Investigative Poetics—his hybrid of the historical and documentary poem— characterizes this mode of writing as a critical form of oppositional poetics: "Investigative poesy is freed from capitalism, churchism, and other totalitarianisms [. . .] in order to describe *every* aspect (no more secret governments!) of the historical present, while aiding the future, even placing bard-babble once again into a role as shaper of the future" [emphasis Sanders] ("Investigative Poetics" 370). Uncontained speech is required for the self-investigation that is a core principle of Investigative Poetics. Such speech stands in contradiction to the obedience required of guru devotion at the same time that it is indebted to the principles of candor that poets like Ginsberg and Waldman championed over the course of their careers.

While I am not arguing that guru devotion is one of Sanders' stated "totalitarianisms," it is, nevertheless, a totalizing discourse (i.e., a mode of speech that does not admit dissent). The disciple is instructed to do as s/he is told by the guru; indeed, Ashvaghosha states that devotion to one's guru takes precedence over all other relationships in the disciple's life. "[F]or the Guru to whom you have pledged your word of honor (to visualize as one with your meditational deity)," Ashvaghosha instructs, "you should willingly sacrifice your wife, children and even your life, although these are not (easy) to give away" (n. pag.). Guru devotion does not acknowledge an ethos of dissent, even if the guru is acting in such a way that would seem detrimental to individuals or the spiritual community at large. Vajrayana commentaries on guru devotion tend to place a great deal of responsibility for a lama's transgressive behavior on the student. Any doubt that arises within the disciple as a result of the guru's actions is, according to Rig'dzin Dorje, speaking for the traditional Vajrayana view of guru devotion, "one of the bogus get-out clauses common to our [Western] culture. We are taught that our momentary feelings should be pre-eminent, and that we must follow them" (89).

However, the highest levels of Tantric practice are kept secret from outsiders, making it considerably difficult to determine whether a disciple's dissent is an expression of substantive doubt or is just another "bogus get-out clause." As Stephen T. Butterfield explains in *The Double Mirror*, a memoir of his years as a Trungpa disciple, "To be part of Trungpa's inner circle, you had to take a vow never to reveal or even discuss some of the things he did" (100). Secrecy can shield high-level Tantric practice, perhaps justifiably, from those who might take teachings from gurus only so that they might attack or slander the practice. Still, such secrecy conflicts with the principles of open, democratic discourse that most Western students bring to Buddhism. Secrecy forecloses upon the possibility of a vigorous exchange of conflicting ideas. In doing so, secrecy privileges homogeneity over difference—and quietism over dissent—leading to the kind of peer pressure that can enable violence toward outsiders, like that which occurred at Snowmass, by threatening those insiders who wish to speak against the grain of the guru's authority. As Butterfield describes Trungpa's closed community of disciples, internal self-policing is just as formidable as external pressure from one's peers: "'May I shrivel up instantly and rot,' we [Trungpa's students] vowed, "'if I ever discuss these teachings with anyone who has not been initiated into them by a qualified master'" (11). Echoing Vajrayana teaching on the disastrous consequences for the student who abandons the guru's closed community of Tantric practitioners, he adds, "Trungpa told us that if we ever tried to leave the Vajrayana, we would suffer unbearable, subtle, continuous anguish, and disasters would pursue us like furies" (11). Principles of secrecy in closed cultures easily can create the conditions for hazing, in which individual members gain "insider" status—and become privileged initiates—by undergoing ritual humiliations. As survivors of their own grueling initiation rituals, insiders of course are often loath to relax initiation rituals for future members. "In the guru-disciple relationship," Butterfield writes, "this self-conscious longing for acceptance, regarded as a form of devotion, operates to intimidate the student into deference, when it would be far more valuable to look like a fool and speak up" (4). Any effort to question the secret society can be perceived as heretical—and, in Vajrayana, can bring with it debilitating psychological and physical consequences. Indeed, Butterfield emphasizes that in traditional Tibetan teachings on guru devotion and Tantra, "breaking faith with the guru must be atoned by such drastic measures as cutting off your arm and offering it at the door of his cave in hopes that he might take you back" (11).

Doubt toward the guru is reflected back at the potentially faithless disciple. According to Rig'dzin Dorje, the possibility that a disciple could pledge devotion to a guru who is flawed is itself a flawed question:

> The question is: "How could you consider this new idea, that you've made a mistake, to be any more serious or valuable than your initial idea, the commitment you made [to the guru], which you thought at the time was to be final and binding? If you have come to doubt that previous moment how can you not also doubt the present moment?" (88)

However, the Vajrayana doctrine of emptiness teaches that all phenomena are empty of an essentialized existence; it would follow, then, that "doubt" could be one of the most valued, even sacred, elements of a healthy guru-student relationship. Doubting Vajrayana essentialism and doubting the essentialized power of the guru could be seen as an expression of a deepening awareness of Buddhist emptiness.[6] Doubt is a prerequisite for the circulation, rather than reification, of power. Rig'dzin Dorje's shifting of responsibility from guru to disciple centralizes power in the guru to an extent that it is incompatible with the contemporary democratic traditions that many students in individualist cultures bring to the guru-disciple relationship. He argues that when a disciple questions the ethics of a guru's actions, this questioning is itself a likely manifestation of the disciple's unchecked tyrannical subjectivism.

Snowmass possibly contributed to the 1977 rejection of Naropa's application for grant funding from the National Endowment for the Arts (NEA). Although public records of the NEA's jury process are not available, it is clear through correspondence between Ginsberg and Merwin, and later between Merwin and an NEA board member, that fallout from the Snowmass incident exerted considerable effect on the institution's reputation. Trungpa's own erratic behavior only made matters worse. It was widely known in the Buddhist community that Trungpa was an alcoholic; he had been drunk the night of the Snowmass incident. In the wake of the 1978 Peoples Temple massacre, Snowmass had become a religious scandal, and, nationally, it was speculated that Trungpa was a cult leader rather than a lama. After all, Trungpa's power was underwritten by the same paternal religious archetypes of hegemonic masculinity that authorized Jones' absolute power over the Peoples Temple: "Power and alcohol go to most men's heads," Peter Marin wrote of Trungpa in a 1979 *Harper's* essay on Snowmass and Naropa, "and if you raise a man from childhood to believe in his own power [as is the case with those, like Trungpa, recognized as reincarnated lamas], it is not surprising that he sometimes abuses it" (53). Questions persisted over whether the NEA grant was rejected because of the quality of the proposal or because of a presumed link between Naropa, as an institution of higher learning, and the attack on Merwin and Naone that occurred at Snowmass. Ginsberg's cryptic response to an interview with Sanders for the Investigative Poetry course's report only obscures the matter further. The application, Ginsberg said, was "all right" but "wasn't quite as pure as [the NEA] needed" (64). Ginsberg's ambiguous use of the word "pure" aside, what matters most in this discussion is that Snowmass threatened the nascent Kerouac School in its earliest years. Naropa's growing reputation as a site for an oppositional poetics was under question because of, paradoxically, a culture of obedience at the heart of its governing Vajrayana Buddhist ethos.

The potential power inequities of Rig'dzin Dorje's explanation of guru devotion recall Hunt's cautionary description of how a dominant culture coopts and maintains control over oppositional discourses. In "Notes on An Oppositional Poetics," she explains how a dominant cultural group recasts dissent from its master narratives in order to contain potentially oppositional discourses. Arguably, no better example exists of the potential for dominance than a male leader, in this case, a guru, whose patriarchal authority is transcendental and whose decisions are presumed never to be wrong. She writes that "dominant culture will transfer its own partiality onto the opposition it tries to suppress. It will always maintain that it holds the complete worldview, despite the fissures. Opposition is alternately demonized or accommodated through partial concessions without a meaningful alteration of dominant culture's own terms" (202). Even when it seems the guru is exhibiting the qualities of a cult leader, the responsibility for the lama's actions is often seen as the student's more than the guru's, insofar as the doctrine states that the guru is infallible; as Hunt might say, the guru "holds the complete world view" and does so "despite the fissures" exposed by the disciple. When asked by interviewer Ngakma Shardröl Wangmo how to distinguish between Vajra masters and cult leaders, Rig'dzin Dorje replied, "It might be more useful to ask, 'At the end of the day, how can I be sure that I am not a cult follower?' Ironically, with the question of cults, the student is the only person who can allow or frustrate the possibility of a cult coming into existence" (104). Guru devotion functions uneasily within the decidedly populist, Naropa-influenced poetics of resistance in Waldman's outrider ideal and in Sanders' practice of "Investigative Poetics." The "people's point of view," from which revisionary history is narrated, risks cooptation when articulated within the ahistorical discursive boundaries of guru devotion. History itself is elided in guru devotion; the lama's authority is transdiscursive and not open to debate. In the absence of historical consciousness, no space for a revisionary history—for resistance—can emerge. The impulse to resist is met by a transhistorical religious authority that cannot be questioned without threatening the blessing bestowed upon the student by the guru.

IV. "This impossible submission to some spiritual dictatorship"

Ginsberg suffered both physical illness and writer's block in the immediate aftermath of Snowmass, especially as it was implied that, as a representative of Trungpa's student-teacher relationships and of Naropa, he somehow was responsible for the erosion of both guru devotion and freethinking inquiry. It is important to note that Ginsberg was not even in attendance at Snowmass when Merwin and Naone were attacked. He was on tour with Bob Dylan and the Rolling Thunder Revue. In John Whalen-Bridge's August 11, 2009 interview with Anne Waldman, which appears in this issue of *The Journal of Beat Studies*, Waldman speculates that Snowmass "would have gone differently" if she and Ginsberg had attended the seminary that year. "I wish we had been there," she says to Whalen-Bridge, "because there was unfortunate harm and misunderstanding that we might have helped circumvent. Yet it [Snowmass] led to interesting conundrum, conversation, argument and different ideological and cultural views: Rugged American Individualism up against ways of presenting Buddhist dharma and teachings and questions of how wisdom travels from the East." Snowmass was fraught for Ginsberg, as an individual poet associated with progressive political causes such as gay civil rights, drug decriminalization, and the anti-Vietnam War movement—all of which affirmed to a great extent the rights of the individual against the totalizing potential of the state. As he explains in the interview with Clark: "I accuse myself all the time, of seducing the entire poetry scene and Merwin into this impossible submission to some spiritual dictatorship which they'll never get out of again and which will ruin American culture forever" (54). Ginsberg's commitment to a guru-student relationship with Trungpa made his position particularly vexing. He affirms to Clark his discipleship with Trungpa, despite characterizing as "very un-American, to say the least" the violent content of Tibetan ritual poems to Buddhist protector deities recited as a group at retreats and teachings (56). Butterfield describes some of these bloody protector chants in his memoir of his guru-student relationship with Trungpa. The student implores the deity Ekajati, for instance, to "eat the hearts of heretics"; similarly, the deities Vajrasadhu and Mahakala are asked to eat the bodies of those who have distorted the Buddha's teachings, and the deity Vetah is beseeched to decapitate "destroyers of the teachings" and to sever their aortas (Butterfield 119-20). Ginsberg admonishes Clark in the interview for politicizing guru devotion; yet this charge comes from a poet for whom the personal voice of candor in a poem is always a public, political gesture. He also argues that Clark's effort to politicize guru devotion is reductive—and, remarkably, for a political poet—he scolds Clark for supporting his rhetorical position with "reference to cultural artifacts like the Bill of Rights" (53). For Ginsberg, it would seem, guru devotion at this time functioned unlike much else in everyday lived experience, as a privatizing act in which the personal is not political at all.

Indeed, the confluence of politics (the protections afforded to the individual by the Bill of Rights) and religion (the student's surrender of the self in guru devotion) is the crux of the dilemma for Ginsberg, as a political poet, in the aftermath of the Snowmass incident, and, I argue, for Naropa as a religious institution committed to oppositional poetics. Clark says to Ginsberg in the interview, "You're talking about your religious feelings. I'm talking about politics, frankly" (54).

Ginsberg began to question the concept of guru devotion, however, after Snowmass. The scandal raised doubts for him about Trungpa. In an unpublished April 4, 1976 journal entry, Ginsberg doubts the efficacy of his subordination to Trungpa and speculates whether guru devotion might be the result of a dangerous transference—that of a deity onto a human being.[7] He wrote, "This submission to Trungpa Guru, this Surrender is it correct, a transfer of God failure debasement to a living Being so at least the Adoration Devotion is to a Real Entity not an Image—And Merwin's War is it mine, 'gainst the vulgar drunken Guru Sangha?—Am I a fool?" (Notebooks). Ginsberg was in a vexing position, caught between his sympathy for the candor and political advocacy of Clark's investigative reporting—the same traits he praises in his poetics—and his devotion to Trungpa. The psychic agitation of Snowmass caused a creative block in him, as he notes in an August 5, 1979 journal entry:

> As time's gone on the last two years, the [Snowmass] conflict's crossed my mind every morning on waking, and I've had difficulty knowing whether I'm lying to myself to cover Trungpa's Hierarchical secrecy, or lying to Clark in not openly and continuously confronting him in his journalistic spitefulness and intrigue. . . . This inhibits my working altogether since I don't want to waste my poesy and readers' time on gossip and spite, or exhibit my own confusion [and] anger with [a] phalanx of irritable critics. (Schumacher 646)

The figural nakedness at the center of Ginsberg's poetics, vital to the oppositional aesthetic of the Kerouac school, now was threatened by the coerced, literal nakedness that triggered the Snowmass scandal. Ginsberg's frustrated ambivalence continued into the next year, as demonstrated in a June 22, 1980 journal entry: "I used to boast no identity! Now why am I stuck with the accusation of a fixed identity as Trungpa's sucker? Am I? [. . .] Why am I torturing myself so? [. . .] Should I renounce Trungpa and retire to my farm?" (Schumacher 649). Ginsberg's emphasis throughout his career on the aesthetic primacy of a poetics based on Buddhist non-duality is reduced to mere "boast" in this journal entry. The poet confesses the temptation to retreat from the politics of guru devotion, a wish that becomes more relevant in later poems that confront his contradictory feelings on the Snowmass scandal.

The guilt in later poems such as "White Shroud" and "Black Shroud"—two poems that continue the sequence begun in "Kaddish"—reflects the strain imposed on Ginsberg's oppositional work by the tension between guru devotion and candor. Most notably, in "Black Shroud," published in 1986, the ease with which the literary establishment coopts the vatic voice of the poet reflects Ginsberg's post-Snowmass anxieties about the Buddhist establishment. The poem opens in the Kunming Hotel in China, where he had been invited in 1984 as part of an American Academy of Arts and Letters delegation. He was in China as an American cultural ambassador, a professional writer simultaneously representing both the American literary establishment and Beat counterculture. The poem stages Ginsberg's anxieties that Beat literature could be coopted, and it serves as a metaphor for the threat of cooptation represented by Trungpa. The dramatic situation of "Black Shroud" reflects Ginsberg's fraught public persona after Snowmass as one of the most visible representatives of Trungpa's guru-student relationships.

"Black Shroud" opens with a scene of intense physical suffering, with the poet kneeling "before the white toilet" and vomiting after eating a tainted chicken sandwich (911). Ginsberg is struggling to disincorporate what has been literally ingested into his body and all that has been figuratively assimilated into his persona as Allen Ginsberg the professional American poet.[8] In these opening lines, Ginsberg traces his vomiting in the poem back to "my mother groaning in Paterson 1937," during the period when Ginsberg, aged 11, was too often forced into the role as one of his mother Naomi's primary caretakers (911). In "Black Shroud," Ginsberg is "retching, a wave of nausea, bowels and bladder loose / black on the bathroom floor"; similarly, in "Kaddish," Naomi is "on all fours in front of the toilet—urine running between her legs—left retching on the tile floor smeared with her own black feces" (*Collected Poems* 911, 226). Ginsberg revisits in "Black Shroud" the guilt over his signing of his mother's lobotomy order in 1947, confronting his regret in dream-images in which the poet is allied with a professionalized medical establishment that would tame a critical component of his oppositional poetics: the undomesticated wild zone represented by Naomi. Naomi's mental illness prompts Ginsberg in "Kaddish" to summon "the final cops of madness" to rescue him; at the same time, he describes Naomi in the poem as the "glorious muse that bore me from the womb, gave suck first mystic life & taught me talk and music, from whose pained head I first took Vision" (*Collected Poems* 230, 231). However, in the dream at the center of "Black Shroud," the poet conflates Naomi's lobotomy authorization with his identification with the coopting influence of the very literary establishment he often positioned himself against. In turn, Ginsberg's alliance with the literary establishment is dramatized against the backdrop of his participation in one of the primary heteronormative institutional practices that would be politically fraught for him, as a gay man—a wedding, the dream-narrative of his cousin's marriage. Dreaming of Naomi's lobotomy as a decapitation perpetrated by Ginsberg himself, the poet worries about how the lies required to maintain his innocence are instead building a "Karma nightmare" (*Collected Poems* 912). As if to confirm Ginsberg's fear of literary cooptation—and to suggest, paradoxically, the materialist protections afforded by cooptation—his publisher assures him in the dream that his *Collected Poems* will be protected from the scandal of his mother's dream-beheading. "Helpful," Ginsberg writes, "alas, too late for me / to undo the murder of my mother, I must confess, I had / confessed, too late to undo confession and truth, I woke" (*Collected Poems* 912). "Black Shroud" ends with a profession of guilt that is overwhelmed, nevertheless, by its ambivalence. The poem offers a wavering dream-confession in which Ginsberg is protected from scandal by his individual allegiance with, rather than opposition to, the literary establishment.

Despite a career as an activist poet for whom the personal poem is a social act, Ginsberg nevertheless privileges a privatized voice when exploring the Buddhist establishment in his post-Snowmass poems. The most visible dramatization of Ginsberg's ambivalence over Snowmass, and of the shift from a public voice to a private one after the scandal, is "Elephant in the Meditation Hall," composed in 1990 and published in *Cosmopolitan Greetings: Poems, 1986-1992*. The poem functions as an accumulating list of twentieth-century religious, political, and literary abuses of power, yet it emphasizes ahistorical generalities over particulars—perhaps the antithesis of the poetics of "minute particulars" that is Ginsberg's inheritance from Blake through Ezra Pound and William Carlos Williams, to name three of his major influences. As a result, the scandals listed in the poem are taken at face value as equivalent to each other: for example, the sexual transgressions of Zen Roshis in San Francisco and Los Angeles are presented as no better or worse than Chinese and Soviet venerations of Mao and Stalin, respectively, or the development of global nuclear armaments. The body of Ginsberg's political work depends on the incorporation of historical particulars to identify the material conditions of oppression and the possibilities of resistance; however, the poem's paratactic logic leaves little room for understanding how power circulates and, by extension, where resistance to abuses of power might arise in different historical eras.

Among the many "elephants" in the meditation hall, Snowmass and the later sexual scandal caused by Ösel Tendzin both play a vital role:

> Vajracharya Trungpa! Dont mention the naked poet at the Halloween
>   Party!
> And the whispered transmission regent died of AIDS (disciple a straight
>   guy sick they say)
> Marxists were right, religion the people's opium! (*Collected Poems* 985)

Ginsberg's use of irony, vital as a counter-discourse in his political poetry, is instead deployed as a mode of quietism in "Elephant in the Meditation Hall." It is a manifestly religious (specifically, Buddhist) poem that incorporates Marx's famous pronouncement that religion is "the opium of the people" to defend transgressive Buddhist teachers against the charge of scandal. Ginsberg's unusual—for him—

ahistorical approach to religious history in this poem actually mystifies Marx's emphasis on the urgency of historical materialism in developing populist resistance. Religion, in this case Buddhism, becomes the opiate of a people's history.

The First Noble Truth of Buddhism—the truth of suffering—is a call to action rather than just a description of human experience in Engaged Buddhism, the activist mode of North American Buddhism most compatible with Ginsberg's poetics of resistance.[9] The path out of suffering articulated later by the Fourth Noble Truth is, for Engaged Buddhism, a matter of combining both inward meditation practice and social action. Yet, in "Elephant in the Meditation Hall," at the very moment when Ginsberg looks inward, his vision recedes into generalized declaratives that decidedly veer from the poetics of concrete particularity that circumscribes his career as a political, and experimental, poet: "Trapped in living nightmare, I made a big mistake I got born, / The world came out of a black hole, whole universe / a scandal, illusion, everyone deluded" (*Collected Poems* 986). The elephant in the meditation hall—the elephant in the room that the poem's title hints it will expose—actually is further obscured as the poem grows more and more skittish about its own rendering of historical particulars. Ginsberg evokes what he terms "Scandals in Buddhafields," but only to subject these scandals to a universalism that swerves from questions of power. The poem eventually is silent about the power imbalances caused by unquestioned devotion to religious, political, and literary leaders: "Scandals in Buddhafields? big mistake in Hemispheres, on moons, Black Holes everywhere!" (*Collected Poems* 986). Ginsberg's guilt over the Snowmass scandal, and his concurrent questioning of guru devotion expressed in his journals, is elided by a strategy of, at best, ambivalence in "Elephant in the Meditation Hall." The poem seems to retreat from history into a universalized archetype of the First Noble Truth—"a cosmic elephant in the meditation planet"—that is too generalized for political efficacy (*Collected Poems* 986). Ironically, as the elephant in the room grows to "cosmic" proportions in the poem, it becomes more and more difficult to name and act upon.

The ironic voice of "Elephant in the Meditation Hall" might seem, nevertheless, consistent with Ginsberg's career-long emphasis on irony as a mode of resistance, where the ironic voice inhabits, and then denaturalizes, dominant discourses. Irony is a critical component in the revisionary impulse of Ginsberg's political poetry. However, in a poem such as "Elephant in the Meditation Hall"—in which the power of the guru is in question—irony only deepens the speaker's ambivalent response to power.[10]

Ginsberg's conception of the materiality of language is, like his use of irony, a crucial mode of opposition throughout his career, and provided a foundation for later poems expressing his post-Snowmass ambivalence. His earlier work crafted an immanent rather than transcendent language for prophecy and, consistent with

Waldman's outrider ideal, was populist in its articulation of resistance. Ginsberg's famous defense of "Howl," from his 1956 letter to Richard Eberhart, explains, for instance, that the poem's central focus is on "mystical mysteries in the forms in which they actually occur here in the U.S. in our environment" (*Howl: Original Draft Facsimile* 152). His 1961 fusion of Western and Buddhist mythos in "Kaddish" swerves from transcendental archetype in favor of materialist representations of desire—political and personal redemption is conceived as a "release of particulars" (220). In the same way, Ginsberg's 1966 anti-war epic "Wichita Vortex Sutra" constructs a language-based vision of the end of the Vietnam War, even as it invokes Buddhist archetype. "I search for the language / that is also yours—" he writes, "almost all our language has been taxed by war" (414). "Wichita Vortex Sutra" superimposes appropriated language from radio broadcasts and newspaper reports onto the voice of a Blakean bard whose task is to redeem a world in which language has been rent by war:

> The war is language,
>   language abused
>   for Advertisement,
>   language used
> like magic for power on the planet [. . .] (409)

    The bard of "Wichita Vortex Sutra" takes war propaganda ironically at its word, reclaiming what he describes as its "magic" power in the service of a redemptive Buddhist mantra that would end the war. Yet Ginsberg's counter-discursive mantra in "Wichita" is embodied, not mystical. In "Wichita," language is a somatic experience: when language is maimed by war, language authorizes the maiming of human bodies. The bard in "Wichita" counters with an "ecstatic language" of "trembling bodies hold[ing] each other / breast to breast on a mattress" (413). "Mind Breaths," composed seven years after "Wichita," affirms the physicality of Ginsberg's language for sacred experience. One of his first significant poems after beginning formal study with Trungpa, "Mind Breaths" is a statement on the concrete, embodied particulars of Buddhist vision. In its dramatization of the sacred experience of Buddhist *shamatha* (mindfulness), the poem is materialist in its representation of the sacred. It privileges nothing more ordinary than the physical body breathing: "a calm breath, a silent breath, a slow breath" that "breathes outward from the nostrils" and serves as a crucial gesture of personal and political empathy in the poem (619).

    However, for Ginsberg, guru devotion presses language into service as a means of limiting dissent, and it operates as a force that would contain the vatic expansiveness of Ginsberg's poetics of resistance. Two poems that speak to

Ginsberg's post-Snowmass ambivalence are "Supplication for the Rebirth of the Vidyadhara Chögyam Trungpa, Rinpoche," which like "Elephant in the Meditation Room" is from *Cosmopolitan Greetings*, and earlier in this volume the tender elegy to Trungpa, "On Cremation of Chögyam Trungpa, Vidyadhara," in which the cremation of his guru's physical body is an occasion for celebrating the lama's teachings on vision, even though the funeral rites are almost unbearably sad for the poet. Ginsberg included "Supplication" is inspired by traditional Vajarayana prayers for the rebirth of gurus, and must be seen as the student's respectful and plaintive plea for the guru to, as Ginsberg writes, "regroup our community" through his rebirth in a human body. "Dear Lord Guru who pervades the space of my mind / permeates the universe of my consciousness," he addresses Trungpa in the poem's opening lines, asking the deceased guru to "Return return reborn in spirit & knowledge in human body / my own or others as continual Teacher of chaotic peace" (*Collected Poems* 1009). As a poem based on the Vajrayana tradition of entreating the deceased guru to take rebirth in human form, "Supplication" is a vital expression, for Ginsberg, of the importance of devotion to the spiritual guidance of the guru. It is a crucial plea for Trungpa to return "to enlighten my [Ginsberg's] labors / & the labors of your meditators" (*Collected Poems* 1009). However, this poem, like "Elephant in the Meditation Hall," offers no strategy for thinking through the contradiction between guru devotion and Ginsberg's career-long emphasis on a poetics of resistance. The poem subsumes Ginsberg's guilt and self-questioning over Snowmass—his fear, expressed earlier, of "lying to [himself] to cover Trungpa's Hierarchical secrecy"—into gestures of artistic and spiritual subordination.

Considered as a poem, a secular artifact, rather than a prayer, the poem's conventional quatrains suggest formalist containment, along with a continuity of literary tradition not usually emphasized in Ginsberg's otherwise experimental work. Two of the poem's six stanzas, the fourth and the sixth, break slightly with their quatrains; each ends with an indented fifth line that, at first glance, could suggest that Ginsberg's language is too expansive for the limited, contained boundaries of conventional form. Such a reading would be in keeping with Ginsberg's reputation as a poet of resistance—as a poet whose work opposes traditional, inherited modes of authority, including those inherited from a canonical past. At closer look, however, these tag lines at the end of the fourth and sixth stanzas coopt language as a vessel for the guru's unassailable authority. Stanza four closes with the proclamation that even in death, Trungpa's authority can heal the wounded sangha even though the guru now exists in a mystical, intermediary afterlife far removed from human experience—"in the sky of your [Trungpa's] mind" (1009). The sixth, and final, stanza of the poem spills into an additional line that expresses its devotion more starkly, naming Trungpa as a protector deity to whom the poet prays:

> These slogans were writ on the second day of June 1991
> a sleepless night my brother's 70th birthday on Long Island
> my own sixty-fifth year in the human realm visiting his house
> by the Vajra Poet Allen Ginsberg supplicating protection of his
> Vajra Guru Chögyam Trungpa Rinpoche (1009)

The poem's authority derives from Trungpa's name, not from Ginsberg's language. Ginsberg ends the poem describing his own language as a series of "slogans"—subservient declaratives, in effect, rather than active speech—that are not directed toward any tactile or concrete phenomena in the poet's historical moment. "Bend your effort to regroup our community within your thought-body & mind-space," he implores Trungpa earlier, in a language of transcendental abstraction (*Collected Poems* 1009). This is not the poet who revises the Hebrew prayer for the dead and the Anglo-American elegy in "Kaddish," nor is this the same poet whose experiments with form produced the revisionary serial haiku of "Nagasaki Days," "American Sentences," "Pastel Sentences (Selections)," and "American Sentences 1995-1997." Instead, "Supplication" is a paean to obedience—more specifically, to the totalizing student-teacher relationship of guru devotion. Devoted to the certainty of the guru's authority, "Supplication for the Rebirth of the Vidyadhara Chögyam Trungpa, Rinpoche" upholds rather than re-envisions inherited tradition.

The untamed vision of "On Cremation" is quieted by ambivalence in "Elephant in the Meditation Hall" and subservience in "Supplication." "Elephant in the Meditation Hall" and "Supplication" suggest that when oppositional poetics creates for Ginsberg unresolvable tension with guru devotion, as occurred after Snowmass, the greatest risk is that his poetic practice might be transformed into a transcendental, and possibly mystifying, discourse in which the historical particulars of dissent so important to his earlier work are overwritten by obedience to a mystical archetype that erases doubt. The secular artifact of the poem, and the secular concerns of populist, historical resistance, are overwhelmed by devotion to the guru as a transhistorical ideal. Lacking concrete referents—privileging the "slogan," as Ginsberg describes it, over his prior experiments with language and form—Ginsberg's poetics of resistance in the presence of the guru is nearly a poetics of deference.

V. "To interrupt and join."

As we research the history of Naropa and its influence on a Beat poetics, it is important to emphasize that this is a history predicated on contradictions and gaps. Given the tension between the experimental impulse of Beat poetry and the obedient sensibility required by guru devotion, the trajectory of Naropa's contribution to a Beat poetics is recursive rather than linear. Michel Foucault's counter-response to Platonic historiography offers a useful representation of this non-linear history. "What is found at the historical beginning of things," he writes, "is not the inviolable identity of their origin; it is the dissension of other things. It is disparity" (79). Foucault's "Nietzsche, Genealogy, History" is one of the foundational texts of the new historicism, and I cite it here because this particular approach to historiography is best poised to explore the fragmented and contradictory intersection of guru devotion and oppositional poetics. Such contradiction is perhaps to be expected: "The forces operating in history are not controlled by destiny or regulative mechanisms, but respond to haphazard conflicts," Foucault argues (88). Naropa's populist revisionary poetics of resistance represents what Hunt has described more generally as oppositional writing's potential for "dispersing" domination (212). Such writing, Hunt argues, "only enhances our capacity to strategically read our condition more critically and creatively in order to interrupt and join" (212). To interrupt—to exert, if only for a moment, and then only as a spontaneous irruption of speech within a dominant discourse—is a speech act that Naropa's outrider tradition is authorized to do by Crazy Wisdom at the same time that it is repressed by the demands of guru devotion in this tradition. When his role as guru is understood in light of a history that includes the Snowmass incident, Trungpa can be seen to have both encouraged and coopted the outlaw impulse of Beat writing to "interrupt and join" the dominant literary and cultural conversations of the postwar era.[11]

The outrider tradition of poetics at Naropa represents a Dionysus to the postwar academic poetry establishment's Apollo—yet this seemingly self-evident analogy only partially describes the complicated relationship between Beat oppositional writing and the authority of inherited tradition. Guru devotion is crucial to understanding the theoretical and spiritual underpinning of the relationship between Naropa, as an evolving institution, and Beat poetics, as a supple and organic participant in the wider landscape of contemporary poetry in the late twentieth century. The facts of what happened at Snowmass are clear. It is not adequate, however, to blame Trungpa's alcoholism or the alleged cult-like tendencies of his followers who attacked Merwin and Naone. Nor is it ethical to blame Merwin and Naone.

A common defense of Trungpa's actions at Snowmass is to explain them as part of the tradition of the "wrathful teacher" in Vajrayana Buddhism. A wrathful guru is one whose teaching methods mimic the lineage of warlike deities in Vajrayana Buddhism—archetypal figures who appear as fierce warlike or demonic figures rather than peaceful bodhisattvas in order to help practitioners forcefully and rapidly cut their attachments to the material world. To describe Trungpa's actions only as those of a wrathful teacher is to evade the historical context of Snowmass, however. Only with historical scrutiny can we determine the difference between, for instance, a transgressive lama whose wrathful teaching is a potential danger to others and, in contrast, an eccentric lama who wrathfully disdains tradition in favor of compassionate, iconoclastic spiritual instruction. As David Michael DiValerio notes, Trungpa himself was aware of the historical particulars of his mode of teaching: "Through his skillful presentation of certain ideas Trungpa created a situation in which it was not just *accepted* that he would act in ways that challenged other peoples' notions of propriety, but it was actually expected of him. The idea that a *siddha* [enlightened master] might display unconventional or eccentric behavior has been around for a long time; Trungpa drew from this precedent and modified it to suit his own needs" [emphasis DiValerio] (677). Any examination of the historical context of Trungpa's teachings cannot ignore that the transcendentalist doctrine of guru devotion contributes to the materialist allure of centralizing power in one person. DiValerio writes, "Trungpa was for his students an unquestioned source of authority. Moreover, for most of his followers, Trungpa was their only source of contact with what they perceived to be the Tibetan tradition [. . . .] Trungpa had a remarkable degree of control over their perceptions, with no real checks or balances on anything he might say" (678).

It is important to examine the theory of power behind what happened at Snowmass; namely, to explore the cultural, political, and aesthetic effects of guru devotion, the concept that gave Trungpa absolute authority and that demanded absolute obedience from his followers. Snowmass is a reminder that Naropa's revolutionary and innovative poetics of resistance is itself founded on principles that also include its antithesis: subordination. As we continue to research the effect of Naropa on a Beat poetics, we cannot subscribe to the notion that Beat literary history is only a revolutionary, liberatory response to the cultures of containment in the postwar United States, more generally, and in contemporary U.S. poetry, more specifically. Instead, given the role of Trungpa in Naropa's early history, and the role guru devotion played in underwriting Trungpa's authority, we should examine Naropa's influence on Beat poetics as one that proceeds from complex movement on a continuum between obedience and transgression.

Notes

Section II of this essay draws upon, and significantly extends, research on guru devotion that first appeared in my *Allen Ginsberg's Buddhist Poetics*. The summary narrative of the Snowmass incident at the beginning of Section III similarly draws upon, and significantly extends, research on Snowmass that appeared in this book. Quotations from Allen Ginsberg's unpublished notebooks and journals appear courtesy of the Department of Special Collections and University Archives, Stanford University Libraries, and Peter Hale and Bob Rosenthal of the Allen Ginsberg Trust. My thanks also to John Whalen-Bridge for permission to quote from his August 11, 2009 interview with Anne Waldman.

---

[1] It is important to emphasize that the purpose of this essay is not to malign the doctrine of guru devotion. I do not mean to diminish the experiences of the many Buddhist practitioners over the years who have deepened their spiritual practice through their devotion to a lama. Nor is this essay an effort to question Naropa's continued presence as a crucial physical and institutional space for literary experimentation since the Kerouac School was founded in 1974.

[2] Nyingma is a lineage in which Trungpa was trained in addition to his primary lineage, the Kagyu School.

[3] Ginsberg later claimed that he assumed Clark would give him the opportunity to revise his remarks before publication in *Boulder Monthly*. Clark countered that no such agreement was made and that he did not encourage Ginsberg to think he could revise his comments before publication.

[4] At the time of Ginsberg's interview with Clark, the 1978 Peoples Temple massacre in Jonestown, Guyana, was still fresh in people's minds as a foremost example of the potentially fatal consequences that could result from abuses of spiritual authority. Peoples Temple initially was one of the most integrated Christian churches of the Civil Rights era, and in its earliest years earned praise for its social justice efforts. However, by the time Jim Jones began relocating the church to Guyana in 1974, it had become a deeply secretive cult in which Temple members were instructed to see Jones as both their adoptive father and the reincarnation of Christ. Dissent from Jones' word prompted abusive psychological and physical punishments. On November 18, 1978, a U.S. delegation led by Congressman Leo Ryan was preparing to fly a group of Temple defectors from Guyana's Port Kaituma airport, just outside of Jonestown, when five members of Ryan's party, including Ryan himself, were shot to death by a group of Jones' security guards who had been commanded by Jones to follow the delegation to the airport and kill them. Once he was informed of the murders, Jones ordered his followers to drink cyanide-laced Flavor Aid and commit what he called "revolutionary suicide." Jones' total control of his isolated followers in Guyana, along with stories told by survivors of coerced poisoning by Jones' security guards, have prompted some to question if suicide is the most accurate term to describe the deaths at Jonestown. "What happened in Jonestown amounted to mass murder, not mass suicide," Tim Reiterman argues. "Jones put all the pieces in place for a last act of self-destruction, then gave the order to kill the children first, sealing everyone's fate" (xi).

⁵ Trungpa was perhaps one of the greatest twentieth-century Tibetan teachers of counatercultural Buddhism in North America and Europe. Buddhist scholar Charles S. Prebish praises Trungpa's unique ability—his "skillful means," in Buddhist terms—to reach practitioners of all levels with his teachings but also cautions that "Trungpa's well-publicized reputation and unpredictability seemed to require at least a bit of caution from all who had not known him previously" (159-60).

⁶ For more on doubt as a potentially sacred Buddhist principle, see the work of Stephen Batchelor, especially *The Faith to Doubt: Glimpses of Buddhist Uncertainty* and *Buddhism without Beliefs: A Contemporary Guide to Awakening*.

⁷ Ginsberg's efforts to merge his Buddhist practice with his Judaism often hinged on his ability to accept that Buddhism is a religion without a creator God. As he writes in a letter to Gary Snyder in 1976, four years after formalizing his training with Trungpa: "Trungpa's teaching of nontheism seems to have penetrated my skull finally. It does seem strange that for 20 years I've been yapping about God. Why didn't you tell me to shut up?" (*The Selected Letters of Allen Ginsberg and Gary Snyder* 182).

⁸ For more on the trope of indigestion in Ginsberg's work, see my discussion of his long poem "Angkor Wat" in *Allen Ginsberg's Buddhist Poetics*.

⁹ The Four Noble Truths, considered to be the first teachings the Buddha gave after his experience of enlightenment, represent Buddhism in perhaps its most condensed form and are central to Buddhist practice: the truth of suffering; the truth of the path that leads to suffering; the truth of the cessation of suffering; and the truth of the path that leads to the cessation of suffering.

¹⁰ For example, Ginsberg's career-long emphasis on irony as a mode of resistance can be seen as his 1974 "Who Runs America?" The sacred interdependence that arises from Buddhist nonduality is reduced, ironically, to totalizing gushes of oil that emerge in "brown smog over Detroit" and culminate in oil that "rings in Mobil gas tank cranks" and "blackens ocean from broken Gulf tankers" as it "spills onto Santa Barbara beaches from Standard of California derricks offshore" (636). His 1978 "Plutonian Ode" re-envisions the Western mythic tradition in a mock-ode to weaponized Plutonium that emphasizes, with acidic political irony, the death drive of the postwar nuclear arms race. Where Ginsberg's American forefather, Whitman, praised technology as an example of American expansiveness and poetic manifest destiny, Ginsberg dramatizes the arms race as a consequence of technological ambition that Whitman never could have foreseen. Ginsberg addresses Whitman in the second line, proclaiming, "At last inquisitive Whitman a modern epic"—yet this is an ode not to technological glory but to a "Radioactive Nemesis" (710). The dispersed, fluid subjectivity shared by Whitman's and Ginsberg's visionary poetics is in "Plutonian Ode" recast as an image of total annihilation; multiplicitous selfhood has no place in a poem that is a mock-ode to the void: "Father Whitman,"

Ginsberg intones, "I celebrate a matter that renders Self oblivion!" (710). "Plutonian Ode" reimagines the Greek lord of the underworld, Pluto, as master of this "matter that renders Self oblivion": Pluto bestows "Rockwell war plants" that "fabricate this death stuff trigger in nitrogen baths" (710-11). Whitman describes his 1876 ode to technological progress, "To a Locomotive in Winter," as an operatic "recitative" (395). "Plutonian Ode" is, in Ginsberg's words, "detonative" (*Collected Poems* 710). The poem functions as a contemporary corrective of Whitman's conviction that American technology is a democratizing principle. In the final section of "Plutonian Ode," Whitman appears redeemed, like a mythic figure from Blake's prophecies, as Ginsberg invokes the sacred Vajrayana practice of Tonglen to "destroy this mountain of Plutonium with ordinary mind and body speech" (713). Echoing Blake, Ginsberg ironically re-envisions Western mythos to demythologize what is, for the poet, the contemporary cultural impulse to make sacred the scientific rationalism of the arms race.

[11] Butterfield says much the same about Trungpa's tendency to simultaneously generate and coopt innovative writing within the Vajradhatu organization. Butterfield argues, "For a dharma system to inspire good poetry, as opposed to political correctness, deep criticism must be invited and engaged, especially if it is heretical. Trungpa himself appeared to invite such criticism; the structural forms that he bequeathed to Vajradhatu invite it and shut it off at the same time" (221).

Works Cited

Ashvaghosha. "*Fifty Verses on Guru Devotion.*" With commentary by Geshe Ngawang Dhargey. Web. 21 Aug 2012.

Batchelor, Stephen. *Buddhism without Beliefs: A Contemporary Guide to Awakening*. New York: Riverhead, 1987. Print.

---. *The Faith to Doubt: Glimpses of Buddhist Uncertainty*. Berkeley: Parallax, 1990. Print.

Berzin, Alexander. *Wise Teacher, Wise Student: Tibetan Approaches to a Healthy Relationship*. Ithaca, New York: Snow Lion, 2010. Print.

Bogart, Gregory C. "Separating from a Spiritual Teacher." *Journal of Transpersonal Psychology* 24.1 (1992): 2-21. Print.

Butterfield, Stephen T. *The Double Mirror: A Skeptical Journey into Buddhist Tantra*. Berkeley: North Atlantic, 1994. Print.

Capper, Daniel. "Enchantment with Tibetan Lamas in the United States." *Journal of Contemporary Religion* 19.2 (2004): 137-53. Print.

Clark, Tom. *The Great Naropa Poetry Wars*. Santa Barbara: Cadmus Editions, 1980. Print.

DiValerio, David Michael. "Subversive Sainthood and Tantric Fundamentalism: An Historical Study of Tibet's Holy Madmen." Diss. U of Virginia, 2011. Print.

Finn, Mark. "Tibetan Buddhism and a Mystical Psychoanalysis." *Psychoanalysis and Buddhism: An Unfolding Dialogue.* Ed. Jeremy D. Safran. Boston: Wisdom, 2003. 101-15. Print.

Foucault, Michel. "Nietzsche, Genealogy, History." *The Foucault Reader.* Ed. Paul Rabinow. New York: Pantheon, 1984. 76-100. Print.

Ginsberg, Allen. *Collected Poems: 1947-1997.* New York: HarperCollins, 2006. Print.

---. *Howl: Original Draft Facsimile.* Ed. Barry Miles. New York: HarperCollins, 1986. Print.

---. Notebooks and journals. Unpublished. Allen Ginsberg Papers, M0733. Department of Special Collections, Stanford University, Stanford, Ca. Print.

Ginsberg, Allen, and Gary Snyder. *The Selected Letters of Allen Ginsberg and Gary Snyder.* Ed. Bill Morgan. Berkeley: Counterpoint, 2009. Print.

Hunt, Erica. "Notes for an Oppositional Poetics." *The Politics of Poetic Form.* Ed. Charles Bernstein. New York: Roof, 1989. 197-212. Print.

Jamgön Kongtrul Lodrö Thayé. *The Teacher-Student Relationship. Translation of The Explanation of the Master and Student Relationship, How to Follow the Master, and How to Teach and Listen to the Dharma.* Trans. Ron Garry. Ithaca, New York: Snow Lion, 1999. Print.

Marin, Peter. "Spiritual Obedience: The Transcendental Game of Follow the Leader." *Harper's* (Feb. 1979): 43-58. Print.

Prebish, Charles S. *Luminous Passage: The Practice and Study of Buddhism in America.* Berkeley: U of California P, 1999. Print.

Reiterman, Tim, with John Jacobs. *Raven: The Untold Story of the Rev. Jim Jones and His People.* New York: Penguin, 2008. Rpt. Boston: E.P. Dutton, 1982. Print.

Rig'dzin Dorje, Nga-la. *Dangerous Friend: The Teacher-Student Relationship in Vajrayana Buddhism.* Boston: Shambhala, 2001. Print.

Sanders, Ed. "Investigative Poetics." *Talking Poetics from Naropa Institute: Annals of the Jack Kerouac School of Disembodied Poetics, Volume 2.* Ed. Anne Waldman and Marilyn Webb. Boulder: Shambhala, 1979. 364-78. Print.

---. ed. *The Party: A Chronological Perspective on a Confrontation at a Buddhist Seminary.* Woodstock, New York: Poetry, Crime, and Culture Press, 1977. Print.

Schumacher, Michael. *Dharma Lion: A Critical Biography of Allen Ginsberg.* New York: St. Martin's, 1992. Print.

Trigilio, Tony. *Allen Ginsberg's Buddhist Poetics*. Carbondale, Illinois: Southern Illinois UP, 2012. Print.

Waldman, Anne. Interview with John Whalen-Bridge. August 11, 2009. Naropa University. Print.

---. "Oppositional Poetics." *Kill or Cure.* New York: Penguin, 1994. 109. Print.

---. "'Premises of Consciousness': Notes on 'Howl.'" *Outrider: Poems, Essays, Interviews.* Albuquerque, New Mexico: La Alameda, 2006. 175-88. Print.

Whitman, Walt. *Leaves of Grass and Other Writings*. Norton Critical Edition. Ed. Michael Moon. New York: Norton, 2002. Print.

Trungpa, Naropa, and the Outrider Road: An Interview with Anne Waldman

John Whalen-Bridge

John Whalen-Bridge met with Anne Waldman in his office above the Allen Ginsberg Library on August 11, 2009, while he was visiting Naropa University, in Boulder, Colorado, as a Lenz Fellow. The campus was just beginning to settle after that year's Summer Writing Program, and Waldman agreed to meet with him to discuss Naropa's "Poetry Wars," the relationship between Buddhism and Poetics at Naropa, and the development of the Jack Kerouac School of Disembodied Poetics.[1] They began by discussing the somewhat Dionysian origins of the Jack Kerouac School before moving on to more recent developments. The interview was updated in November and December 2012.

John Whalen-Bridge: Let's begin with the Tibetan Buddhist teacher who started it all, Chögyam Trungpa. The documentary about his life *Crazy Wisdom* (2012) is making its way through the Buddhist film festival circuit, presenting the "bad boy of Buddhism" to a new generation.[2] The Naropa story begins with Trungpa. Did you ever have a problem with his "bad boy" behavior?

Anne Waldman: No. I come from a world of artists and writers, and my parents came out of a bohemian background as well, with alcohol fueling a lot of creativity. Trungpa Rinpoche was what we often called an "activity demon"—he accomplished much of great benefit to others in such a short lifespan. He left a profound legacy through his books and his students. I never felt angry, but I did feel bereft when he died. I also felt sympathetic, having known in my own world people infused with brilliance, suffering, creativity, addiction, and "crazy wisdom mind"—or whatever his particular gifts as a meditation teacher were.[3]

JWB: It isn't a great model, is it? Addiction?

AW: Sometimes it accompanies wisdom. I don't know if I can speak to whether he died of alcoholism. I've heard how things were at the end, almost theistic stories of his body staying in *samadhi*–in meditation posture–for many days. I don't know if that is possible for a normal addicted body. I just don't know.[4]

JWB: Were you around for the Naropa Poetry Wars?

AW: I was in Boulder, and I was affected by the aftermath. The incident took place at the three-month-long seminary held that year in 1975 at Snowmass, Colorado.[5] Neither Allen Ginsberg nor I were at the seminary. Had we been there, I think it would have gone differently. I think we would have intervened. In public situations that required intervention, Allen had a way. He was skillful, and he was very good at pacifying chaos. He was also very diplomatic and kept a level head in the middle of... a political demonstration an orgy or Halloween party! [laughs] I wish we had been there because there was unfortunate harm and misunderstanding that we might have helped circumvent. Yet it led to interesting conundrum, conversation, argument, and different ideological and cultural views: Rugged American Individualism up against ways of presenting Buddhist dharma and teachings and questions of how wisdom travels from the East. How does it crack American style, habitual patterns, and spiritual materialism? Could you be a Buddhist and an artist in the twentieth century? The Poetry Wars brought things to the point where you had to talk about them. We had to talk about what was Buddhism. I remember Ed Dorn and Tom Clark discussing Trungpa as the "yellow peril." But they were also interested in challenging Allen Ginsberg's authority and position as a major cultural figure. W.S. Merwin stayed with Buddhist practice. He stayed through the seminary, and then he decided and said as much: Trungpa wasn't the teacher for him.

JWB: People want to take a position. This is an interesting thing about Tom Clark's book. Ginsberg had to respond somehow. He was a spokesman. Gary Snyder refused to say something, not because he was a fan of Trungpa, but because didn't want to say anything that would hurt Allen. He was fiercely loyal. So I'm sure there are all kinds of things he would have liked to have said for *Shoes Outside the Door*.[6]

AW: There were a lot of versions of the story. It is really like a *Rashomon* tale. Ed Sanders' book *Investigative Poetics* (1976) actually investigated the situation more thoroughly than Tom Clark's *The Great Naropa Poetry Wars* (1980) did.

JWB: I haven't seen the Ed Sanders' book—copies keep disappearing from libraries![7] In retrospect, would you say the events were a blip on the screen, or did they have something to do with the evolution of Naropa?

AW: What interested me was the coming together of these two strands in my own life: the poetry and Buddhism. One could become a Buddhist and not have been involved with this whole situation. The "Wars" became huge. It got to the point that even when Allen and I traveled internationally, this incident would invariably come up as a question at the end of an event or reading during the Q and A. It was one of those knots that required a kind of "negative capability" and the ability to sit in the situation and see the discourse without being able to reason it out—no "irritable reaching after fact or reason."[8] It was difficult to take sides. I didn't defend Trungpa Rinpoche's behavior, however. Trungpa was also human, with human faults and obstacles.

JWB: Here at Naropa, the faculty members come from different Buddhist backgrounds. Some are from different schools of Zen, for example. But I get the sense that you are a Tibetan Buddhist practitioner in Trungpa's tradition. Is that right? Can you say a bit about particular Buddhist approaches at Naropa and which influences meant the most to you?[9]

AW: I was already leaning into Buddhism from an early age. And had encounters and teachings from Nyingma teachers. When I first went to India in the early seventies, I was fortunate to meet Kalu Rinpoche, Khyentse Rinpoche, and Dudjom Rinpoche.[10] All remarkable teachers. I felt a particular karmic connection to Chatral Rinpoche, with whom I first took refuge vows. He was more rugged and outside the tulku linage system.[11] His own teacher, Sera Khandro Kunzang Dekyong Wangmo (1892-1940), was a woman.[12] He gave me permission to continue on my own path of poetry and creating community and cultural activism. He encouraged me to stay on the path at Naropa, which was an experiment in community and contemplative education. It was still the early years. In 1973 I was supposed to go to the Vajradhatu Seminary.[13] When cheap tickets to India became available, I went on a pilgrimage with poets John Giorno and Michael Brownstein.[14] John was already focused on Buddhist dharma and was a student of Dudjom Rinpoche. So I chose the trip over the seminary, which is interesting. The trip opened up opportunities to meet these powerful teachers. Subsequently, of course, a lot of those teachers came to the U.S. of A. Visiting India is life changing, in any case.

When I was first at seminary with Trungpa Rinpoche, in 1980, I was resistant. I didn't take the final samaya vows. These are the "promises" that bind student and teacher together in Tantric Buddhism. I later took the Shambhala warrior vows, which are vows to one's own mind and community and an allegiance to various practices that benefit others, and to the lineage that keeps them alive. In one ceremony, you would kneel into the guru's crotch, a typical bowing ritual gesture in many traditions, and a humorous way of seeing a very simple ceremony involved with touching a calligraphy brush with ink to one's tongue. Ink—which is essentially mineral and earth-connected—is considered the blood of the warriors.[15] My connection to Trungpa as a teacher came largely through the Shambhala teachings. His vision of Naropa as encouraging and supporting the creation of a more enlightened society is essentially my practice. Naropa wasn't just another job; it felt like a spiritual project.

JWB: Did you feel like you had a 100 percent confidence in this man when push came to shove, or did you feel like you had *enough* confidence in this man?

AW: I had enough confidence. It was interesting to find where my part was in all this. I met Trungpa in 1970, and we founded the school in 1974 after I had been in India (1973) for the first time. I was interested in an alternative to straight academia, and toward the practices of more spiritual and utopian communities. Naropa mirrored a tribal situation: these different roles developing within an expanding culture. There were people working with accommodation and hospitality, artists and poets and educators finding where their energy could best be used; there was a task for everyone. I felt very comfortable with this. Allen and I were basically handed the poetics school to create, with input from Diane di Prima and others. We were given incredible permission. "The Academy of the future is opening its doors" is an apt line from John Ashbery. We had been seductively invited into the mix the summer of 1974 and then presented a view of an experiment in education that could go on beyond our lifetimes and might benefit people – especially younger people – in the future. Trungpa Rinpoche understood poetry as a path and calligraphy as a path – we read our poetry together. He told Allen not to be so angry! He came to America wondering, Where are the poets? Take me to the poets. No, I would find it hard to critique his path even if I didn't always "see" the methods clearly or appreciate his behavior.

JWB: Were you around when Joni Mitchell came through?

AW: Joni Mitchell came through Boulder in 1976 and was present at one of Trungpa's talks, as I recall, and then met with him privately, and we went out afterwards with a few friends to one of the clubs up on the hill. It was the time where there was a frisson and glamour about it all. She was genuinely interested, however, a very subtle mind, as I was later to experience on the Bob Dylan Rolling Thunder tour. Also generous. She gave me a dulcimer to accompany my poetry. Trungpa was magnetizing many creative persons.

JWB: She spoke in an interview about her experience at Naropa, and, of course, there is her song "Refuge of the Road" from the album *Hejira* (1976).[16] The song was quite popular—but people are surprised to hear that it was written about Trungpa. In the interview, she said that when she met with him, he did something magical involving forceful breathing—and for three days she had no sense of self. Her self-conscious nervousness dropped away, and she quit using cocaine.

AW: He could definitely shift the frequency with people. My first meeting with Trungpa was when he was quite inebriated, although completely lucid. I was going with a poet friend to pick him up at the airport in Vermont and then drive back to Tail of the Tiger in Barnet, his burgeoning dharma center in Vermont. He was mumbling about Casper the Friendly Ghost as a kind of *Sambhogakaya* manifestation because of these little holograms at Disneyland.[17] [laughs] But he was magnetizing.

There was a seminar on the writings of Milarepa for two weeks at Tail (later called Karmê Chöling), after which I went to visit the playwright, Sam Shepard.[18] After that I was supposed to go to Cuba on a trip organized by the Yippie activist Jerry Rubin and his wife. So I was stopping on the way with friends in Vermont. I had met Kunga Dawa (aka Richard Arthure) at an artist party in New York. Kunga Dawa was one of Trungpa's first Western students, and he spoke about Trungpa Rinpoche being in the U.S. I had already met the great Mongolian teacher Geshe Ngawang Wangyal when I was 18—I felt "zapped" when I met Geshe Wangyal.[19] I felt his mind, I looked into his face, and it was like a vast mirror. I was told before I walked into the room, I should not wear lipstick; Geshe must be approached in the proper way.

JWB: You were told not to wear lipstick, was it the "royal treatment?"

AW: I was told not by the monk but by one of the self-conscious Western male students. When I met Trungpa Rinpoche, he hit me, he slapped me in the chest, and said something like "You're too 'New York.'"

JWB: A Lin-chi moment? Like the Chinese Ch'an master who whacks students?[20]

AW: A Lin-chi moment. It did something in my head. Yes, I am "New York" identified – the speed and sharp edges and ambition to change the world—but I related this incident to something earlier he had said to me about New York—that it's a "holy city." At the time I was thinking I wanted to leave the city and move to the country. It was the seventies, and everyone was moving out of New York, getting out of the city and back to the land, "back to the garden."[21] But he told me to stick with New York. He said New York is the holy city, the charnel ground. And I did, and I continued to work on the Lower East Side. Within a few years, Naropa became a viable reality.

JWB: It always seemed to me that Trungpa had two tracks. The line in the Dhammapada would be: it's good in this world, it's good in the next, and whether or not there is a next, it's good in this world. So put that out of your head. It seemed like this world, okay Shambhala. If we say your life should have magic in it, it's Shambhala.

AW: In European countries, schools are church-based and run, particularly in Italy. Shambhala draws on certain kinds of models that are uncomfortable for people: the model of a court of enlightened Kings and Queens. But the view is to work in these times on an enlightened society, how to design governments by considering what is human; how to work in the world. Why does democracy have failings? How do we make sense of the clash between civilizations and worlds we are seeing?

JWB: For most people in the organization now, is the idea of Shambala a human invention or is it as Chogyam Trungpa said, "Looking in the mirror, I can see the kingdom"?

AW: Both are true. Shambala is dharma. If you try to be historically factual about Buddhism, particularly Buddhist Tantra, where those teachings are coming from and when do they appear, one must ask: is this the historical Buddha giving those teachings or do they come in from some other plane of existence?

JWB: What do you think about the word *progress*? If we talk about spiritual progress or literary progress, do you have a sort of a big picture for your own career, for example, your 25-year project?

AW: I guess that is when I've returned to certain texts and practices. For example, every time I do the *Werma* practice,[22] I feel like there is something more I get, something that clicks, why this is working or not working. It's still always a struggle. I'm not so good at visualization. *Werma* is a Shambala practice: the Roar of the *Werma*. I'm probably not even supposed to talk about these things, but I'm not divulging anything. These particular practices are like poems: they are liturgy, litanies, text that you recite, mantra, visualization.

JWB: I am reading a lot of science and Buddhism books, and there is a fast and loose solution that is sort of the party line. It's a relaxed sense of science that says: if you can't prove that it's not true, we are not going to give it up. That is not what science is. His Holiness the Dalai Lama is very careful about that in *The Universe in a Single Atom*. He says there are three possible relations, and he is not claiming that Buddhism is scientific, but some people are. I think it is one thing to want to move scientific inquiry into the area of contemporary practices but another thing to deny that you have to make a leap from scientific rationalism to something else.

AW: Do you believe in magic?

JWB: I believe my personal experience, but my personal experience is limited.

AW: I have had prophetic dreams. I had a dream about time being a spiral—not linear or narrative. Certain kinds of dreams seem more like visitations and come at a particular time. I talked to Chogyam Trungpa about a couple of them. A kind of Yeshe Tsogyal figure was appearing to me and instructing me, showing me the map of the night sky which became a kind of fabric, an image I subsequently employed in the long *Iovis* work and in an another investigative project of my own. In another dream, she came in the guise of a tortilla lady with an oven.

JWB: You know it was Yeshe Tsogyal?

AW: I felt this connection. My root teacher Chatral Rinpoche had a connection to Sera Khandro. There is lineage connection to female teachers through Chatral Rinpoche. I discussed with Chogyam Trungpa this notion of feeling some connection. He said it was very likely that this is some kind of auspicious dream, not just an ordinary dream. Not that any dreams are ordinary.

In the Buddhist tradition, you do Kalachhakra practice with dreams that come at dawn. You are instructed as part of the Bardo practices to pay attention to your dreams, to use dreams, to enter into them and have conversations with the figures that appear. For me it's a poetic realm. My Manatee/Humanity project had some of that *terma* quality—I am always interested in the description of what *terma* is and what a *terton* is—*Terma* can be a ripple on the water or some cloud formation, the way a tree moves or the way the crux of the tree looks. The elements of phenomenality and our perception of them trigger a *Sadhana*. It's all very illusory: the light of that particular day, what the weather is, the color of the light. All these things play together to present an image of phenomena.

JWB: Inspiration is one thing. But the idea that a certain presence exists in the way that someone exists down the hall, that's another idea. But your feeling wasn't just that you were reading books about this person and wanted to write a great work of poetry to include one of your eighteen ideas.

AW: I felt guided by the consciousness of some kind of a non-human elemental —I'm interested in this—what are the microbes talking about? There is so much going on simultaneously in all ten directions of spaces. Buddhist cosmology is a mind state for me. I'm not going to worry about whether Mt. Meru is in reality the center of my world. But in certain kinds of practices and certain mandalas, I can feel that center in my own consciousness.

JWB: For me, there has been sort of an ongoing civil war for decades that is a real hindrance. It sounds like you had a relationship with a teacher who was happy to allow you to come to terms with things so that it didn't become a problem. You mentioned several teachers: Chatral Rinpoche and Trungpa Rinpoche. Within Tibetan Buddhism you have the guru model. You have guru yoga and *50 Verses of Guru Devotion*, which is a kind of voluntary enslavement. Now His Holiness the Dalai Lama has come along and said on the front page of *Snow Lion* that people are going a bit too far with this. But I'm in a community of practitioners where devotion becomes related to fund-raising, which brings up some suspicion for me. We've talked about people who were very suspicious about Shambahala. This is institutional religion whether it's the Catholic Church or this or that. The ideology and the service of the institution and the spiritual technology in the service of enlightening the individual can sometimes seem to be in conflict.

AW: This is really the rub. For this female body with somewhat feminist views, it's a constant challenge: institutionalization, patriarchy, the role of primarily male teachers, nuns having to sit below the monks. While Tantric Tibetan Buddhism does not allow for reinvention, there is room for a certain kind of spontaneity. Certainly some of these practices, which came *terma*-like out of Chogyam Trungpa's mind, are more like poetry. It interests me that these things can come about in our world time. We're not just reifying the Qur'an, so to speak.

JWB: Each year, Naropa hosts a Summer Writing Program. If we look at the programs for the last few years, what would you say have been the emerging trends? Is "contemplative poetics" a developing area of interest, or are there emerging trends that will in the future define Naropa to a similar degree?

AW: The program continues to honor its experimental and postmodern lineages in the New American Poetry, which includes Black Mountain, the Beats, The New York School, and Black Arts, and there are also classes in [William] Blake, James Joyce, and Gertrude Stein. We didn't develop out of an English Department; consequently there is much more freedom. We've given up "tracks" and embrace the hybrid as a more interesting model. Emphasis on feminism, on writing as a healing art (somatic poetics) grounded in the body. There's greater ecological emphasis. A focus on symbiosis. And so on.

We have developed a new cohort model for study. And continue to support activism in cultural projects in the community. Working in schools, prisons, with the elderly. There will be a Warrior's Exam, modeled on the Buddhist method of having students display their knowledge in a public setting for the writing students. There is a new team of younger writers guiding much of this, supported by the core faculty, which is exciting.

JWB: During the 2009 Summer Writing Program, I participated in a panel on "Poethics," and there was some discussion among panelists about the politically activist movement within Buddhism known as "Engaged Buddhism."[23] Maybe we could talk about the how political activism gets discussed in the writing program and on the Naropa campus. I like to use the phrase "Engaged Aesthetics," which contains the notion that literary art is responsible both to society and its problems and to the demands of literary art. Does this phrase describe what you mean by "poethics"?

AW: I would say so to some extent. But I would refer you to Joan Retallack's *The Poethical Wager* (2003), which describes an aesthetics of complexity that leaves things to chance, and yet advocates taking responsibility for what happens. The mind of an artist or thinker or writer is attuned to the circumstances of our world and culture. There are different skillful means or actions required in one's work. For many years one of the strongest inspirations for working at Naropa has been the idea of working in community and the view of poetry by necessity coming into public space. This inculcates almost a dharmic view of the power of language, speech, and thinking and that it's important to be synchronized beings in our world and in our cultures as we are more connected and have more information about what exists in other realities. Other universes even, the 3-brane world[24] but ultimately a vow of sanity to not pollute our world further. To help "wake the world up to itself" through the arts, through poetry.

For many artists, the practice of art is a very lonely path and, just as in spiritual practice, you need retreat time and time away, time to really look at your mind and figure out how many directions you are going in and make decisions about how the work needs to take shape in the world, but there's also coming into community. I find that each project I do is very different, and yet I have a consistent tone of urgency that is always with me. In my current project, *The Iovis Trilogy: Colors in the Mechanism of Concealment*, on which I have been working for over 25 years and am trying now to bring to closure [published by Coffee House Press in 2011] there has been a consistent consciousness or authority of the poem over this long time period. I look at early sections written in the eighties and more current "cantos" written in 2009. There is a shifting reality—considering the terms of engagement in light of our shifting planet dynamics—the wars, the genocide, the climate change, the new weapons and technologies—yet a consistent aspiration toward the light in a "still wild place," which is the imagination. I think of this project as exemplifying a distinct poethics.

JWB: What's the difference between Engaged Buddhism and, say, the psychological engagement of Henry James' "Live all you can"?

AW: Engaged Buddhism requires that you benefit others. When I read Henry James I feel tremendously benefited by his sentences, his grammar, and his astute psychology, although some of the issues he writes about, for example sexual issues and subtle issues around relationship and caste and wealth or lack of it in the privileged world of the Boston Brahmins, feel dated. "Live all you can" was limited for females as he describes time after time – look at his complex heroines.

From a literary perspective, it seems that much poetics activity has had to take refuge within the academy. Many radical inventive writers are in tenure-track positions, now, a far cry from the lives of the Beats. The academy is a wonderful place for certain kinds of discourse and conversation that might not be supported by the mainstream culture. But this new experimental culture within the academy raises questions about privilege. Naropa is a different kind of beast. The economics are a constant struggle. There is no cushion; you are more exposed, less protected. So people are required to participate in ways that go beyond "career" and so-called comfort zones. And we are constantly inventing ourselves here.

JWB: Would you say that political engagement and contemplative aesthetics (and experimental writing) are waiting out a problem within the universities?

AW: Right, exactly. So I am back to this relative world about engagement and where it takes place and occurs. It's so important that our audio and video literary archive survive. It is an oral treasure. Chögyam Trungpa Rinpoche talked about some sort of archive that will need to be out of America: for all the wisdom traditions, all the spiritual traditions. When the dark ages truly arrive with even more decimating "New Weathers," as I call them, and ideological struggle, our gnosis will need sanctuary. Many political spokespeople who make decisions on the future of this planet don't accept evolution. They don't acknowledge that the earth is four-and-a-half billion years old.

JWB: What are some of your most overtly political forms of poetic composition?

AW: The *Iovis* project takes on war and investigates patriarchy. In Book III, I've included writing I did in the middle of protests held during the [George W.] Bush administration, especially during the inauguration events in Washington, D.C. and later on the streets of New York City during the Republican Party convention at Madison Square Garden before his dreadful second term. I was out on Seventh Avenue and at Union Square, down at the piers, and people were getting bashed on the head and rounded up by police. I was catching moments of samsara as they flew by. That seems as relevant to me as some moment or phrase that's looking at putting my head in the yoke at a Hindu shrine in Calcutta where animal sacrifice

Robert Duncan, Anne Waldman, unknown male, and Chögyam Trungpa Rinpoche —— June 1976, Boulder, Colorado. Photo c. Allen Ginsberg Estate.

Vidyadhara Chogyam Trungpa Rinpoche drove down from his favorite view on Bald Mountain for Rendez-vous with me in Boulder. He'd been ill, rumor'd to 've been "visiting the Dakinis" "Where?" I asked. "Right there," pointing to the window sill above the sofa. "What do they say?" I continued. He replied that sometimes they criticized him for teaching Vajragens too openly, sometimes told him to teach even more. That day he was uniformed as ideal Shambhala society, April 12, '85." —Photo with annotation by Allen Ginsberg, © Allen Ginsberg Estate.

takes place. Thinking about Mohenjo-Daro or the cult of cattle, you see on the coins images of cattle, with wooden yokes, and you see this same yoke in a contemporary Hindu temple. Then you see the dharmic yoke coming up in the water in the old Buddhist adage of the rarity of a human coming into that yoke, and then you see the yoke on the streets of New York when people are being handcuffed and tied up. In particular, there was a moment when the police cast out orange nets and "yoked" the demonstrators to haul them in. Those kinds of fascinating luminous details travel through lifetimes in the mind.

"In the mind of the poet all moments are contemporaneous" is a paraphrase of Pound. The point is that these things travel. Things are symbols of themselves; you know where you are, but at the same time the imagination is carrying these images that arrive from way back and become part of the fabric of the text. So I am talking about text in space, text in public space, text in performative space, text in historical, archeological space. And text from dream space. Many parts of *the Iovis Trilogy* are performative, as an epic by definition is. I want the feeling of being active and out walking around like Apollinaire or Frank O'Hara, in addition to the alchemical scriptorium. Every encounter is some kind of dharma gate opening.

JWB: In addition to making poems, you make poets. Naropa's Jack Kerouac School of Disembodied Poetics is one of three or four places that stands out in the country as a poetics factory.

AW: Factory? [laughter] Poetry is not such a good "product" so to speak! What is its value?

JWB: You hesitate over *factory* and words like *institution*, but it seems to me that part of the maturation of American Buddhism is recognizing that "beginning mind" is not enough. Perhaps that is a heresy, but when we think about making things work over time, one has to have some kind of institutionalization.

AW: I always invoke the "temporarily autonomous zone" or TAZ from Hakim Bey, where one is less invested in the institutionalization of creativity than in the liberation of utopian potentials.[25] Something important has already occurred here. We have had an amazing meeting of minds, an experience of *tendrel*—auspicious coincidence—of things coming together as they did with the founding of Naropa, the Kerouac School, and all the other things –ideas, people, talent – that began that first summer in 1974. This has been enough to spur inspiration and activity in others, and around the world. It was an historic cultural intervention. It wasn't until the winter of 1976 when the year-round school began that I felt more seriously lured out here and curious enough to see what this at least 100-year project would be, and I did want it to continue. In the summer of 1974 there had been the meeting with John Cage, Diane di Prima, Allen Ginsberg, and myself, where Trungpa Rinpoche famously proposed we consider a poetics school within this experiment of Naropa. That was my assignment and it continues to this day. But I have no illusions about how it might falter and struggle and needs committed careful intelligence and an open heart. It needs protection from very different kinds of agendas.

So I returned to Boulder in 1976 to roll up my sleeves. Already classes were happening: small gatherings in cold rooms at what is now the Shambhala Center on Spruce Street. I was inspired by the Black Mountain experiment, which I heard about through the histories and accounts and writings of John Cage, the art of Robert Rauschenberg, the performance of Merce Cunningham, and through the poetry of Charles Olson and Robert Creeley. Black Mountain College was a school for people coming back from the war on the GI Bill and one of the first colleges in that part of country to admit black students, but it was also seen as a radical weird experiment, much like Naropa.

I had also attended the Berkeley Poetry Conference in 1965, and that was certainly an inspiration.[26] The vision of a poetic *sangha*, which is Sankrit for spiritual community. And I also had the years at The Poetry Project at St. Mark's Church in-the-Bowery, which I had helped found in 1966, sponsored originally by a grant from the Office of Economic Opportunity under President Lyndon Johnson. The purpose was to work with "alienated youth" on the Lower East Side of Manhattan. The message, as with the instance of Black Mountain and its paucity of women faculty, was to include more women, inspire more diversity.

Iowa had the singular creative writing program at that time. When I started to think about a year-round degree-granting program, I was very curious about their structure. We were not accredited until 1985, which was quite a journey. I was also thinking about the Bohemian model and the School of the Night, a group of sixteenth-century Englishmen—poets and scientists—that included Christopher Marlowe and George Chapman, and which may have formed a kind of literary underground. So, yes, seeing what communities of poets that would gather, discourse and exchange; younger writers sitting at the feet of older writers, the apprentice model, which still goes on in Europe to some extent. Paris, Prague, Viennese cafés. It is only recently that there are thoughts of creative writing programs abroad. You would have arts schools, but as a poet, you would seek out an elder and meet in a café. So, this was some of the thinking that we began this project with, how to maintain some of that early spontaneous spirit, of meeting mind to mind with another artist—an elder—historically and otherwise. Both Allen and I were wary of institutionalization and certain kinds of deadlines and requirements, and selling the program, the kind of language used in advertising and also the consideration of how to evaluate creative students. For a while we had commentary for students and that had to be translated into grades. Allen was always very late with his grades. In fact, I think once it took him a year to hand them in.

I've watched the school change over the years. Streamlined, more standardization. A hierarchy of decision-making I don't always agree with. Top-down authority. Even if it never achieves Ivy League status, however, there is still more need now for a place such as this in a world that has grown darker in myriad ways. It is important to be able to work firstly with the mind, to still the mind, to synchronize it. To break through habitual obsessive patterns. To act with care, kindness, and compassion. But with intellect and discriminating awareness. To respect others. To stay curious and investigative. And to be innovative, inventive with language, and to honor our predecessors who struggled with form, with genre, with imagination, with a world gone mad with war.

JWB: Can you say a bit more about what the present need is, and how you think Naropa can fill it? How are things going?

AW: The present need is largely economic, as ever, but things are going well with the new re-organization. The five schools of Naropa of which the Kerouac School is one are more empowered in the overall structure.[27] And there are now some fellowships for students and new faculty hires. More online publications and the like. The summer programs have been gathering 200 students regularly and the sense of mutual support is inspiring. The level of discourse is extremely high as well. I am feeling optimistic about the future and better benefitting our core students. We still need more support for the preservation of the archive. I'm co-editing an anthology on "cultural rhizomes" at Naropa. We have a brilliant CD of readings and performances (*Harry's House*, Fast Speaking Music 2012) recorded in our little recording studio where the music anthologist and filmmaker Harry Smith lived. Michelle Naka-Pierce, who is an accomplished graduate of the Kerouac School, is the new director of the core program, while I continue to be the artistic director of the Summer Writing Program.

JWB: But these are issues of creating an institution out of a bunch of people who chose a way of life because they do not want to put up with peoples' rules.

AW: Yes, and being part of this larger university, we realize we are not the only culture. But we have always been seen as somewhat of a subculture with our strange name—and that comes up for argument every few years: why can't we get rid of this "Jack Kerouac School of Disembodied Poetics" since it's outlived is use, it's no longer relevant. I went back to Chogyam Trungpa's comment when this came up years and years ago, that it's bad luck to change the name of a horse in midstream. I also think the name is broad and interesting and magnetizes in the world. It magnetizes, and it's a bit of a conundrum: what does disembodied mean, why would you select this name.

JWB: I met Allen Ginsberg in 1986 the morning after he first lectured in Gary Snyder's writers series at U.C. Davis. He said, "Do you know why we named it the Jack Kerouac School? It was a joke 'cause he was *dead*, it was a *joke*!"

AW: That's surprising. But I think he was referring to the "disembodied" that always provokes query. I also think he was trying to inoculate me against academic humorlessness while I was still a babe. It was a compassionate jab. There was that playful sense of the name, but it's not just a joke. Using Kerouac's name, in fact, was not a joke at all. He was a writer who was a magnetizing presence and influence on Allen, the quintessential American mongrel/hybrid: an immigrant football hero, a reader, thinker, and an original kind of mind from outside the academic mainstream, a traveler to fellaheen worlds who examined with meditative attention the grammar of his own thinking and mind and tried to catch it. Who was pierced by samsara, the sense of impermanence, and realized the first Buddhist noble truth of suffering. He had warrior qualities, but the tragedy of his life, which is common in our culture and world, evokes incredible sympathy and empathy.

I threw in the word *disembodied* because we didn't have a site, a desk, a building, stationery, a telephone, finances, or the usual accoutrements to be a school. But we did have a vision and a view, and a community and our own experience to draw on.

We want to have desks and buildings, but at the same time we don't want to over- reify this identity of "poet" or say this is the career track that we have here and this is what you have to do to get somewhere. In addition to a serious commitment to writing and scholarship, the training is about being a human being in artistic community, with attention to the larger world as well. Treading with respect and wanting to be helpful to the world.

JWB: This points to the momentary god of the disembodied transcendent phase rather than institution, buildings, constitution, by-laws, endowment…

AW: Yes, but of course what we do is embodied. It takes a body to make this writing, to sing our songs, to be effective in the world with our hands, our limbs, our minds and imaginations. It's this negative capability of the view that always interests me; now you see it, now you don't. Don't get attached to ideas about things; deconstruct notions moment to moment. We don't reify this identity of "poet" or say this is the career track that we have here and this is what you have to do to get somewhere. I think this is often a source of frustration and argument: why aren't we bringing in more people who talk about how to publish? Why don't we bring in agents?

JWB: One of your books is entitled *Outrider* (2006). Does the school teach an outrider ethos, and, if so, what does that mean?

AW: It means trusting one's own imagination and creative impulse, strengthening one's own mind, being open to new forms of experiment and poetics and not being susceptible to pre-existent power structures or patriarchal master-narratives. In a way, at best, it is a non-compromised vision. Women artists have had to struggle hard for a place at the table, so to speak; thus some of my thinking on this comes from the sense of finding the appropriate space for a new "body poetics." It also implies not falling into cliques or factions or wasting time with envy and malice. The outrider ethos includes others – and the writing of *other* places and cultures—it means not limiting yourself to just what's fashionable. And breaking new ground. There's a protective notion here as well. So invoking that sense of alternative possibilities from more conservative poetry tropes as well, and also the "both both" of "negative capability" which opens the mind to surprise, spontaneity, long years of investigation, cultural activism and intervention, and a refreshed language. Outriders rode along on the edges of the herd—not totally outside it.

JWB: So for your outrider folk, what's unprofessional, and what are you telling your students not to do?

AW: Competition is a problem in the professional careerist world. I think you've maybe picked it up being here at Naropa that it's a fairly noncompetitive environment. There is a lot of mutual support and collaboration which is stressed over individuals finding their own ways. So that's another quality of the outrider: they are like-minded. There are ways to work in the world that will benefit one another, the work, the reception of the work. You can create these communities for support. You start there rather than the model of lone person who endlessly sends poems to the *New Yorker*, not in communication with a close writer friend who can look at their work. Of course the writing program provides that, you do have community, you do have conversations about what you love and what you love to do, that's important. I think that is part of the Ethopoetics.

There is also a sense of diversity within the community. I'm constantly encouraging students to look into other languages and cultures and get out of the American culture's careerist mode as writer and to be aware there are choices on this path and these choices are self-empowering. The gift culture is also important, the sense of each exchange as artistic exchange rather than monetary.

JWB: What would you like to see Buddhism in America do?

AW: That's a big question because I don't know all the different ways it's come in. The primary streams in my world are Zen and Tibetan. I guess the important thing is to wake people up. I could see cadres of meditators working in mediation, for example, a whole branch of the UN devoted to a peacemaking practice . . . I've had recurring dreams that are very Armageddon-like. We are living underground and can't practice except in secret. The texts, the implements—whether it's damarus or vajras—cannot be displayed or we could be arrested. I remember once having my bag opened at the airport when I had a Vajra and bell in my purse and I had to explain what they were. This was before 9/11.

We also need to pay attention to our speech, how we speak to one another. Trungpa Rinpoche instituted the practice of elocution. Sometimes we would be roused out the bed at 2 in the morning and have to go through these exercises: "I feel sorry for the Queen of England." I can hear Trungpa's voice saying, "No, no, no! I feel *sorry, sorry, sorry…*" over and over. This was at seminary in 1980. I was pregnant. Can you imagine what someone might think if they were to look at what

we are doing at this Buddhist seminary in the middle of the night working with Oxonian English: "Cathy's hair is black. Her complexion – no! no! *complexion, complexion...*" [laughter] Trungpa's view was that speech and discourse would get so degraded that part of our job would be to speak well. That's an odd teaching.
JWB: Do you think *50 Stanzas of Guru Devotion* is bad advice for Americans?
AW: That is such a big question. I can barely practice this myself. Part of my job is to always see the other side, so dealing with the patriarchy in Buddhism is a phenomenal investigation or exploration or teaching. It is very hard for me to get solid. Buddhism might have to change, as the Dalai Lama has said, around issues of authority, gender, science even. I will come into situations and feel that something is wrong and this is not the real deal so I also trust my intuition as well. So there is that kind of barometer. And a healthy skepticism. And one needs always to separate out the enlightened qualities from the neurosis. Many of *Vinaya* rules were culturally driven and culture has shifted. It will be interesting to see how emerging women teachers will influence the tradition.
JWB: Thank you so much.

Notes

[1] The phrase "poetry wars" comes from Tom Clark's *The Great Naropa Poetry Wars*, his expose about the events at a 1975 Halloween party. Eliot Weinberg's take-no-prisoners report, "News from Naropa," was published in *Works on Paper: 1980-86*, 27-41.

[2] The film *Crazy Wisdom* presents Trungpa as a controversial teacher of Buddhism, but if anything the film downplays the degree to which his methods challenged conventional notions of how a Buddhist teacher should behave. Trungpa Rinpoche (1939-1987), sometimes called "the Vidyadhara" by his students, was one of the early teachers of Tibetan Buddhism in the west, known especially for his methods of presenting Buddhism to countercultural Americans. William Burroughs once referred to him as "the whiskey lama" because of his heavy drinking, and he made no secret of his womanizing. He cultivated relationships with writers, especially Allen Ginsberg and Anne Waldman, but he was heavily criticized by some. Kenneth Rexroth claimed that Trungpa was the worst thing to happen to American Buddhism (Weinberger 38).

He had a flair for the English language beyond that of any other Tibetan teacher, and he captivated countercultural students with what might be called his Dionysian Buddhist pedagogy: a willingness to test conventional boundaries—as if waging a Dadaist revolution—in order to subvert the bonds of ego. Much of the writing about Trungpa comes from students and tends towards hagiography. However, the best account of his life is *Dragon Thunder: My Life with Chögyam Trungpa* by Diana J. Mukpo (Trungpa's ex-wife) and Carolyn Rose Gimian.

[3] The iconoclastic "crazy wisdom" tradition has a venerable history within Tibetan Buddhism. See Georg Feurstein: "The crazy wisdom message and method are understandably offensive to both the secular and the conventional religious establishments. Hence crazy adepts have generally been suppressed. This was not the case in traditional Tibet and India, where the 'holy fool' or 'saintly madman' has long been recognized as a legitimate figure in the compass of spiritual aspiration and realization. In India, the avadhuta is one who, in his God-intoxication, has 'cast off' all concerns and conventional standards" (105).

[4] Waldman refers here to the Tibetan practice of *thukdam* (Wyl. thugs dam), the form of bardo meditation in which a great master, having experienced medical death, keeps the kernel of consciousness within the body for a period of time, during which *rigor mortis* and putrefaction do not occur. For a close description of an accomplished lama's *thukdam*, see the following account: *A brief account of the passing of Kyabje Tenga Rinpoche from Benchen Monastery Community*. Web. 21 Dec. 2012.

[5] The first "Vajradhatu Seminary," an intensive 12-week course of meditation and textual study, was held in 1973. Trungpa presided over each seminary from 1973 through 1986, except for 1977. Trungpa died in 1986.

[6] *Shoes Outside the Door*, written by Michael Dowling, is a history of the San Francisco Zen Center and Zen in the United States.

[7] A writer in the Jack Kerouac School told me that the book kept disappearing from the Allen Ginsberg Library at Naropa. The writer volunteered a photocopy to replace the missing volume—several times. In October 2009, I attempted to look at a copy again, this time traveling to the Library of Congress. The embarrassed librarian reported that the copy was missing.

[8] Ginsberg often cited Keats' notion of "negative capability," a state of mind in which one could hold "opposite, contradictory thoughts…without an irritable reaching after fact and reason" (Raskin 142).

[9] Tibetan Buddhism (also called Vajrayana or Tantric Buddhism or Northern Buddhism or Esoteric Buddhism) is a form of Mahayana Buddhism that developed in India but then moved to Tibet and other Himalayan countries, where it flourished long after Buddhism's decline in India. There are four primary lineages in Tibetan Buddhism: the Nyingma, Sakya, Kagyu, and Gelug sects. Trungpa was primarily associated with the Karma Kagyu sect.

[10] Nyingma is one of the four primary lineages of Tibetan Buddhism. "Rinpoche" is an honorific title that means precious gem, and it is given to those who are considered highly realized practitioners, as well as to abbots of monasteries. Kalu Rinpoche (1905-1989), Dilgo Khyentse Rinpoche (1910-1991), Dudjom Rinpoche

(1904-1987) were luminaries of Tibetan Buddhism who had to flee Tibet in the wake of the mid-twentieth century Chinese invasion. They were each extremely important in transplanting Tibetan Buddhist teachings in Western countries. The reclusive Chatral Rinpoche was born in 1913 and is regarded as one of the highest living masters of Dzogchen meditation. These teachers, and Chatral Rinpoche, are all luminaries of Tibetan Buddhism who left India for Tibet.

[11] A tulku is a recognized reincarnation of a previous Buddhist master. A tulku is believed to be the repository of highly developed spiritual powers, is given special privileges, and may even inherit property from a previous incarnation. The tulku selection process—a kind of test to see if the child can identify possessions from the previous life, is represented in the Martin Scorsese film *Kundun* (1997).

[12] She was reputedly a "treasure revealer" and a *dakini*. Treasure revealers discover sacred items and teachings that are akin to spiritual time-capsules—teachings given by an eminent person but for which the world is not yet ready. A *dakini* is a female angel. See Jacoby. For a biography of Sera Khandro Kunzang Dekyong Wangmo (Web. 21 Dec 2012). Also see Jacoby.

[13] The 1973 Vajradhatu Seminary was held at Jackson Hole, Wyoming, November-December 1973, led by Trungpa.

[14] The pilgrimage was organized by American Hindu students, with the tickets provided by Dharma Deppo, a guru Neem Karoli Baba (d. 1973). Neem Karoli Baba, a Hindu guru devoted to the monkey-god Hanuman and who had many American students, was also the teacher of frequent Naropa visitor Ram Dass (Richard Alpert, born 1931), author of the 1971 spiritual best-seller *Be Here Now*. Alpert was also a psychology department colleague of Timothy Leary at Harvard during the period of the LSD experiments. Alpert left Harvard to pursue other interests.

[15] Trungpa developed a set of teachings, connected with the mythical Shambhala kingdom, that are not strictly Buddhist, although they involve meditational practices and a strong sense of engagement with the social world. See Trungpa's *Shambhala: The Sacred Path of the Warrior*. The current website for Shambhala training centers lists about 200 worldwide: http://www.shambhala.org/centers/.

[16] The opening lines to "Refuge of the Road" are "I met a friend of spirit / He drank and womanized / And I sat before his sanity / I was holding back from crying / He saw my complications / And he mirrored me back simplified" (http://jonimitchell.com/music/song.cfm?id=7).

In the 2006 interview for *Reader's Digest* with Mary Aikins, Mitchell said, "[Trungpa] was the bad boy of Zen. I wrote a song about a visit I made to him called 'Refuge of the Road.' I consider him one of my great teachers, even though I saw him only three times. Once I had a fifteen-minute audience with him in which we argued. He told me to quit analyzing. I told him I couldn't—I'm an artist, you know. Then he induced into me a temporary state where the concept of 'I' was absent, which lasted for three days. [Later], at the very end of Trungpa's life I went to visit him. I wanted to thank him. He was not well. He was green and his eyes had no spirit in them at all, which sort of stunned me, because the previous times I'd seen him he was quite merry and puckish—you know, saying 'shit' a lot. I leaned over and looked into his eyes, and I said, 'How is it in there? What do you see in there?' And this voice came, like, out of a void, and it said, 'Nothing.' So, I went over and whispered in his ear, 'I just came to tell you that when I left you that time, I had three whole days without self consciousness, and I wanted to thank you for the experience.' And he looked up at me, and all the light came back into his face and he goes, 'Really?' And then he sank back into this black void again." [Aikins 134-35]

[17] According to the Trikaya (three body) theory of Mahayana Buddhism, the Trikaya Sambhokakaya (or, "enjoyment body") form of Buddha-manifestation is available to higher-level practitioners in states of visionary experience, whereas the historical Gautama Buddha would have been a Nirmanakaya manifestation. The third body is the Dharmakaya, which refers to enlightenment as such, which is free of conceptual limits or boundaries.

[18] Milarepa (c. 1052-1135 CE) was a great poet/yogi from Tibet. Early in life, at the insistence of his enraged mother, he learned magic in order to kill the uncle who had cheated them of their fortune. Regretting this evil act, he studied with the teacher Marpa, who made him build, tear down, and rebuild a stone house four times in order to purify his karma.

[19] Having come to the United States from India in 1955, Geshe Ngawang Wangyal (1901?-1983) may be considered the pioneer of Tibetan Buddhism in North America. The title "geshe" designates high-level monastic training at least as arduous as the attainment of a doctorate. Wangyal was of Kalmyk origin and had the further distinction of having to flee *two* communist regimes. He left Russia during its civil war, and then he fled India after the Chinese invaded and stepped up their occupation through the 1950s. In 1958 he established a monastery in Washington, New Jersey, and in the 1960s and 1970s he taught at Columbia University. His students in the United States, including Robert Thurman and Jeffrey Hopkins, have been among the most influential scholars of Tibetan Buddhism.

[20] Lin-Chi (d. 866 CE) is the Chinese teacher who is considered the founder of Rinzai Zen Buddhism. See *"The Zen Teachings of Master Lin-Chi."*

[21] The phrase "back to the garden" is from Joni Mitchell's song "Woodstock."

[22] The Werma Sadhana is a sadhana meditation practice unique to Shambhala lineage. It is based upon a Shambhala terma received by Chogyam Trungpa Rinpoche at Casa Werma in Mexico in 1980.

[23] The term "Engaged Buddhism" was first been popularized by Thich Nhat Hanh, a Vietnamese Zen Buddhist monk and spiritual leader, in his book *Vietnam: Lotus in a Sea of Fire* during the period of the Vietnam War (1959-1975). He used it to describe the interpretation of Buddhism as a path of mindful social action and reconfigured the idea of "enlightenment" in ways that were clearly social and even political. His interpretation can partly be understood as a modernist attempt to reverse the image of Buddhism's historical "quietism" and passiveness toward public life.

[24] Some string theorists believe that reality consists of multiple dimensions (as many as 9 or 11). The word *brane* is short for *membrane*, and the 3-brane world is a reference to our universe, which we perceive as having only three dimensions because the other "stringy" dimensions are curled up—six dimensions curled up within every point of space as we know it.

[25] Hakim Bey is the pseudonym of Peter Lamborn Wilson (b. 1945), an anarchist writer who developed the concept of "temporary autonomous zones." These are highly charged communal environments that not undergirded by authoritarian control structures because they do not last more than a few years, i.e., they are "temporary."

[26] This event, organized by Thomas Parkinson (professor of English at U.C. Berkeley), Donald M. Allen, Robert Duncan, and Richard Baker was held from July 12–24, 1965. The participating poets were Robin Blaser, Robert Creeley, Robert Duncan, Allen Ginsberg, Joanne Kyger, Ron Loewinsohn, Lenore Kandel, Charles Olson, Gary Snyder, Jack Spicer, George Stanley, Lew Welch, and John Wieners. Terence Diggory, eds. "Berkeley Poetry Conference" in *Encyclopedia of the New York School Poets*. NewYork: Facts on File, 2009. 47-49. Print,

[27] The other four schools are the Graduate School of Psychology, School of the Arts, School of Humanities and Interdisciplinary Studies, and School of Natural and Social Sciences.

Works Cited

Aikins, Mary. "Heart of a Prairie Girl." Interview with Joni Mitchell. *Reader's Digest*. Canadian Ed. April 3, 2006. 126-154. Print.

Ashvaghosha, *Fifty Verses on Guru Devotion*. With commentary by Geshe Ngawang Dhargey. Web. 21 Aug. 2012.

Clark, Tom. *The Great Naropa Poetry Wars*. Tiburon Belvedere, California: Cadmus, 1981. Print.

Crazy Wisdom The Life & Times of Chogyam Trungpa. Dir. and Prod. Lisa Leeman. Alive Mind Cinema,a division of Kino Lorber Films, 2012. DVD.

Dass, Ram. *Be Here Now*. San Cristobal, N.M.: Lama Foundation; New York: distributed by Crown, 1971. Print.

Dowling, Michael. *Shoes Outside the Door: Desire, Devotion, and Excess at San Francisco Zen Center.* Berkeley, California: Counterpoint, 2002. Print.

Feuerstein, Georg. *Holy Madness: The Shock Tactics and Radical Teachings of Crazy-Wise Adepts, Holy Fools, and Rascal Gurus*. New York: Paragon, 1991. Print.

Jacoby, Sarah. "To be or not to be Celibate: Morality and Consort Practices According to the Treasure Revealer Sera Khandro's (1892-1940) Auto/biographical Writings" in Sarah Jacoby and Antonio Terrone (eds). *Buddhism Beyond the Monastery: Tantric Practices and Their Performers in Modern Tibet*. Leiden: Brill, 2009. Print.

Lin-chi. *The Zen Teachings of Master Lin-Chi*, translated by Burton Watson (with new preface), New York: Columbia UP, 1999. Print.

Mukpo, Diana J. and Carolyn Rose Gimian. *Dragon Thunder: My Life with Chögyam Trungpa*. Boston: Shambhala, 2006. Print.

Myers, D. G. *The Elephants Teach: Creative Writing since 1880*. Chicago: U of Chicago P, 2006. Print.

Nhat Hanh, Thich. *Vietnam: Lotus in a Sea of Fire*. Foreword by Thomas Merton and afterword by Alfred Hassler. New York, Hill and Wang, 1967. Print.

Raskin, Jonah. *American Scream: Allen Ginsberg's Howl And the Making of the Beat Generation*. Berkeley: U of California P, 2005. Print.

Retallack, Joan. *The Poethical Wager*. Berkeley: U of California P, 2003. Print.

Sanders, Ed. *Investigative Poetics*. San Francisco: City Lights, 1976. Print.

Trungpa, Chögyam. *Shambhala: The Sacred Path of the Warrior*. Ed. Carolyn Rose Gimian. Boulder, Co: Shambhala, 1984. Print.

Waldman, Anne. *The Iovis Trilogy: Colors in the Mechanisms of Concealment*. Minneapolis: Coffee House, 2011. Print.

---. *Outrider: Essays, Poems, Interviews*. Albuquerque: La Alameda, 2006. Print.

Weinberger, Eliot. *Works on Paper: 1980-86*. New York: New Directions, 1986. Print.

The Miraculous and Mucilaginous Paste Pot: Extra-illustration and Plagiary in the Burroughs Legacy
Davis Schneiderman

1. Burroughs Redux

The critical resurgence for William S. Burroughs' work was perhaps unsurprisingly timed to his 1997 death. Less than six months later, Timothy S. Murphy's provocative argument for Burroughsian possibility, *Wising Up the Marks: The Amodern William Burroughs* (1998), inaugurated a new era of theoretically focused critique. On either side of Murphy's text were three primary-text works of what were then considered relatively "minor" forms for Burroughs—letters and interviews including Oliver Harris' *The Letters of William S. Burroughs: 1945-1959* (1993), Allen Hibbard's *Conversations with William Burroughs* (2000), and Sylvère Lotringer's *Burroughs Live* (2000). These works—and particularly Harris' *Letters*—created the pre-conditions for Burroughs criticism to finally, and perhaps fundamentally, separate from the occasionally overpowering myth of the "Author" as expressed in traditional Romantic terms.

As Philip Walsh and I noted in our introduction to the first collection of new Burroughs criticism, *Retaking the Universe: William S. Burroughs in the Age of Globalization* (2004), the specter of the man looms large: "Whether as novelist, essayist, painter, filmmaker, recording artist, mystic, countercultural icon, queer hero, science-fiction guru, junkie, or media theorist, William S. Burroughs (1914-1997) casts a larger-than-life shadow over the second half of the twentieth century." Two recent films, meant to varying degrees for popular audiences, *William S. Burroughs: A Man Within* (2010) and *The Beat Hotel* (2011), delightfully explore this direction, and there will no doubt continue to be a vibrant readership attracted to the Burroughs myth.[1]

Nonetheless, while the critical move toward Burroughs' work, as opposed to his myth, was also bolstered by Jamie Russell's *Queer Burroughs* (2001)—the first text to attempt a full assessment of representation of sexuality in the Burroughs oeuvre—it is Harris who has opened a provocative material-based direction in his recent revision of Burroughs' manuscripts, *Junky: The Definitive Text of Junk* (2003), *The Yage Letters Redux* (2006), and *Queer: 25th-Anniversary Edition* (2010), as well as in his thorough critical reexamination of the relation between Burroughs' work and epistolary in *William S. Burroughs and The Secret of Fascination* (2003). Harris' texts consistently present the secret of Burroughs' production as no secret at all; rather, the "letter" becomes the mundane economic reality of Burroughs' method, and Harris ably focuses on what is "present" in each text, rather than what is merely "represented" through metaphorical analysis.

This effective focus on the genetic elements of Burroughs' works is essential not only for the deconstruction of the myopically mythopoeic elements of this criticism, but also for the way such study tracks with the user-generated interventions that characterize the use of cutup-related processes in the 21st century. These include everything from quotidian social networking and sharing behaviors (the image filers of Instagram or the forking strands of Facebook commentary) to fan-based participations in specific series (*Star Wars Uncut*, composed of 15-second fan-made reshoots of the original). A cursory scan of the internet produces so many user-interventions in creative spaces that it becomes impossible to consider this aesthetic as any more exceptional than we might think of smart phones as ancillary to land lines.

The critical turn, beyond Harris, has oscillated between readings of Burroughs that further seek to investigate his metaphorical writing practice—the significance of the "meaning" in this work—and readings that move further into the direction of production analysis. The first strand remains of interest in its application of (often) post-structuralist theory as a mechanism to liberate Burroughs' work from the purely authorial past. Take Christopher Breu's "The Novel Enfleshed: *Naked Lunch* and the literature of materiality" (2011) as an example of this critical strand. Breu offers a Lacanian reading where "the literature of overaccumulation is a product of a context that these writers find themselves structured within…the figuration of the body… intertwined with late capitalist production, consumption, and signification practices" (202). This is a compelling work of traditional theory: it presents an argument for the significance of Burroughs' work according to particular themes abstracted by the critic. Murphy's *Wising Up the Marks* offers a homologous critical position, and the contribution of these texts is precisely in the models they provide: how might we think of Burroughs' work beyond the tropes of the mythopoetic. Many (but not all) of the contributor essays in my own *Retaking the Universe* would also fit this model. If Burroughs' work is said to imagine alterity, these works help with the projection.

The second strand—genetic analysis that focuses on the genesis of literary works—may be typified not only by the sustained study of the cutups such as *Edward Robinson's Shift Linguals: Cut-Up Narrative from William S. Burroughs to the Present*, which attempts to provide a history of the use of the process, but also by essays such as "Implicating the Confessor: The Autobiographical Ploy in William S. Burroughs' Early Work" (2010) by Alex Wermer-Colan, which attacks critics who may have been too quick to believe what Burroughs' texts "say"—the trap of the intentional fallacy—in the formation of early reception theories.

This is not to say that these are two completely distinct or mutually exclusive poles of criticism, as the second would be completely unthinkable without the first. The genetic work exemplified by Harris requires access to archival materials and the unhealthy interest (which I partially share) in revealing either the provenance of cutup works or the complications that their previous receptions have engendered. Put another way, traditional theory—the application of symbolic readings to text—is more common than genetic analysis.

Nonetheless, this essay will embrace the second strand for several reasons, and I present my argument in reverse order of its appearance. First, a brief reading of Burroughs' cutup production will maintain focus on the "material present" of the text through a crucial example of his small-press cutup oeuvre: the repeated use of the September 17, 1899 *New York Times* front page. This is a genetic project that will ultimately trace practices, but not provide revelations. Such practices will prove of interest to readers interested in copying as a material procedure. The copy always comes from somewhere, but that somewhere is usually not a special place of privileged origin but a site that mirrors, transforms, or distorts as it duplicates, upending the notions of originality that might otherwise be mapped onto the "first use" of a text.[2] This paper will demonstrate several uses of this September 17, 1899 date (and will present a theory in a footnote on its meaning from another scholar), but it will remain *incapable of and uninterested in determining exactly what the date itself means*, lest it fall surrender to the intentional fallacy.

Second, the intention here is to locate Burroughs' work—typified by the above practice—into a larger trajectory of user-interaction with text that extends further back into literary history than is commonly thought. This work demonstrates not roots but connections that go beyond the commonly accepted origin point of early twentieth-century historical and literary avant-garde and Modernism. *That* genetic argument has recourse to the counter-discourses of Marcel Duchamp's divided square constructions, Tristan Tzara's automatic poems, and John Dos Passos' "Camera Eye" segments in the USA novels, and these relationships would come as no surprise to anyone familiar with Burroughs scholarship. These linkages have been a hallmark of such scholarship for many years and have been no doubt bolstered by Burroughs' work with Brion Gysin, who had direct connections to the French avant-garde.

Burroughs' association with the Beat aesthetic—a problematic and complex relationship due to the methodology and anti-Romanticism of his work—allows him, also, to be linked to both sides of the aesthetic we today conflate as "Modern." On the one hand, Burroughs may be read as a traditional High Modernist, in league with Joyce or Stein or even Mann. This argument equates linguistic experimentation with classical erudition and plays into Burroughs' pedigree from Harvard and his oft-spoken interest in T.S. Eliot. Such recourse to traditional Modernism often considers Modernist art as an extension of the classical tradition, and that for all its experimentation, may remain deployed, perhaps, to show us the *real* below the textual surface.[3] Opposing this (before its scholarly conflation with traditional Modernism) is the avant-garde, or those whose works are anti-Romantic and yet often critical of "reason" and increasingly industrial homogeneity. On this side, Burroughs may be linked with the likes of Tzara and an anti-Modern avant-garde, as these figures once stood in at least partial opposition to the literary experimentation of High Modernism, which might still be located within the bounds of earlier Romantic ideologies. Today, these two hands clasp together to articulate the term "Modernism," and Burroughs scholarship might be placed, uneasily, in either corner of this critical space.

This essay's supposition is that the cutups share strong practical and material affinities with an earlier and pre-Modernist mode of user-intervention into texts, a rarely reported phenomenon derived from reader-originated portrait insertions into an English history text by the Reverend James Granger in the late 1700s, called, alternately, "Grangerization," and for our purposes, in its expanded form, "Extra-Illustration." Nonetheless, the purpose of this investigation is not to sever Burroughs from the Modernist tree.

Instead, this work will present the cutups (a term including fold-ins and other related aleatory methods) as a simultaneously aesthetic and socio-political exercise—with important yet under-analyzed implications for contemporary Authorship reflective of our current moment precisely because the present moment is *not* solely the flowering of mid-twentieth century experimentations. Burroughs and his collaborators produced astounding investigations for their time period, but let us not make their output into the divine (but scrambled) Word. The technologies Burroughs explored—typewriter, film, and tape recorder—presented opportunities for his practice, as YouTube may present opportunities for ours. The nineteenth century, as I will demonstrate, offers its own extraordinary possibilities.

2. The Miraculous and Mucilaginous Paste Pot

As much as the social and economic position of the author (following Pierre Bourdieu's analyses [4]) might be said to determine the material production of a text, the implication of Harris' studies (and, elsewhere, in the work of Anthony Enns), is that the availability of printing technology functions as a control and limit to processes of reproduction and the aesthetics derived from these processes. Laurence Sterne's *Tristam Shandy*, for instance, published in 9 volumes (1760-1767), includes in Volume 3 the famous "marbled page." This page, which *Shandy* calls the "motly emblem of my work," is different in all 4000 editions,[5] demonstrating an awareness of the relative *impossibility* of representing the text differently in each edition, except when that representation comes at what we can only assume was considerable expense, and which, as a marbled page, proved to be opaque. Through this opacity, the reader is able to see a marker of the text's singularity but is not, in any conventional sense, able to "read" its markings.

Such a gambit reminds us of the divide between the lovingly constructed "unique" book object that marks itself as individuated and the mass produced text that defies our ability to intercede *physically* in its contents. The book may be the province of the mind—we are free to mentally construct our own images to accompany written work, free to imagine landscapes, characters, the exact shape of Richard III's hump, *ad nauseum*—yet the copyright regime generally forbids the manipulation of a book's physical contents by the end user, at least until the current digital revolution.

Accordingly, *Shandy* expresses the tension between mass production and individuation. The practice of extra-illustration, a type of bibliomania, expresses one pre-Modernist response to this tension. The practice originated, as Newberry Library Reference Librarian and extra-illustration scholar Jill Gage explains, with the publication of the Reverend James Granger's *A Biographical History of England, From Egbert the Great to the Revolution...* (1769), a catalogue of the known portraits of prominent figures in English history. Before long, collectors began interleaving their prints as a way to display and arrange their own collections of material. Gage notes: "Illustrating one's Granger was such a rage that in 1775 the publisher Thomas Davies published an edition of Granger's book interleaved with blank sheets to make the tipping in of portraits easier; the appearance of the already interleaved book contributed to the belief that Granger himself advocated the practice" (Gage, "Re: Extra-illustration..."). The craze grew from the insertion of merely illustrative portraiture toward extensive visual and literary additions of other source texts (including the interleaving of newspaper and magazine clippings).

Enter the figure of Chicago journalist and trade publisher, John Mansir Wing, a major benefactor of the Newberry Library. As Burroughs was the most dedicated practitioner of cutups, Wing was perhaps the most dedicated practitioner of extra-illustration. Wing worked steadily from the late 1800s to his death in 1917 on over 363 extra-illustrated editions, re-plated with new bindings and cover pages. Gage sees Wing (or "Mr. Wing," as he is called by the current Newberry staff) as an endearing character self-consciously constructing his persona as a man of letters, especially once he began working for the Newberry in 1912.[6] His affections were for history and parody (in the tradition of Rabelais); he was a skeptic of the press, as well as organized religion, and his work displays an often wicked sense of play. For instance, he extra-illustrated the fifth edition of Granger's *A Biographical History of England...* (1824) before 1899, in the early years of his extra-illustrating practice, no doubt as a meta-comment on the endeavor and on Granger's response to the practice. The Reverend was not happy that the practice seemingly derived from his History or the fact that it had acquired the appellation "Grangerization" in its early years.

Wing deploys his critique by including an 1803 portrait of Granger at the start of Wing's re-plated text, followed by an engraving of Granger's letter (on parsonage stationary) from December 30, 1769. Granger's words, re-appearing in Wing's edition, are worth quoting:

> I find that the Iconomania, a new Disease prevails much in London. One Symptom of it, in which it differs from all other kinds of madness is, that it delights in maiming of <u>old Books</u>; and what I am much concerned to hear is, that some of them are of such value, that none but an idiot was ever before known to have willfully done them the least Injury. I have great Reason to believe that the Rage of this Distemper will soon be over.

Granger's concern for the seemingly unassailable physical character of the printed word should be unsurprising given his clerical status and the still widespread sanctity of the written word even in our own age. What differs between Granger's outrage and today's widespread practice of digital and mechanical manipulation is the *physical* transfer capabilities of the Georgian period. The portraits that became subjects for Grangerization had to be removed, physically, from earlier printed books. As with Burroughs' analogue cutups, this physical transfer suggests the "Disease" that the Reverend diagnoses, which "delights in maiming <u>old Books</u>." The language here is particularly telling: one does not simply disassemble a book in order to "Grangerize." Rather, one must be *infected* with "Iconomania," becoming an "idiot" (a commonly deployed term for the "feeble-minded"). Tellingly, it is only Granger's great "Reason," born from the Enlightenment principles underlying his religious beliefs, which provide a bulwark against this plague. While this is perhaps a stretch of Granger's verbiage, it is not beyond inference to say that those who extra-illustrate are not only delinquent in their recognition of economics ("such value") but are also spiritually depraved ("it delights in maiming"). Further, his "Iconomania" (opposed to the later term, "bibliomania") becomes an affront to the civilized values of society inscribed onto the material body of the book.

For Wing, especially in his later years, extra-illustration became an obsession deployed against Granger's "Reason," similar in intensity to Burroughs' cutup practice. Burroughs, as noted almost everywhere in the Nova/Cut-Up trilogy (*The Soft Machine* [1961, 1966, 1968], *The Ticket that Exploded* [1962, 1967], and *Nova Express* [1964]), sought to expose the "real" or perhaps even "sur-real" proceedings of the cosmos through his cutup influenced cosmological conspiracy theories: "I doubt if any of you on this copy planet have ever seen a nova criminal"

(*Nova Express*, 50). Yet following Harris' logic, it is a mistake to read the Nova Mob from his 1960s cutup work as mere metaphor. The economic and social factors of production in Burroughs' texts generated their content; the cutup sources Burroughs had access to, for instance, as an educated white male cutting Rimbaud and Shakespeare, or as an expatriate with easy access to the *International Times*, would in large part determine the product. In this way, the cutup serve as both prophecy (releasing the future) and prophylactic (revealing the mechanism of control). If you didn't get it, if you dissented (as Gregory Corso did at the publication of the first cutup collection, *Minutes to Go* [1960]), you were compromised. For Burroughs, you were either a "Shit" or a "Johnson," and so the cutups, well reduced in appearance by the time the Shit/Johnson dichotomy appears in *The Place of Dead Roads* (1983), prove to be a potent entry point into a line of thought that may be aligned with Wing's eccentric practice.

For example, Wing's edition of *Table Traits* by John Doran, extended from two to fifteen volumes through extra-illustration, echoes the vitriol of such "straightforward" Burroughs' texts as "A Thanksgiving Prayer" or any of the savage parodies of the Nova/Cut-Up trilogy. Wing's colophon offers a Burroughsian litany, describing how the text was produced over a roughly two-and-a-half week period (1905-1906), with "the labor giving zest for many a good dinner and moving his bowels with comfort, while the outside world struggled and stumbled on—

The reformers reformed:
The Preachers swallowed their bread with loud voices:
The Money-makers fought:
The Politicians grafted:
The Poets liquefied and metagrabolized their brains:
....
The maggots and infusoria of society joined the socialists...

And so on, closing with, "All being more or less constipated by the mollification of their '*intestinum rectum*,' because of their insane desire to become known as somebody among fools." Wing could be "blue" in his own way, and he was prepared in this practice to gear up the vitriol.

Wing rejects being known as "somebody," and his invectives against those in power (the litany of hypocrites, above) and against standard notions of genius and originality are no less severe than that in the cutups. Burroughs and Gysin's manifesto for partisan activity, *The Third Mind* (first published in English in 1978), offers similar rebuffs against those who practice the linearity Wing duly rejects. Wing's inward turning from the bustle of the outside world perhaps differs from Burroughs' direct assault on sensory and syntactic lines, but the role of the

"Author"—a person we might assume to be, if successful, "somebody among fools"—becomes sublimated in both cases to the producer authorizing not "original" work in the Romantic mode of authorship, but by the relative *anonymity* of extra-illustration outside the lemming box of genius (despite Wing's own authorial posturing).

A notable Wing extra-illustration titled *Habits of Men and the Makers of Both* (1990) (also a Doran text, called *Habits and Men* on the Wing title page) pushes the practice well beyond the relatively simple introduction of portraits into a printed text, and extends Wing's own antics in a direction of commercial interaction akin to Burroughs' mass media critiques. Gage considers the text to be composed of Wing's "junk mail"—and so we find a difference between *Habits* and earlier extra-illustrated editions. The first pages of *Habits* (Volume VIII) are studded with the expected inserts—an image of "A man of the Sandwich Islands, Masked"; a matted cut-out of a well-dressed chap with the handwritten caption "Namely Calves"; a portrait of James Boswell—before we are confronted with a black-and-white catalogue picture for "Fleece Lined Gloves." A few pages later, a hand-written title introduces "Habits and Men/Stockings/Chicago-1910," a full-color 1909 "Silk Hosiery for Gifts" catalogue from Marshall Field & Company. Striking in its full insertion, without the interspersed commentary of the *Habits* text, these 21 catalogue pages (plus cover) speak to a regime of thoroughly twentieth-century extra-illustration and would look quite at home in Warhol's work a half-century later or in the pages of a recent major conceptual literature anthology *Against Expression: An Anthology of Conceptual Writing*, edited by Craig Dworkin and Kenneth Goldsmith.[7] This prolonged junk mail interlude in *Habits* says as much about the material available to Wing as it does to the economic conditions of his text's production. As if anticipating a response generated by the use of such "low" cultural products, the same mass-market detritus to which Burroughs would frequently turn, Wing's title page quotes a 1910 warning of his obsession in *The Connoisseur* (London): "Extra illustrating, or 'Grangerizing' as it is sometimes called, is a seductive [sic], but when carried to its logical conclusion, a prolonged and costly pursuit—" (my emphasis). As easy as taking a Stanley knife to a newspaper, Wing pastes ad copy to a *serious* book on the habits of men, defusing the criticism of *The Connoisseur* by demonstrating "budget" extra-illustration. Burroughs deployed a similarly democratizing praxis despite the occasional contrary statement[8] in the use of newspaper texts.

3. The two-fold danger

Burroughs was initially sanguine about the ability of *all* cutups to effect their word magic—their ability to transform reality in some way—but within a short time from the "discovery" of the process in the summer of 1959, he advocated a more thorough separation of results. In a Sept. 5, 1960 letter to Allen Ginsberg, he notes: "The cut up method is a tool which I am learning to use after a year of intensive experiments. There is no reason to keep cut up material that is not useful to the purpose....It depends on the material cut and the purpose in cut" (*Rub Out the Word* 44). Like Wing, the further Burroughs delved into his method, the more refined and intricate the process became. Wing may have introduced "junk" materials in *Habits*, but it would be an error to assume that such interleaving was arbitrary for either practitioner.

In fact, Burroughs remained an enthusiastic cutter of "factual" newspaper material, particularly in his small-press work for publications such as Jeff Nuttall's *My Own Mag* (1963-1967); Burroughs was a regular contributor and eventually had a two-page feature at the end of several issues, called "The Moving Times." In a one-page feature called "Afternoon Ticker Tape" (issue 6, under the banner headline "The Burrough," as opposed to the title "The Moving Times" in issues 5 and 7)[9], we find a newspaper-style collage of typical cutup prose. An example graph: "The Committee has already bred a race of sheep. Serve 'peace with one/ another'. Sexless providence supported by the rich. Policemen jumped out/on them. Nobody knew whence he came. The policemen a long time ago applied/."

The "mystery" of the text was revealed to some extent the next year in the archival typescript of a piece called "St. Louis Return" (housed at Columbia University), published in a 1965 issue of *The Paris Review* (though originally written for *Playboy*) and reprinted later in *The Burroughs File* (1984, 79-89), where the narrator, speaking to the character "B.J.," comments upon the obscurity of "Afternoon Ticker Tape":

> Relevant material I cut out and paste in a scrap book. For example last winter I assembled a page entitled <u>Afternoon Ticker Tape</u> which appeared in <u>My Magasine</u> [sic] published by J. Nuttall of London. This page, an experiment in newspaper format, was largely a rearrangement of phrases from the front page of the New York Times, Sunday September 17, 1899, cast in the form of code messages. Since some readers objected that the meaning was obscure I was particularly anxious to find pints [sic] of intersections, a decoding operation you might say relating the text to external coordinates: <u>From Afternoon Ticker Tape</u> [sic] "Most fruitful achievement of the Amsterdam Conference a drunk policeman" And just here in the St. Louis Globe Democrat for Dec. 23, I read that a policeman in Dellwood has been suspended for drinking on duty slobbed out drunk in his prowl car with an empty brandy bottle ....Unable to contain himself B.J. rolled on the bed in psychophantic convulsions "I tell you boss you write it and it happens. Why if you did'nt [sic] write me I wouldn't be here."

Burroughs uses newspaper text for the strength of anonymity[10] —not coded to any particular author in what he would often call the "Shakespeare squadron." The relative generality of newspaper text provides an empty vessel that he can fill with meaning *after the fact*. Additionally, a comparison of the version of "St. Louis Return" published in *The Paris Review* (and *The Burroughs File*) with the archival typescript reveals an important syntactical variant. In the typescript, the assumed template for *The Paris Review*, the phrase reads: "Since some readers objected that the meaning was obscure I was particularly anxious to find pints of intersection…" [sic]. In *The Paris Review/The Burroughs File* version two additional words are added so that the sentence reads: "Since some readers objected that the meaning was obscure *to them* I was particularly anxious to find points of intersection…" (82, my emphasis).[11]

The "to them" insert speaks to the editorial mechanism at work between the archival typescript from 1964 and the published version in 1965. Since the misspelling of "pints" has been corrected to "points," we can assume that the insertion of "to them" is the product of a deliberate editorial hand. One possibility: in the earlier Columbia typescript, the narrator responds to criticism that cutups are perhaps obscure in meaning, yet by the time of publication, the added qualifier suggests that any deficit of meaning is to be found on the part *of the reader*. The process, in other words, is sound, yet the audience must be trained in its workings, which would explain the necessity of cutup pieces merging practice and theory. "St. Louis Return" falls into this category—inter-leaving cut material and "explanation," whereas Wing's extra-illustrations offer their commentary through juxtaposition only. Herein lies the most significant achievement of the cutups random method—not to reveal any specific meaning through juxtaposition of past materials, but to produce, for Burroughs as much as for the trained reader, the future. This procedure, if we follow Harris, is more than a metaphor.[12]

4. September 17, 1899 over New York

September 17, 1899, according to the *New York Times*, was a relatively uneventful news day (with a far right-column lead story on events leading toward the Second Boer War), and probably, because of this dearth of significant alacrity, Burroughs managed to mine effective cutup phrases from the Gray Lady's apparently mundane substance. During the summer of 2005, my research assistant Jennifer Murphy spent an exhaustive period tracing this Ur-date through archival Burroughs material from the Columbia University Rare Book and Manuscript Library and the McCormick Library of Special Collections at Northwestern University Library. She found that the date is repeated not only in "Afternoon Ticker Tape" but also in other small press texts of the period.

Yet from the initial *New York Times* page, Murphy discovered the following lines repeated through the Columbia and Northwestern archival compositions: "the two-fold danger," "the South Atlantic squadron," "or had even an opportunity to do so," "A long time ago," "Electricity is in the air," "Police Sergeant," "decided that the rich should support him," "refused to sign the contract," "Last Tuesday was the regular day for signing," "price for the remaining months," "is like one man," "lad, born and raised," "Stein's," "books opened," "South Africa," "Other Well-Known People" (from a headline), "confusion at Waterloo Station," "Foreign Blind Association," "they are all valueless I know from some of our blind," "Almost Completely Deserted" (headline), "the United States Consulate is improving," "ends the last day of this month," "active preparations for war," "have sailed for South Africa," "of peace or war," "British ultimatum," and perhaps most significantly for Burroughs' cutup cosmology, appearing as a member of the Nova Mob in the Cut-Up/Nova trilogy: "the Bradley-Martins."

Tracing the usage of such phrases through Burroughs' texts is a maddening procedure—and other single words were perhaps used with significance—but regardless of whether an entire phrase can be identified in future cuts, we can never be sure of the precise reason for usage. Yet if we are to take Burroughs' Sept. 5, 1960, letter to Allen Ginsberg seriously, believing that a definite editorial mechanism was put to work, we must assume that these phrases result from more than a random knife-blade.

A piece such as "The Coldspring News" (found in published form at Northwestern, in three columns, presumably the same as the 1965 version in *The Spero*), appears to use only the possible intersection phrase "a long time ago" (twice)—a phrase not so uncommon as to be definitively drawn from the *New York Times*. Yet the physical markers of this text, mimicking a newspaper page, would imply a greater connection between the two usages. When approached structurally, the usage of cutup phrases changes from the application and discovery of merely one-to-one correlations (every instance of "September 17, 1899" for example), to a process of rhizomatic mapping. The *Times*'; famous slogan "All the News / That's Fit to Print," becomes the slyly worded "All the News That Fits, We Print" with the "September, 17, 1899" date at the head of the page. Simultaneously, and more importantly, the three-column layout gradually distorts the linearity of the narrative toward a material praxis. We lose "linearity" as we proceed to the third column.

For example, the first column of this page-ready archival "The Coldspring News," slugged "On The Back Porch / Of His Farm," finds Bradley Martin accosted for cattle rustling by neighboring ranchers; significantly, Martin is accused of changing the brand before selling the stolen cattle (a charged later mimicked in the section called "First Recordings" from *The Third Mind*). The second column, slugged "Waiting The Survey / Line Quite Some Years," maintains a token sense of narrative movement, using recognizable phrases and characters from the first column, and most notably commenting on the accusation of re-branding stolen cattle, certainly an analogue for accusations that the cutups are theft: "Look folks don't own what they thought." The third column takes the pattern of a "full" cutup, using the familiar markers of Burroughs' work in this vein, including many phrases that establish the fungibility of setting: "Silent grocer shops cobblestone streets and the lake like bits of silver paper..."

This gradual distortion of traditional narrative assumes significance beyond the left-to-right column drift. Looking visually at the page, with a concordance prepared by Murphy for the other affiliated September 17, 1899 archival texts (henceforth called the "1899 cluster"), we see that the first column is free of cutup material from the "1899 cluster." The second transitional column contains a smattering of phrases that also appear in "The Moving Times," "The Last Post," and "Your Day," totaling approximately 27 of the column's approximately 350 words. The third column, which further distorts linear narrative, contains 131 words that appear in the other texts (from approximately 350 in the column, although, almost certainly, considerable chunks of the remaining text are cutups from other sources). The material implication shows that as the three-column narrative trends further into its aleatory mechanism, the "1899 cluster" that appears to organize this specific critique assumes a greater presence; while it is difficult to know in what chronology these archival pieces were composed (the Columbia University finding-aid lists the relevant folder of "Experimental Prose. Tangier. ca. 1964"), visual scans of their cross-correlations maintain the importance of the third column "1899 cluster" storehouse within each piece.

In "The Last Post," a relatively short cutup selection (later expanded into "The Last Post *Danger Ahead* in *Lines* magazine [1965]; reprinted in *The Burroughs File*), the third column is repetitive[14] of material in the third column of "The Coldspring News": "A distant soldier never / came out at recess time / that afternoon I watch / the torn sky bend with / the wind white white white / white a blinding flash / white as far as the eye can see."

These are examples of the usage. "Your Day," tellingly followed by the subhead, "So we'll take all the [sic] pieces of all your days and stir them / into one day / Sept 17, 1899," unsurprisingly contains almost all of its "1899 cluster" in the third column, with text shared between the archival "The Moving Times" and "The Coldspring News," as well as a considerable amount drawn from the *New York Times* front page.

The Columbia archival typescript of "The Moving Times" offers a similar process,[15] with the third column, provocatively slugged "September 17, 1899 / Dead Start Drew September 17,1899 Over New York," sharing text with "Your Day," "The Coldspring News," and for the most part, the *New York Times*. To further confuse the issue, the second and third columns of a *separate* published edition of "The Moving Times" in the Columbia archive (from *My Own Mag*) matching the Northwestern University archive (oversized),[16] both not analyzed by Murphy, contain different text from this Columbia archival typescript. In fact, the third column of the published *My Own Mag* / Northwestern copy, both slugged "Last Gun Post Erased In/A Small Town Newspaper/September 17, 1899," shares considerable text from its first section with the aforementioned third-column of the Columbia typescript iteration of "The Moving Times." A correction of the word "form" in the Columbia archive to "from" in the *My Own Mag* / Northwestern edition would seem to imply a composition chronology. Further, *The Burroughs File* version of "The Moving Times" (150-151), which claims prior publication in the *VDRSVP, Nova Broadcast Sheet* (1969) presumably, the same as the Northwestern copy, as well as an unlisted appearance in *My Own Mag* (issue 5 [1964]: 3-4), contains a majority, but not all, of the text from the *My Own Mag* / Northwestern versions, yet cuts between columns and pages *completely* reorganize the content between this and the other two published editions.[17] What do all of these usages have in common, if anything?

In all four iterations (three different versions—1: Columbia typescript, 2: *My Own Mag*/Northwestern copy, 3: *The Burroughs File*) of "The Moving Times," the first two columns have date slugs much more recent to the time of apparent composition: February 6, 1964, and "November 18 & 19 1963" (sic) in the Columbia archival typescript; February 10, 1964 and January 17, 1947 in the *My Own Mag*/Northwestern editions (with the first column of the second page provocatively listed as "1964 1947 1899 Jan. Feb. Sept.), which are shared, without dates on the second page, by *The Burroughs File* version. Consistent across these three versions is the use of the "1899 cluster" in the third column, which, while changing in content from the Columbia typescript to the two other iterations, maintains its primacy at the start of the material text in the columns. By maintaining the use of the cluster in the third column, these texts signal not only usage-as-placement, but also usage-as-process.

Burroughs' familiar injunction in column one of the Columbia typescript, "Read across / columns. Fill one column / on another page with / cross column readings. / Fill the other two columns / with your future time / guesses and so on. ...," allows "The Moving Times" to remain always in motion and play in the middle column, as it does in the *My Own Mag*/Northwestern, and *The Burroughs File* versions, with the Janus verb "to fix." For Burroughs' work, September 17, 1899 becomes a date that is not idly "fixed" in the past, but a materially movable parcel through which he can "fix" (re: repair) the stultifying linearity of the written word by continually recasting the detritus of the newspaper layout.

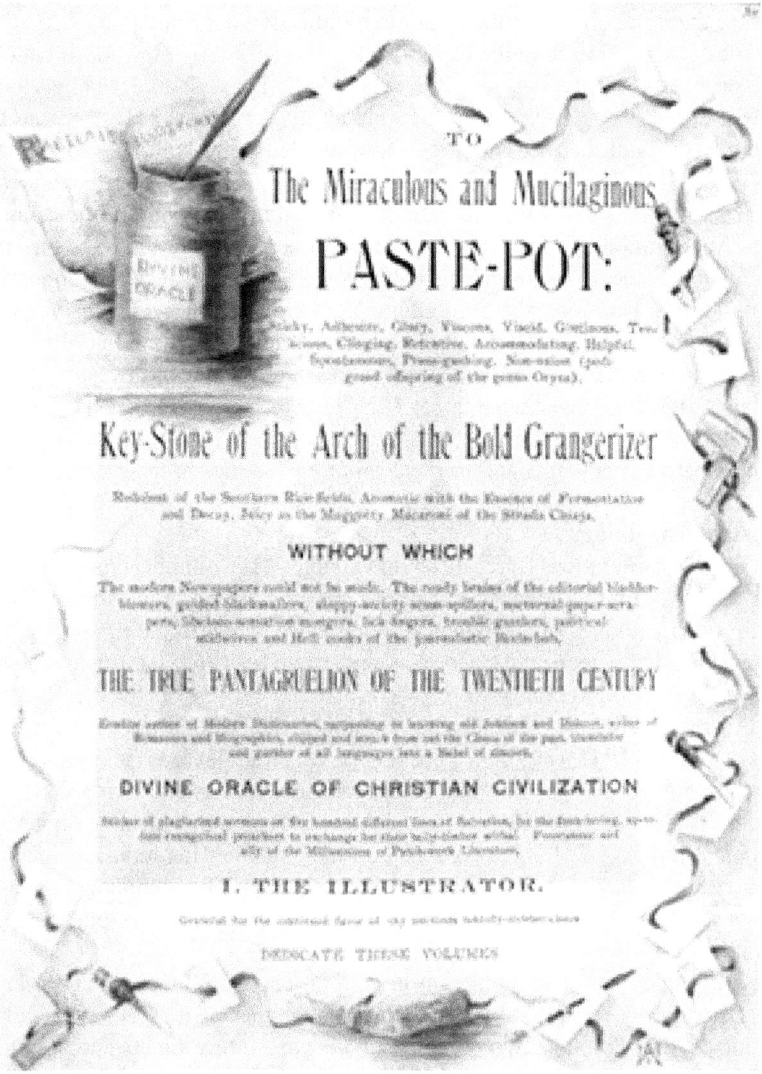

This dedication page by John M. Wing is to his extra-illustrated volume of *The Comédie Humaine of Rabelais*. London, 1864. Copy at the Newberry Library extra-illustrated by John M. Wing, 1904.

According to Jill Gage, reference librarian at the Newberry Library, this photographic frontispiece appears in many volumes extra-illustrated by Wing, yet only after 1905. Wing first contacted the Newberry in 1899 and died in 1917. Gage's excellent article "With Deft Knife and Paste: The Extra-Illustrated Books of John M. Wing" provides additional detail.

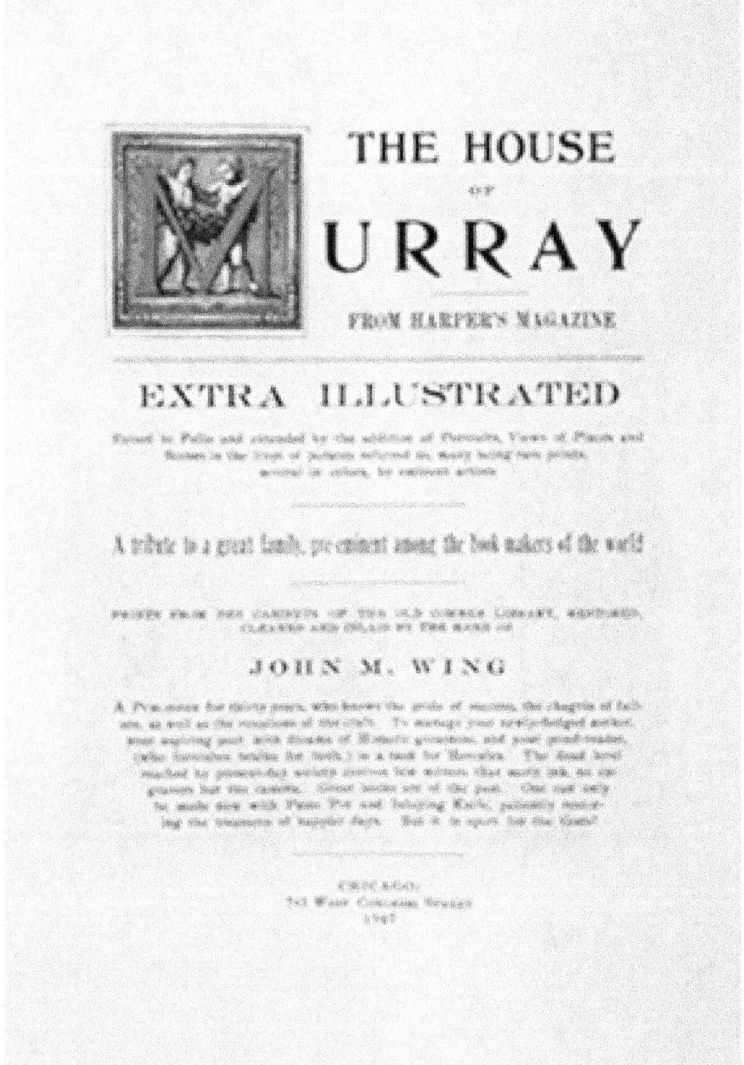

This dedication page by John M. Wing is to his extra-illustrated volume: Espinasse, F. "The House of Murray" from *Harper's Magazine.* Sept. 1885. Copy at the Newberry Library extra-illustrated by John M. Wing, 1907.

William S. Burroughs' "The Coldspring News." 1p. (photocopied). San Francisco Earthquake 1.35 (1968):13 (?). Jan Herman archive, Box 6. McCormick Library of Special Collections, Northwestern University Library. Presumably, a reprint of poster in *The Spero*. 1.1 (1965): 15-16. This image contains color-coded notes tracing the appearance of phrases from the "1899 cluster" and their reappearance in other Burroughs cutup texts referenced in this essay. The cluster is used in many more cutups than those discussed in this essay.

5. Dead stars heavy with his dusty answer

Aside from the striking visual trace—the "1899 cluster"—of the compositional process in these examples, we find even more clearly the multi-generational praxis of the cutups at work. Was the September 17, 1899 *New York Times* page cutup a single time during one furious session with a Stanley blade so that the resulting text, whichever of these it might be, could be cut again into the next piece, and so on? Or did the *New York Times* function as a recursive word bank, from which Burroughs could draw whenever he needed to access some version of the "1899 cluster" to push towards the material processing of text that would characterize his cutup practice?

The question of whether the "original cut" produced a series of "daisy chain" texts, versus the possibility of returned cutting to the *New York Times* fountainhead, might only be answered through a more thorough (and perhaps pointless) search of material records. How many copies of the *New York Times* page did Burroughs procure? How, exactly, did he procure the text? In a March 6, 1964 letter to Dick Seaver, Burroughs thanked Seaver for providing the page, although the motivations for his request and how many copies Seaver provided remains unclear (Harris, private e-mail). And after procurement, did Burroughs re-type and/or carbon the initial cutup of material for future cuts, or did he warehouse the useful phrases in a cutup bank, perhaps his many scrapbooks, where they could be used again and again (as with the popular magnetic poetry later based on the method)? The answers to these questions would no doubt provide more questions, for like the shattered body of Osiris, Burroughs lacunae have been spread through countless archives, old musty books shops, and private hands.[18]

And this distribution, perhaps, is the key legacy of the Burroughsian canon. Aside from remonstrations too often taken as metaphor ("retake the universe," etc.), the material bequest of the word-hoard and its attendant dispersal through a news pulp labyrinth of small press publications—impossible to fully catalog and difficult to collect—actually authorizes the work's larger critique of authority. To use the newspaper and scrapbook format (making his production as ethereal as the zine and the hard-copy newspaper, easily disposable) suggests that the ego-based construction of authorship—where writers produce *only* tangible, fixed-form books to be distributed through easily accessible channels—is merely a reduplication of a textual system that inscribes author and reader within a larger socio-economic system of "original" production. For Burroughs to break with the power of the word, he needed to break with the power of the copy, and so to copy freely, pushing the available technology so that any search for "origin" (as in the work of the poststructuralists) becomes a tellingly futile exercise.

The extra-illustrated editions of Wing and others (when taken beyond the requirements of mere portraiture collection) produced a largely private critique of this system. Wing, never hesitant to declare the death of conventional genius ("Great books are of the past. One can only be made now with the Paste Pot and Inlaying Knife" [*The House of Murray*]), ready to interleave his own portrait with an edition of Rabelais (which Gage thinks to be itself an extra-illustration), presents a pre-Modern (or early-Modern) critique of individual construction through the reclusive practice of his Old Corner Library. His work, produced by a man of means and leisure, might still be construed as a defense of an earlier notion of genius, perhaps in the same way that Holbrook Jackson's amusing *Anatomy of Bibliomania* (1932, 1947, 1950), a partial imitation of Robert Burton's *Anatomy of Melancholy* (1621), justifies excessive citation of borrowed material.[19] Even so, by the time Wing begins pasting the Marshall Field's catalog into *Habits and Men*, it is clear that his process has shifted toward Burroughs' "low-culture" practices.[20]

Wing might have never placed his extra-illustrated texts into public circulation, no doubt constrained by the lack of reproduction technologies and his inward philosophy on the process of creativity; yet Burroughs, an author who simultaneously published with well-known presses and the lowest budget mimeographed magazines, was able to interweave his cutup process into the folds of a world which, through the increasing reproductive technologies of the twentieth century, could no longer be contained within the pages of private volumes.

These differences, which may be elaborated upon under further study, suggest not merely *difference*, but a series of multi-generational genetic practices that unseat, to varying degrees, the intentionality of the author through the mechanisms available to the reader at a particular moment. These practices share a set of antagonisms directed toward the passive reception of texts, while resisting any unifying principle beyond the broad principle of user-generated praxis. This principle, surely, didn't begin with Wing (or Granger) or Burroughs (or Gysin) any more than it began with Tristan Tzara, busy with newspapers and scissors. A *Washington Post* review of the Folger Library's "Extending the Books: The Art of Extra-Illustration" (2010) makes the same point: "[P]eople have been dressing up the word, decorating the text and inserting indelible reminders of their corporeal existence into documents for centuries" (Kennicott). Taken as a loose tradition, these practices have enabled the present aesthetic of mash-ups and remixes and recut movie trailers and fan fiction and macro memes and Lolcats and the thousands of other works constructed and uploaded and shared during the time it took you to read this essay. Don't take my word for it, but do, please, take my words, if you like.

As many as you like.

I offer sincere thanks to the Newberry Library's Jill Gage, for her kindness, generosity, and infinite knowledge on all things extra-illustrated. Her enthusiasm for Wing is more than contagious, and I am lucky to have benefited from her aid on this project. Thanks also to Jennifer Murphy, the most organized and perspicacious student I have had the honor of working with; her archival analyses proved invaluable to the preparation of this essay, and all of the initial "September 17, 1899" legwork stems from her good offices. I owe special gratitude to Oliver Harris and Tomasz Stompor.

Notes

[1] Full disclosure: I engaged in one day of minor script consulting on *William S. Burroughs: A Man Within*.

[2] These arguments about copying and its anxieties are explicated in much greater detail in Marcus Boon's *In Praise of Copying* (Harvard 2010), a book cleverly available for free download, which I read long after writing this essay and once Boon and I had begun collaborating on research connected to Burroughs and Brion Gysin's *The Third Mind*.

[3] Consider Gilles Deleuze and Félix Guattari's well-known critique of Burroughs' later work as *fascicular*—or false—in *A Thousand Plateaus*.

[4] Pierre Bourdieu (1930-2002), a French sociologist, explores taste (among other ideas) in relation and as a product of social position, arguing that both interiority and external structures contribute to one's position as an aesthetic producer. The relevance here may be oversimplified: one does not make art solely because of one's "feeling;" one makes art through the means available due to one's position in the field of artistic production. This is a rejection of ideas of the "total" artist and an argument for a more nuanced and less Romantic view of how art is actually produced.

[5] The previous chapter closes with: "for without *much reading*, by which your reverence knows, I mean *much knowledge*, you will be no more able to penetrate the marbled page (motly emblem of my work!) than the world with all its fagacity has been able to unraval the many opinions, transactions and truths which ftill [still] lie mythically hid under the dark veil of a black one" (168). Sterne's publisher R. and J. Dodsley actually inserted two different marbled pages for each individual print (pps. 169 and 170). In Chicago, the Newberry Library's copy (cited above) contains cacophonous bubbles of yellow, pink, white, and green that glow like the projections of a 1960s acid test. No doubt the colors have faded over the centuries, but the fact that the original press run of approximately 4000 copies each contains two separate, unique, marbled pages speaks to *Shandy*'s position as a text that recognizes its status under the sign of the printing press, and thus, the sign of replication.

⁶ Wing's name appears on the bindings of (most) of the over 360 editions in the Newberry collection, and the 6000 regular editions from his Old Corner Library were secondary, for Wing, to the donation of his extra-illustrated works. In fact, the first communications between the Newberry Board and Alexander J. Rudolph (assistant librarian of the Newberry from 1894-1911) about the possibility of acquiring Wing's collection, focused almost entirely on the extra-illustrated volumes (Gage). Art Miller, the Lake Forest College archivist who worked at the Newberry several decades ago, remembers that much of this work was not taken seriously at the time, and Gage notes the laughter of her fellow librarians at Wing's fascination with phallus worship.

⁷ Warhol's "Crazy Golden Slippers," from a 1957 issue of *Life*, skirts the boundary between ad and art (although perhaps largely in retrospect). *Against Expression*, and other works of conceptual literature, present certain texts that are complete re-situations—unchanged found, recorded, transcribed, transformed, material lifted from its source and re-printed in a literary space. Aside from Wing's image insertions, his new title pages also speak to this re-purposing of existing book-space. The anthology *I'll Drown My Book: Conceptual Writing by Women* (Les Figues) includes an excerpt of Susan Howe's *A Bibliography of The King's Book or, Eikon Basilike*, which opens with Howe's interpolated title page. Tom Phillips has spent the last decades in a much more elaborate overwriting of a previous book with his *A Humument: A Treated Victorian Novel*.

⁸ From *The Third Mind*: "If fragments of newspaper be the 'poorest' material for cutups, these treasures of world literature as rendered in English are, presumably, the 'richest'" (89). This is a reference, perhaps with irony, to using canonical Western texts as cutup material

⁹ "*My Own Mag*" is now available online at *Realitystudio.org*. This is a welcome development for scholars and enthusiasts, yet it also presents significant bibliographic challenges. Jed Birmingham's column post "*My Own Mag*: A Bibliographic Nightmare" expresses the difficulties with clarity and cites Ian Sinclair's convincing correction to previous incorrect numberings. My archival research, therefore, originally used a different numbering than *Realitystudio.org*. I have retrofitted to adopt the latter's ordination.

¹⁰ An area for further research regards the analogy between extra-illustration and scrapbooks and cutups and scrapbooks. "St. Louis Return," claims Burroughs in a November 9, 1964 letter, derives from a scrapbook about T.S. Eliot assembled by Rives Matthews, an old St. Louis neighbor of Burroughs: "What has kept me so occupied derives from your scrap book and visiting card tray which gave me an idea for a new method of presentation namely the scrap book format, pieces of old letters, texts, photos, etcetera" (170). *Ports of Entry: William S. Burroughs and the Arts* by Robert A. Sobieszek, offers high-quality reproductions of some of Burroughs'

approximately "twenty small agenda-, sketch-, and notebooks (filled) with his own typescripts, bits of newspaper headlines and stories, columns from *Time* and *Newsweek*, account of disasters…" (45). These are full-on multimedia affairs, especially in contrast with earlier text-based notebooks, such as that reproduced as *Everything Lost: The Latin American Notebook of William S. Burroughs* (Ohio State, 2008) covering July-August 1953.

[11] This same wording, and this same passage, appears in the piece "Precise Intersection Points" in *The Third Mind* (133-137), which is otherwise different from "St. Louis Return."

[12] Briefly, I argue in the paper "Everybody's Got Something to Hide Except for Me and My Lawsuit: DJ Danger Mouse, William S. Burroughs, and the Politics of 'Grey Tuesday'" that cutups reverse the "ideas" before "expression" vector protected by copyright. Once this prophetic element rises from the text, the expression begins at the articulation of the cut, but the idea, or meaning of that expression, is not determined until a later time. Copyright law, of course, makes no room for such un-writing.

[13] These include archival pieces slugged "The Coldspring News" (published 1965), "Other Voices" (typescript only), "The Last Post" (typescript. only) "Your Day" (typescript only), and one of the many pieces called "The Moving Times" (typescript, raw material for *My Own Mag* 5), and, almost certainly, an undetermined number of additional texts. The date closes the final section of *Nova Express*, "Clom Fliday," with "September 17, 1899 over New York" (179), and provides the linchpin for the repeated shoot-out between characters Mike Chase and William Seward Hall in *The Place of Dead Roads*. The date also appears in a number of reprinted small-press texts of *The Burroughs File*, including the excerpt from "A Distant Hand Lifted" (34-38), "*The Last Post Danger Ahead*" (53-55, which shares some text with the archival "The Last Post"), from "The Coldspring News" (67-71, a different version than the archival piece), "Who is the Walks Beside You Written 3rd?" (72-78), "St. Louis Return" (79-89), "The Moving Times" (150-151), and several instances within "Pages from the Cut-Up Scrapbooks" (153-183). Certainly, there are other uses in Burroughs' vast oeuvre.

[14] With two small variations: the word "*watched*" in "Coldspring" becomes *watch* in "The Last Post;" "[W]hite as the eye can see" in "Coldspring" becomes "white as far as the eye can see" in "The Last Post."

[15] Only the first ms. page is available in the Columbia archive, although the text would *appear* to continue.

[16] The second page of both of these different-sized published pieces lists two addresses for "contributions:" Burroughs in Tanger, and Nuttall in London, implying that this piece appeared originally in *My Own Mag* (housed at Columbia), and

that the reprint may be from *VDRSVP, Nova Broadcast* (Northwestern). For our purposes, I will refer to these pieces collectively as "*My Own Mag*/Northwestern."

[17] The only entry in Joe Maynard and Barry Miles' *William S. Burroughs: A Bibliography: 1953-1973* for *VDRSVP* is indeed a text called "The Moving Times," a "[S]ingle larger sheet of newsprint," from 1969 (159). The entry (C232) notes two publication points: 1) a tipped-in offering to Kaleidoscope 17 (Milwaukee, 1969) and 2) as a folded newspaper sheet in *San Francisco Earthquake* 5 (1969). There is no mention in Maynard and Miles of prior publication in *My Own Mag*.

[18] This completely ignores the question of the "meaning" behind the usage, a question Tomasz Stompor addressed in a presentation to the European Beat Studies Network (2012) titled "'Larval Entities': William S. Burroughs' Concepts of Time," which offers a productive genetic point that the three-column layout was a necessity of the foolscap paper size, followed by this hypothesis: that the 1899 year is linked to the "inscription of the date as usually seen on the friezes of arches and portals" (6). He adds that Burroughs' frequent references to these cities—New York, Gibraltar, and St. Louis—in this order is linked to visible date inscriptions on the Dewey Arch in New York City, the left-most of the three-arched Southport Gates in Gibraltar, and "speculatively" the Gateway Arch in St. Louis. (Stompor)

[19] Burton: "I was ever wont to intermix with mine own work some ornaments from the works of others, and I have laboriously collected this fardel out of divers writers, and like him, *sine injuria*, I have wronged no writers, but given every man his due; and thus citing and quoting mine authors, I am no thief…I have taken, not stolen" (23).

[20] The methodology is also different, and would benefit from further study: extra-illustration is an intervention in already-printed books, whereas the cutups are interventions within already-printed texts and author-produced typescript pages. Wing wrote his own title pages, yet these were specific to the works under expansion. So far as we know, he did not repeat these exact wordings in his title pages, despite the repetition of sentiments (or the insertion of the letter from Granger); Burroughs, as this essay notes, reproduced the same text with abandon.

Works Cited

Bergvall, Caroline, Laynie Browne, Teresa Carmody, and Vanessa Place, eds. *I'll Drown My Book: Conceptual Writing By Women*. Los Angeles: Les Figues, 2012. Print.

Birmingham, Jed. "*My Own Mag:* A Bibliographic Nightmare." Web 12 Dec. 2012.

Boon, Marcus. *In Praise Of Copying*. Cambridge, Mass.: Harvard UP, 2010. Print.

Breu, Christopher. "The Novel Enfleshed: *Naked Lunch* And The Literature Of Materiality." *Twentieth Century Literature* 57.2 (2011): 199-223. *Academic Search Premier*. Web. 10 Dec. 2012.

Burroughs, William S. "Afternoon Ticker Tape." *The Burrough*, in *My Own Mag* 6 (1964): page 6. *My Own Mag* archive box, L Eng Serial. McCormick Library of Special Collections, Northwestern University Library. Mislabeled as issue #16. See "*My Own Mag*." *Realitystudio.org*. 12 Dec. 2012.

---. *The Burroughs File*. San Francisco: City Lights, 1984. Print.

---. *Burroughs Live: The Collected Interviews of William S. Burroughs, 1960-1997*. Ed. Sylvère Lotringer. Los Angeles: Semiotext(e) Double Agent Series, 2001. Print.

---. "The Coldspring News." 1p. (photocopied). *San Francisco Earthquake* 1.35 (1968):13 (?). Jan Herman archive, Box 6. McCormick Library of Special Collections, Northwestern University Library. Presumably, a reprint of poster in *The Spero*. 1.1 (1965): 15-16.

---. from "The Coldspring News." In *The Burroughs File*, 67-71.

---. *Conversations with William S. Burroughs*. Ed. Allen Hibbard. Jackson: UP of Mississippi, 2000, Print

---. "A Distant Hand Lifted." *In The Burroughs File*, 34-38. Geoffrey D. Smith, John M. Bennett and Oliver Harris, eds. Print.

---. Smith, Geoffrey D., John M. Bennett and Oliver Harris. *Everything Lost: The Latin American Notebook Of William S. Burroughs*. Columbus: The Ohio State UP, 2008. Print.

---. *Junky: The Definitive Text of "Junk."* Ed. Oliver Harris. USA: Penguin, 2003.

---."The Last Post." In "Experimental Prose. Tangier. ca. 1964." T.ms. 1p. (carbon). Spec MS Coll Burroughs. Columbia University Rare Book and Manuscript Library.

---. "The Last Post *Danger Ahead*." In *The Burroughs File*, 53-55. Print.

---. *The Letters of William S. Burroughs: 1945-1959*. Ed. Oliver Harris. USA: Penguin, 1993. Print.

---. "London, 5 Sept, 1960. Letter To Allen Ginsberg." T.l.s. 2p. MS Coll Ginsberg, Columbia University Rare Book and Manuscript Library.

---. "The Moving Times. 3-column dates: February 6, 1964; November 18&19, 1963; September 17, 1899. In "Experimental Prose. Tangier. ca. 1964." T.ms. 1p. (carbon). Spec MS Coll Burroughs. Columbia University Rare Book and Manuscript Library.

---. "The Moving Times." *My Own Mag 5* (1964): 3-4. In "Burroughs, William Seward, Tangier, 20 May 1964, To Allen Ginsberg." Following "written on copy of *My Own Mag*." 2 p. Spec MS Coll Burroughs. Columbia University Rare Book and Manuscript Library. Listed as No. 8. Also in 2 over-sized pages. *VDRSVP, Nova Broadcast*, San Francisco, 1969(?). 3-column dates: February 10, 1964; January 17, 1947; September 17, 1899. Herman, Box 15, Folder 2. McCormick Library of Special Collections, Northwestern University Library. See "*My Own Mag.*" *Realitystudio.org.* 12 Dec. 2012.

---. "The Moving Times." In *The Burroughs File*, 150-151.

---. *Nova Express*. (1964) New York: Grove Press, 1992. Print.

---. "Other Voices." In "Experimental Prose. Tangier. ca. 1964." T.ms. 1p. (carbon). Spec MS Coll Burroughs. Columbia University Rare Book and Manuscript Library. Print.

---. "Pages from the Cut-Up Scrapbooks." In *The Burroughs File*, 153-183. Print.

---. *The Place of Dead Roads*. New York: Holt, Rinehart and Winston, 1983. Print.

---. *Queer: 25th-Anniversary Edition*. Ed. Oliver Harris. New York: Penguin, 2010. Print.

---. Morgan, Bill, *Rub Out The Words: The Letters Of William S. Burroughs 1959-1974*. New York: Ecco, 2012. Print.

---. "St. Louis Return" [London? 1965]. T.ms., 6, 2p. (carbon; draft of Fall 1965, *Paris Review* article). Ms Coll Miles. Columbia University Rare Book and Manuscript Library.

---. "St. Louis Return." *The Paris Review*. 35 (1965): 50-62. Later published in *The Burroughs File*, 79-89. Print.

---. "Who is the Walks Beside You Written 3rd?" In *The Burroughs File*, 72-78. Print.

---. "Your Day." In "Experimental Prose. Tangier. ca. 1964." T.ms. 1p. (carbon). Spec MS Coll Burroughs. Columbia University Rare Book and Manuscript Library.

Burroughs, William S. and Allen Ginsberg. *The Yage Letters Redux.* Ed. Oliver Harris. San Francisco: City Lights, 2006. Print.

Burroughs, William S. and Brion Gysin, et al. *Minutes to Go.* Paris: Two Cities Editions, 1960. Print.

Burroughs, William S. and Brion Gysin. *The Third Mind.* New York: Seaver Books/Viking, 1978. Print.

Doran, John. *Habits and men and the makers of both.* Vol. VIII. Boston: Francis A. Niccolls & Co, n.d. Copy at the Newberry Library extra-illustrated by John M. Wing, 1910.

---. *Table Traits.* Boston: Francis A. Niccolls & Co., 1854. Copy at the Newberry Library extra-illustrated by John M. Wing, 1906. Print.

Deleuze, Gilles Guattari, Félix. *A Thousand Plateaus: Capitalism And Schizophrenia.* Minneapolis : U Of Minnesota P, 2005, c1987. Print.

Dworkin, Craig and Kenneth Goldsmith. *Against Expression: An Anthology of Conceptual Writing.* Evanston, IL: Northwestern, 2011. Print.

Enns, Anthony "Burroughs' Writing Machines." In *Retaking the Universe: William S. Burroughs in the Age of Globalization*. Eds. Davis Schneiderman and Philip Walsh. Sterling, Virginia: Pluto Press, 2004: 95-115. Print.

Espinasse, F. "The House of Murray." *Harper's Magazine*. Sept. 1885: 503-522. Copy at the Newberry Library extra-illustrated by John M. Wing, 1907.

Gage, Jill. Conversations with the author, 2005-2006.

---."Re: Extra-illustration questions...for your expertise." E-mail to author. 3 Aug. 2006.

Gage, Jill. "With Deft Knife and Paste: The Extra-Illustrated Books of John M. Wing." *RBM: A Journal of Rare Books, Manuscripts, and Cultural Heritage.* 9 (2008): 118-126. Print.

Geiger, John. *Nothing is True Everything is Permitted: The Life of Brion Gysin*. New York: The Disinformation Company, 2006.

Granger, John. (First published 1769). *A Biographical History of England from Egbert the Great to the Revolution, Consisting of Characters, Dispersed in Different Classes and Adapted to a Methodized Catalogue of Engraved British Heads, Intended as an Essay Toward Reducing Our Biographies to a System, and a Help to the Knowledge of Portraits*. London: William Baynes and Son, 1824. Copy at the Newberry Library extra-illustrated by John M. Wing, pre-1899. Print.

Harris, Oliver. *William S. Burroughs and the Secret of Fascination*. Carbondale, IL: Southern Illinois UP; 2003. Print.

---."Re: Also, WSB question." Email to Davis Schneiderman. September 24, 2012.

Jackson, Holbrook. *The Anatomy of Bibliomania*. (1950) New York: Avenel Books, 1981. Print.

Kennicott, Philip. "Extending the Book: The Art of Extra-Illustration." *The Washington Post*. 11 March 2010. Web. 12 Dec. 2012.

Maynard, Joe, and Barry Miles. *William S. Burroughs: A Bibliography: 1953-1973. Unlocking Inspectors Lee's Word Hoard*. Charlottesville: UP of Virginia, 1978. Print.

Murphy, Timothy S. *Wising Up The Marks: The Amodern William Burroughs*. Berkeley: U of California P, 1997. *New York Times*. 17 Sept. 1899: A1.

Phillips, Tom, and W.H. Mallock. *A Humument: A Treated Victorian Novel*. New York: Thames & Hudson, 2012. Print.

Robinson, Edward S. (2011) *Shift Linguals: Cut-up Narratives from William S. Burroughs to the Present*. Amsterdam: Rodopi, 2011. Print.

Russell, Jamie. *Queer Burroughs*. New York: Palgrave, 2001. Print.

Schneiderman, Davis. "Everybody's Got Something to Hide Except for Me and My Lawsuit: William S. Burroughs, DJ Danger Mouse, and the Politics of 'Grey Tuesday.'" *Plagiary: Cross-disciplinary Studies in Plagiarism, Fabrication, and Falsification.* (online). 1.13 (2006): 1-18. Plagiary 2006 (print). 1 (2006): 191-206.

---."Gysin the THERE." *American Book Review.* 27.5 (2006): 30. Print

Schneiderman, Davis and Philip Walsh. Eds. *Retaking the Universe: William S. Burroughs in the Age of Globalization.* London: Pluto, 2004. Print.

Sobieszek, Robert A. and Burroughs, William S. *Ports Of Entry: William S. Burroughs And The Arts.* Los Angeles: Los Angeles County Museum Of Art; 1996. Print.

Star Wars Uncut. starwarsuncut.com. 21 Jan. 2013.

Sterne, Laurence. *Tristram Shandy: The life and opinions of Tristram Shandy, gentleman.* Vol. 3. London: R. and J. Dodsley, 1761. Print.

.Wermer-Colan, Alex. "Implicating The Confessor: The Autobiographical Ploy In William S. Burroughs' Early Work." *Twentieth Century Literature* 56.4 (2010): 493-529. *Academic Search Premier*. Web. 10 Dec. 2012.

Did Beatniks Kill John F. Kennedy?
Rob Johnson

Section I

At the 1960 Republican Party convention held in Chicago, former President Herbert Hoover, 85 years of age and in his sixth decade of attending these conventions, took to the stage accompanied by the tune of "Happy Days Are Here Again" and declared that America was in a "frightening moral slump" of crime, juvenile delinquency, and corruption. And who was to blame? Communists, beatniks, and eggheads:

> During the 14 years since the war, communist conspiracies and their fronts have poured the Marxist poison into our people. They insist that love of country, pride of a people in their history, their ideals, and their accomplishments, is wicked nationalism. Ever since the war, the communist fronts and the beatniks and the eggheads have conducted a national chorus of denunciation of this wicked nationalism.[1]

The speech was lost on the distracted convention-goers, who belatedly and mildly applauded it, but the phrase "communist, beatnik, egghead"—often wrongly attributed to FBI director J. Edgar Hoover—has become a staple of Beat scholarship.[2] Lost in his speech, and oddly *beat* in its sentiments, however, was Hoover's further call for a "rebirth of a great spiritual force" in America.

Setting aside the category of eggheads, which would be, and has been, the subject of a study of anti-intellectualism during the Cold War,[3] I want to explore this conflation of "communist" and "beatnik." As is well known, the blame begins with *San Francisco Examiner* columnist Herb Caen, who in a 1957 column complaining about the influx of "beat" characters into the North Beach area of San Francisco coined the term "beatnik," creating the diminutive of *beat* by playing off the name of the Russian satellite "Sputnik."[4] So the term *beatnik*, a distinct pejorative, quickly replaced in the minds of many the key understanding of *beat*, which has a pre-Beat Generation history, but its association with this group of writers is traced to Jack Kerouac, who in 1948 coined the foundational term *Beat Generation* and was a radical individualist with little interest in a collectivist society.[5] In September 1960, writing to Allen Ginsberg following Ginsberg's return from a communist-sponsored literary conference in Chile and Ginsberg's meeting with Fidel Castro in New York City that same year, Kerouac stated that "what Jesus said about astonishment of paradise, seems to me much more on the right tracks of world peace and joy than all the recent communist and general political hysteria rioting and false screamings. Cuba Shmuba . . ." (*Selected Letters* 268). He would maintain, in a series of defensive articles dating from this time period such as "Lamb, No Lion," that *beat* meant beatific, certainly not "communist," and that "The Beat Generation is no hoodlumism . . . My favorite Beat buddies were all *kind*, good kids, eager, sincere" (*Good*, 51, 53).

However, by the time of Hoover's speech, given at a convention that would nominate Richard M. Nixon as its presidential candidate, Kerouac's definition of Beat had been significantly erased by the epithet "beatnik," which the public had come to associate with communists. The word had also come to stand in for every anti-establishment, juvenile delinquent, commie, and rock-and-roll hoodlum type in America. *Beatnik* continued to hold this distinction, arguably, until it was replaced by the epithet *hippie*, following the Human Be-In in San Francisco in 1967. *Beatnik* was a reigning pejorative term for dangerous societal malcontents, therefore, on the morning of November 22 in 1963 when John F. Kennedy was gunned down on the streets of Dallas. Following the disbelief and shock of the moment, the question that inevitably followed was, "Who shot Kennedy?" It's still a question being debated today, of course, but that day, in 1963, who shot Kennedy was a question initially answered along lines deeply divided by politics and ideology.

On the left, the speculation as to the identity of the killer was voiced most famously by Chief Justice Earl Warren: The president's "martyrdom," he said when informed of Kennedy's death, was directly caused by "the hatred and bitterness that has been injected into the life of our nation by bigots" (qtd. in Piereson 92). In other words, Kennedy was killed by Dallas rednecks opposed to Kennedy's civil rights agenda, his supposed "coddling" of Communism, his support of the United Nations, and other "liberal" causes. Warren, half-jokingly, had warned Kennedy to go around Texas, not through it. Others were more serious, including Billy Graham, who also attempted to warn Kennedy against visiting Dallas (Kashner), and Senator William Fulbright, who told Kennedy, "It's too dangerous. I wouldn't go there, don't you go" (Melanson 63). "Impeach Earl Warren" billboards had been up in Dallas for months before Kennedy even arrived, Jewish-owned stores had recently been vandalized, and right-wing tracts were being circulated in the public schools accusing Kennedy of being a communist. Kennedy himself was greeted with a full-page newspaper ad in the *Dallas Morning News*, bordered thickly and ominously in black, telling Kennedy, the commie lover, to go home. Jackie Kennedy was upset by the advertisement, and JFK tried to calm his soon-to-be widow by joking, "Oh, you know, we're headed into nut country today" (Piereson 58).

"Nut Country" could well have been the title of one of the best novels about the Kennedy assassination, *Strange Peaches* (1972) by Edwin "Bud" Shrake, a

Dallas-based writer at the time of the assassination who has been labeled a "Texas Beat" by literary historian Steven L. Davis. Shrake was very close to the action in November 1963: he was even dating Jack Ruby's headlining stripper Jada. Shrake also knew Jack Ruby fairly well and was eyewitness to, as Texas literary historian Don Graham says, the "weird" world that was Fort Worth and Dallas before and after the assassination (28). But Shrake did not just know the underground: he was drinking buddies with super-rich oil barons and Texas powerbrokers such as Clint Murchison and even knew the reclusive billionaire H. L. Hunt (Davis 112-113). Shrake's alter ego in the novel, John Lee, bridges these two worlds in unique fashion: he's a Dallas-born actor who plays a longhaired nineteenth-century era cowboy on a popular TV show, *Six Guns Across Texas*, and when he's not filming the show and is back in Dallas, he keeps the hair long. Apparently, in Fort Worth and Dallas in 1963 you could be a freak with long hair as long as you were also wearing a cowboy hat.

In the novel, Lee, the longhaired freak, is thus still able to hang out with the most powerful men in Dallas on the eve of the assassination. At a private hunting club, where exotic animals are released into the gun sights of waiting "hunters," he hears talk that Kennedy is a communist, the CIA is a communist front, and that Kennedy should have invaded Hungary and did not (122). Lee himself is called a communist at a chamber of commerce "Breakfast Brigade" talk when he criticizes the business community's funding of the *Dallas Morning News* ad against the president (271). The people of Dallas, including Lee's mother, have been fully brainwashed against Kennedy by his arrival on November 21: "Ohhh, the world is in such bad shape," his mother tells him. "Every day you read the worst things in the papers. The President is being friendly with the Russians. I just don't see how the people can let him do that. Crime keeps going up. Why, we've started locking our house. You read about these nigras and beatniks roaming around" (134).

Lee, often mistaken for a beatnik himself until he's recognized as a cowboy actor, covers the Kennedy motorcade while making a film about the "real" Texas and witnesses the assassination looking through a Bolex lens on a 16 mm camera. Moments before Kennedy is shot, though, he makes eye contact with the President, "and a communication flashed from him to me that said *there you are you freak what a time you must have among these people I like you for it don't give up*" (281, emphasis Shrake's). When Kennedy is shot, Lee sees pieces of his skull fly out the back of his head and knows he is dead. The crowd starts looking for the shooter, and spotting John Lee, the "freak" with long hair, someone yells, "Grab that longhaired guy! Get him!" "Officer, get that long-haired fellow!" "What's your name, Buddy." "Wallace." "What's your business here?" "I came to see the President." "What kind of work do you do" "I'm a cowboy." "Okay, move along"(284). Subsequently, Lee spots two Dallas men in business suits openly celebrating Kennedy's death. The presence of a policeman stops him from assaulting them, and he and his friends are ashamed that they had not "worked off our rage with blind violence against those we knew deserved it" (288).[6]

Those we knew deserved it: the "right wing bastards," the crew-cut John Birchers holding their assassination celebrations, the anti-Kennedy anti-communist anti-civil rights anti-Castro business men and chamber of commerce types, the oil men such as the Murchisons and Hunts—this is who Shrake points the finger at in the immediate aftermath of the assassination, much as Earl Warren blurted out that Dallas was full of "bigots." But that characterization hardly had time to form before, suspiciously, news media were already reporting that Kennedy's killer had been caught, and that, yes, he was a known "communist." The Dallas Chamber of Commerce members, the members of the Petroleum Club, the Baptist ministers, all must have allowed themselves a brief sigh of relief before nodding their heads with certainty. Oswald was himself assassinated a few days later leading to endless speculation regarding his political motives and possible accomplices. And it all had to be sorted out in the massive Warren Commission Report, released in 1964.

The Warren Commission interviewed 552 persons about what happened that day and the days before the assassination, making November 22, 1963 arguably one of the single most researched days in the history of the world. They interviewed police officers, plumbers, strippers ("Is there a difference between an exotic dancer and a striptease dancer?")[7] —everyone in every walk of life who had pertinent information, creating an amazingly deep view of Fort Worth, Dallas, and the United States as a whole during this period. And this is where the question that forms the title of this essay comes in – "Did Beatniks Kill JFK? – because if one does a search of the on-line text of the Warren Commission Report and all of its appended reports and exhibits and put in the term *beatnik*, this label, initially derived from a philosophical conversation in 1948 between two aspiring novelists, Jack Kerouac and John Clellon Holmes, is an enormously useful and resonant concept for creating the profile of an assassin the commission seems invested in describing: a non-conformist, unemployed, and unkempt loner with communist or leftist sympathies—the Lone Gunman Theory (abbreviated LGT by assassination researchers). The commission's single-minded approach, therefore, de-emphasizes many other plausible profiles of a gunman who was perhaps Mafia-connected, a Castro agent, or connected to one of the Dallas businessmen described by Bud Shrake who so visibly demonstrated their hatred of Kennedy—among other possible profiles of an assassin at the time. In the Report, *beatnik* is clearly shorthand, culturally current, that steers perception away from some or all of these other possible assassins. Moreover, a crafted image of Oswald as a beatnik helped underpin the Commission's findings that Oswald was a communist by conflating (as described earlier) communist with beatnik.

This is particularly true in the Report when it comes to Oswald's appearance—his clothing, haircut, and hygiene. If the Left thought the killer had to have a crew cut, the average person interviewed by the Warren Commission apparently thought the opposite: he had to be a scruffy beatnik in appearance. Interview after interview reveals this, even though the real Oswald was clean-cut, clean-shaven, and neat in appearance. However, in the days before the assassination, Oswald was sighted all around Texas—in Alice, San Antonio, Freer, and Pleasanton—and in most cases he was described as dirty and should be unkempt and fitting the stereotype of the beatnik communist (Courtwright). He was frequently seen in the company of other beatniks as well, according to several informants. In Mexico City, for example, where Oswald was trying to obtain a visa to visit Cuba, he was spotted by two embassy employees in the company of "two other beatnik looking boys."[9] An eyewitness in Dallas who spotted Oswald on a firing range just prior to the assassination also says he was with a man whose hair was worn in a "beatnik style."[10] One of the most controversial informants, Perry Russo, who testified in District Attorney Jim Garrison's Kennedy assassination investigation while under the influence of sodium pentothal, claimed to have seen Oswald at a party in New Orleans where the assassination was discussed, and that Oswald "looked like a typical beatnik, extremely dirty, with his hair all messed up, the beard unkempt, a dirty t-shirt, and either blue jeans or khaki pants on. He wore white tennis shoes which were cruddy and had on no socks"[11] — the very image of a beatnik popularized by *Life* Magazine in photo spreads such as the pictures of a beatnik pad that accompanied Paul O'Neil's November 30, 1959 *Life* magazine article "The Only Rebellion Around" or in *Mad* Magazine, or on TV's *Dobie Gillis*, for that matter. When investigators showed Russo a picture of a clean-shaven Oswald, he asked them to draw a beard on him, then said, "Yes, that's him." Later, at the Detective Bureau in New Orleans, Russo spent six hours working with police artists on a sketch of Oswald, objecting throughout that Oswald didn't look "dirty and disheveled" enough (Lambert 71). In the service of turning Oswald into the stereotypical beatnik and communist, it didn't matter that the real Oswald, by almost all accounts, looked nothing like a beatnik.

Even witnesses who do not report Oswald looking "dirty and disheveled," make it a point to say, unprompted, that Oswald "was not a beatnik," as a man who sat next to Oswald on a bus out of Laredo, Texas, said of him, apparently surprised at Oswald's lack of cooperation in terms of his physical appearance.[12] At times, interviewers for the Warren Commission try to push informants to call key characters in the assassination "beatniks." The following exchange takes place between a Mrs. Voshinin and Warren Commission interviewer Jenner regarding a man she knew named George de Mohrenschildt, a friend of Lee Harvey Oswald in Dallas:

> Mr. Jenner: Was he [de Mohrenschildt] unconventional?
> Mrs. Voshinin: Uh--what does that mean exactly?
> Mr. Jenner: He didn't dress normally--
> Mrs. Voshinin: That's true; yes.
> Mr. Jenner: He would come to church in shorts?
> Mrs. Voshinin: Exactly.
> Mr. Jenner: Sort of a beatnik?
> Mrs. Voshinin: Well, no; not beatnik--but he was definitely nonconformist. He would just love to do exactly what people would, you know, object to.

Today, no one would confuse George de Mohrenschildt with a beatnik, and it's a sign of the times that the Warren Commission interviewer applies this label, apparently searching for a term that generically applies to anyone who is in the slightest degree unconventional, leftist in their politics, eccentric, or foreign-born. In fact, de Mohrenschildt was a petroleum geologist who was friends with the Bouvier family (Jacqueline Bouvier [Kennedy] called him "Uncle George") and future president George H. W. Bush and was also an associate of some of the most conservative and powerful oilmen in Texas, including Clint Murchison and H. L. Hunt. Later, he was identified as a CIA operative (Waldron and Hartmann, *Ultimate* 451-453). Either these facts did not matter to the Warren Commission interviewer or he was unaware of them. It was enough that de Mohrenschildt was an atheist who talked provocatively about politics at times. Mrs. Voshinin's labeling of de Mohrenschildt as "non-conformist" as opposed to "beatnik" is actually more precise and is a more fruitful link to Oswald as well: Oswald, like de Mohrenschildt, was often described as "loving to do exactly what people would, you know, object to." Moreover, Mrs. Voshinin apparently at least knew what a real beatnik looked like, if the investigator did not.

In fact, Fort Worth and Dallas did have bona fide beatniks at the time of the Kennedy assassination—famously so, in the wake of the full Warren Commission investigation. In 1960, the mayor of Fort Worth had even signed a proclamation declaring a city-wide "National Beatnik Day," and *Life* magazine ran a picture of the signing ceremony, which shows the balding mayor flanked by a man in a beret and goatee and a woman dressed in dance tights, among others. In February 1960, *Life* also photographed two beatnik candidates running for Democratic party precinct chairman in Fort Worth, "Big Mike" Calloway and Peter "the Hero" Gill. At their rally in downtown Fort Worth, a banner read, "Kick the cows out of cowtown and let the cats in to swing." Gill campaigned on a platform of "free espresso, dancing ladies, and beatniks all over the place." Calloway promised to improve the conditions in flophouses for winos ("Politics").

The center of beatnik culture in Fort Worth and Dallas, and where Gill and Calloway organized their ultimately unsuccessful campaigns, was a coffee shop called The Cellar. The place is infamous in Kennedy assassination annals, for it was at The Cellar that Kennedy's secret service agents reportedly partied until the wee hours of the morning the day of the assassination. The owner of The Cellar, a controversial, Van Dyke-bearded character named Pat Kirkwood, who is still a legend in Dallas, was known as the "Daddy of the Beats" in the Fort Worth-Dallas area.

The Cellar was located below street level in downtown Fort Worth, a walk-down bar just blocks from the Hotel Texas, where the Kennedy entourage stayed the night before the assassination. Secret Service agents began the evening drinking at a bar called The Press Club and were spotted by the press doing so. Not content to drink just during legal hours, the agents then went to The Cellar. The Cellar didn't have a liquor license and therefore could stay open all night. It was quite a colorful bohemian night spot.[14] The waitresses wore bikinis or lingerie along with cowboy hats, and patrons were entertained by rock bands, comedians (including a young Dallas DJ named George Carlin), and if they were lucky, by Cannibal Jones, also known as Bongo Joe, who recited free form poetry while beating rhythms out on a 55-gallon Texaco oil drum (Crouse and Beal).

The club was infamous, and its reputation had reached all the way to Washington, D.C., apparently. CBS news anchor Bob Schieffer, then a young Fort Worth reporter, says he was approached by a Secret Service agent while covering Kennedy's trip to Dallas and was asked if he would take a group of agents to the club, about which they had heard wild rumors. He obliged and spent a long night drinking with the agents, a story he only recently revealed in his 2004 memoir subtitled *What I Couldn't Tell You on TV*. Now, while technically The Cellar couldn't serve alcohol, it was well known that it did, in neon-green drinks spiked with Everclear, a pure grain alcohol. Pat Kirkwood, the owner of The Cellar, managed to convince a host of investigators and policemen following the assassination that he served no drinks to the agents that night, but he later admitted, "[T]hose guys were bombed. They were drinking pure Everclear" (Waldron and Hartmann, *Ultimate* 716). This just a few hours before they were assigned to guard the President of the United States. Warren Commission investigators couldn't get the agents to admit they had been drinking anything other than "fruit drinks and coffee," but they did admit they had been at the beatnik nightclub until 3:30 a.m. That was enough for one investigator, a Mr. Rankin, to lay into James J. Rawley, a senior Secret Service officer on duty that day:

> Now other people, as they went along there, even some people in the crowds, saw a man with a rifle up in this building from which the president was shot. Now, don't you think that if a man went to bed reasonably early,

and hadn't been drinking the night before, he would be more alert to see those things as a Secret Service agent, than if they stayed up until 3, 4, 5 o'clock in the morning going to beatnik joints?[15]

Therefore, Rankin is angered not only by the agents drinking while on duty and their questionable state of readiness on the day of the assassination (how did they miss seeing a rifleman atop a building bordering the parade route?) — but also by the particular site of their drinking, a club frequented by dangerous beatnik types. "It would seem to me," Rankin continues in the Report, "that a beatnik joint is a place where queer people of all kinds gather anyway, and that the mere fact that these men did leave their post of duty might be an indication to someone that the President was not being protected, and might leave an opening for them to go there and try to do something."[16]

Beatniks didn't kill John F. Kennedy, maybe, but if you were looking for a candidate to do it, a "beatnik joint" might be a good place to look. Why not simply broadcast to every "queer" character in Fort Worth that the president is unguarded because his agents are quite publicly knocking back Everclear fruit drinks and ogling college-aged women in lingerie at 4 a.m.? Although this scenario sounds outrageous, there's more truth to it than one might expect. From 1960-1961, police had been called out to The Cellar almost 100 times for complaints ranging from disturbing the peace to gang fights. In the summer of 1961, the club was closed down for a brief period, but the bongo drums were back by August of 1961 ("Fort"), and the club re-opened for business. Strippers from Jack Ruby's mob-connected nightclub The Carousel were also known to frequent the club. It was hardly a place for Secret Service agents to be seen drinking until near dawn the day of a presidential parade being held in a city that had no love for John F. Kennedy. Anything could happen in The Cellar, and according to Secret Service agent Abraham Bolden, it did. In a recent memoir, Bolden recalls that at the time of the shooting it was well known that the agents were drunk that night and that they were entertained at The Cellar by a party of strippers, probably sent over by Jack Ruby from his Carousel Club. One of the agents apparently lost his Secret Service ID badge that night at The Cellar, with serious consequences: it may well have been the badge that showed up in the possession of the "mystery man" on the grassy knoll by Dealey Plaza, a still unidentified man who escaped investigation by flashing Secret Service credentials (Bolden 104-105). Considering that the House Select Committee on Assassinations in its 1976 report concluded that at least one shot "probably" came from the grassy knoll, this person's identity is of great interest—and his cover might have come from a Secret Service ID surreptitiously lifted from an agent's coat earlier that morning in a beatnik nightclub.

The Warren Commission investigators, therefore, had good reason to be critical of the agents' choice of nightspots. An inconvenient truth about their behavior that night, however, is that for anyone who has studied it, Kennedy's sometimes reckless personal behavior—his reported affair with mobster Sam Giancana's mistress, his friendship with mob-connected Frank Sinatra, his reported drug use, including Mary Meyer's account of dropping LSD with the president (see, for example, Seymour Hersh's *The Dark Side of Camelot* [1997]; *Brothers: The Hidden History of the Kennedy Years* [2008] by David Talbot; and *Mary's Mosaic* [2012] by Peter Janney)— resonates with images of underworld figures and avant-garde musicians, such as Bongo Joe.[17]

Perhaps that's why the "freaks," therefore, sensed some sympathy from Kennedy, as John Lee does in *Strange Peaches*, interpreting Kennedy's eye contact with him to mean, "Yeah, you're a freak, but keep doing what you are doing." Kennedy, as the son of the powerful Joseph P. Kennedy, was hardly a "freak," but the fact that he was a Catholic alienated a large number of Protestant Americans nationwide. He was tolerant, accordingly, of difference. In Mexico City, June 1962, Kennedy's motorcade was halted by a man whom the Secret Service agent in charge, Gerald Behn, said "had the appearance of a typical beatnik." When the "beatnik" came around to Kennedy's side of the car, Behn hit him and knocked him down. Kennedy, who apparently didn't think the man's appearance was enough to arouse this violent response, reprimanded the agent for hitting the "beatnik."[18] Kennedy also knew something about the Beat Generation. Kennedy joked that a "naked lunch" was what he wanted, although the reference to the still-banned Burroughs novel was lost on Sinatra (Jacobs and Stadiem 91). Then, too, Jackie Kennedy was at least as hip as her husband. During the 1960 campaign, she was photographed by Jacques Lowe reading *The Dharma Bums* while on-board the Kennedy family private jet; she told *Reader's Digest* she read everything from "Colette to Kerouac" (McNally 294). Jack Kerouac told his editor Ellis Amburn that Jackie had even invited him to the White House, although when Amburn asked Kennedy about it, she coyly refused to confirm or deny the meeting: "We asked many writers to the White House" (Amburn 358). In Eisenhower-era America, the Kennedys' taste in literature and their personal style was remarkable enough in some corners of America to brand them as suspiciously unconventional. The fact that Kennedy didn't wear a hat at his wintry inauguration, and his brother Robert often didn't wear ties at meetings was enough to upset some people in 1960. Robert Kennedy, according to Ben Bradlee, looked like a "Brooks Brothers Beatnik" (Hilty 192). When Jackie wore a sleeveless sundress to a Good Friday service in Palm Beach, everyone thought "it was a little too free-thinking and beatnik," recalls *Vogue* editor Hamish Bowles (Leight).

Text of handbill distributed in Dallas, November 1963:

THIS MAN is wanted for treasonous activities against the United States.

1. Betraying the Constitution (which he swore to uphold). He is turning the sovereignty of the U.S. over to the communist controlled United Nations. He is betraying our friends (Cuba, Kalanga, Portugal) and befriending our enemies (Russian, Yugoslavia, Poland).

2. He has been WRONG on innumerable issues affecting the security of the U.S. (United Nations-Berlin wall-Missle [sic] removal-Cuba-Wheat deals-Test Ban Treaty, etc.)

3. He has been lax in endorcing [sic] Communist Registration laws.

4. He has given support and encouragement to the Communist inspired racial riots.

5. He has illegally invaded a sovereign State with federal troops.

6. He has consistently appointed Anti-Christians to Federal office. Upholds the Supreme Course in its Anti-Christian rulings. Aliens and known Communists abound in Federal offices.

7. He has been caught in fantastic LIES to the American people including personal ones like his previous marriage and divorce.

Lee Harvey Oswald in handcuffs

Still, no one would seriously call Kennedy a beatnik. Or a beat, for that matter. Except perhaps ultra-conservative novelist and philosopher Ayn Rand in an article titled "J.F.K--High Class Beatnik?" published in the Bible of the conservative movement *Human Events*. Rand's September 1, 1960 article is a response to Kennedy's "New Frontier" speech, a decidedly youth-oriented one that in the tones of a counter-cultural indictment of the status quo asks young Americans to make the choice "between the fresh air of progress and the stale, dank atmosphere of 'normalcy'--between dedication or mediocrity." Kennedy, Rand argues, seeks to set himself as "an advocate of some 'new' home-grown version of fascism." So who is Kennedy, she asks. Is he a bright young man, or is he "the figure of an irresponsible young beatnik, a high-class beatnik, who, with unlimited means at his disposal, chose the power game, as others choose hot-rod racing--for kicks."

Kennedy, who appears to have read a lot of his own press, responded to Rand and the other writers in the section of *Human Events* titled "Kennedy's Liberal Promises," which described him, he says, quoting, "'as the farthest-out liberal democrat around.'" He used this as a laugh-line when he accepted his party's nomination in a speech delivered September 14, 1960: "While I am not certain of the 'beatnik' definition of 'farthest-out,' I am certain that this was not intended as a compliment." Kennedy might have turned Rand's comments into a joke, but the intent behind her essay—the first political essay she ever published—is extremely serious: In 1960 America, you are either for or against us, she seems to say. Kennedy, the young Irish-Catholic candidate can thus be "othered" by connecting him to every anti-establishment label that comes along with outsider status: he's a juvenile delinquent, a hot-rodder, and, most importantly, a "beatnik." Rand didn't even have to call him a communist; calling him a beatnik carried that baggage for her. Her argument is not unlike the crude generalization made by John Lee's mother in *Strange Peaches*: "nigras and beatniks" are roaming the land. Rand's characterization of beatniks as juvenile delinquents and Kennedy's humorous aside thus provide a snapshot from 1960 of the public perception of the Beat Generation and its lack of seriousness in the very serious landscape of politics: As Allen Ginsberg says famously in his poem "America," "Everybody's serious but me" (32).

Section II

The Beats had already been labeled "Know Nothings" and apolitical by Norman Podhoretz and others, and one way Beat scholarship can correct this view is by focusing on Beat writers' responses to the latter years of the Eisenhower administration, Kennedy's brief but historic administration, and his assassination. In fact, by the late 1950s, Beat and Beat-associated writers had become decidedly political in their writings, nowhere more so than in their response to the Cuban

Revolution, the Bay of Pigs, and the subsequent Cuban Missile Crisis during the Kennedy administration. In *The Cubalogues*, published in 2010, Todd Tietchen argues that America's policy towards Cuba in the late 1950s and early 1960s was crucial in moving Beats and sympathetic scholars into the political realm. Poets LeRoi Jones and Lawrence Ferlinghetti, and sociologist C. Wright Mills all spent time in Cuba following the Revolution and wrote in protest against the disinformation spread by the American government about the Revolution and against an American foreign policy that was forcing Cuba into the arms of the Soviet Union. In "Cuba Libre," Leroi Jones describes how he completely changed his worldview after traveling with Castro's revolutionaries and began his journey into the black nationalist movement; C. Wright Mills was hounded to death by FBI agents after publishing his sympathetic but not uncritical account of the Cuban Revolution, *Listen, Yankee* (1960) (Wakefield 5); Allen Ginsberg met Castro at a gathering in a Harlem hotel room in 1960 and the revolutionary leader shook hands with him, acknowledging Ginsberg as a famous poet and fellow traveler (Morgan 320). Many writers and intellectuals—including Ginsberg, Ferlinghetti, and Norman Mailer—were members of the Fair Play For Cuba Committee, a group founded in New York in 1960 dedicated to countering American propaganda about the Cuban Revolution. By the time Kennedy was assassinated, some Beat writers were among the most political writers of their time. Ginsberg alone penned enough political poetry and prose between 1957 and 1963 to fill a small volume, including "Death to Van Gogh's Ear!"; the essay "Poetry, Violence, and the Trembling of the Lambs (1959); "Subliminal" (written just after the Nixon/Kennedy debates); "Bay of Pigs"; and several untitled political poems in his journals. His correspondence with his father Louis during these years is filled with lengthy political analysis of world events, analysis that today appears cogent, well informed by his international travels and by the alternative press (particularly I. F. Stone's newsletter), and even-handed: in these letters to his father, Ginsberg is harshly critical of both Kennedy and Nikita Khrushchev right up to the moment of the assassination (Ginsberg, *Family* 148, 164,190).

The reaction to the news of the assassination by the three most famous Beat writers—Kerouac, Ginsberg, and Burroughs—very much reflected the politics and ideology of the individual writers. Kerouac, famously apolitical, was asked by Sterling Lord to write an article on the Kennedy assassination but declined the offer, saying he didn't "know anything about it" (*Letters* 385). Later, in a 1964 interview, he blamed Lyndon Baines Johnson for Kennedy's murder and said "they're going to get [Barry] Goldwater now" (Maher 441). Both Burroughs and Ginsberg subscribed early on to conspiracy theories about the assassination involving the CIA or the Mafia. Burroughs said the JFK assassination had "all the earmarks of a CIA and Mafia job combined." He was particularly amazed by the poor work performance of the Secret Service: "the people who were supposed to be protecting Kennedy didn't know their business, obviously" (Bockris 167-168). Ginsberg, in his poetry, mentions the CIA ("Capitol Air") and the Mafia ("Bayonne Turnpike to Tuscarora") as prime suspects behind the assassination, but he also advances the theory first publicly announced by Earl Warren on the day of the assassination—that race hatred motivated Kennedy's killers. In an interview with the magazine *The Burning Bush* just four days after the assassination, Ginsberg was critical of race consciousness— be it on the part of Blacks, Jews, Nazis, anyone—and said such consciousness "is built on the same stuff that killed President Kennedy" (Miles 332), implying that Kennedy's support of civil rights or his Catholicism were connected to his death. After all, in 1956, Ginsberg himself had written in his poem "America" that his "ambition is to be President despite the fact that I'm a Catholic" (*Howl* 33).

Recently declassified documents more or less confirm Ginsberg's and Burroughs' theories about CIA and Mafia involvement in the assassination. The Mafia almost certainly was trying to kill Kennedy, and following the Church Committee's report in 1975 it has been public knowledge that the CIA had recruited members of the Mafia to kill Fidel Castro, a fact that makes Burroughs' belief that the two organizations were working together quite prescient. As in one of the most recent exhaustive studies of the assassination, *Legacy of Secrecy: The Long Shadow of the Kennedy Assassination* (2008), Lamar Waldron and Thom Hartmann argue that it was the Mafia bosses' involvement in CIA-sponsored assassination plots against Castro as well as their knowledge of a planned coup in Cuba to be executed on December 1, 1963 that led them to believe they could kill Kennedy with impunity: any investigation of the JFK assassination would have to suppress information about top-secret plans to kill Castro and overthrow the Cuban government, information which, if it were made public in 1963 or 1964, could well have led to nuclear war between the United States and the Soviet Union over Cuba. Instead, Mafia bosses believed the subsequent investigation of Kennedy's assassination would focus on a lone gunman, a patsy such as Lee Harvey Oswald (Waldron and Hartmann 42-57). The plots to kill Castro were kept secret until the end of the Nixon administration and Oswald remained, officially, the lone gunman.

Even the political prophet Allen Ginsberg could not have imagined the complexity of these most recent assassination theories. In fact, Ginsberg was oddly quiet about the assassination and never wrote a full account of his own reaction to it. We don't know why he did not write such an account, but he had been harshly critical of Kennedy before he was even elected. By 1959, Ginsberg had become one of the most politically prescient poets in the United States. "I am the defense early warning radar system," he wrote in 1957 ("Death to Van Gogh's Ear"), referring to the over-the-horizon radar built in part by the supplies he helped ship to Alaska when he worked as a merchant seaman just after the "Howl" reading in 1955 (Schumacher 231-237). Eerily, in October 1959, while accompanying his brother Eugene to the doctor's office, he glanced at a *Look* magazine article "about 1960 presidential races, Kennedy's politicianing and shiftiness" and had a sudden vision of Kennedy slain: "He has a hole in his back. Thru which death will enter" (*Journals* 111). In heated letters to his father in which Ginsberg attempts to educate him about Kennedy's disastrous decisions leading up the Bay of Pigs, he says, "if anybody gets hanged better it should be Kennedy at this point rather than Castro." He later writes his father that supporting either Kennedy or Khrushchev is a "Why anybody in his right mind should want to take SIDES in this suicidal contest of Stupidity I'll never understand" (*Letters* 190). In the poem "Bay of Pigs," dated "April 13, 1961--Paris," he is less evenhanded and calls Kennedy a "boy man advertising fruit caught starting a war / denying his responsibility in crazy headlines" (*Journals* 200).

However, by the time of the assassination, and not long before it, Ginsberg had come to the conclusion that his bitterness over politics was destroying his soul and his writing. "Pound went mad trying to make up just laws for ignorant men," he warned himself in an untitled poem dated December 1960 (*Journals* 170). His experiences in India, where he spent many hours learning to meditate, culminated in a spiritual awakening that occurred on board a train in Japan in 1962. "I'm telling you the cold war's over, hurrah. All we really got to do is really love each other," he wrote Peter Orlovsky in late 1963 (Morgan 376-377). He was becoming the Allen Ginsberg of the 1960s, dedicated to non-violence and love. His poem based on this awakening, "The Change," was going to press in Ed Sanders' *Fuck You* magazine the very day of the assassination (Sanders, *Fug* 1).

When Kennedy was shot, Ginsberg had only recently arrived back in America from India and was living in San Francisco. The week before the assassination, he had participated in the first anti-Vietnam protest on American soil, staged outside a San Francisco hotel where the "First Lady" of Vietnam, Madame Ngo Dinh Nhu (from 1955-1963, the official hostess to the unmarried president of South Vietnam, her brother-in-law Ngo Dinh Diem,), was staying. He was already the bearded hippie icon of the 1960s, dressed in Indian garb, dedicated to non-violence, and telling fellow protestors as he told a journalist, "Anger and fury of left wing will only drive the humanoid bureaucrats and cops into deeper humanoidism. Be kind to cops" (Miles 330-311). Neal Cassady delivered the news of Kennedy's assassination to Ginsberg as he was eating breakfast. Cassady asked him what he thought would happen now, and Ginsberg said, "The country will go into a tailspin" (Miles 331). That afternoon he performed at a poetry reading in the Haight-Ashbury, and that night he went to a party at Lawrence Ferlinghetti's house. The evening was subdued, Ginsberg, "very kind to everyone,". . . " appeared almost courtly," and according to folksinger Eric Anderson (who was present at the party), one would never have known the president had been shot (Anderson 378).

Ginsberg, Lawrence Ferlinghetti, and Gregory Corso—among other Beat writers—all wrote poems about the Kennedy assassination, an event of such pathos that it challenged aesthetic response. Reflecting the mood portrayed in Anderson's recollection, Ginsberg's poem, "November 23, 1963: Alone," does not directly discuss the assassination, and Neal Cassady continues about his business of betting on horses. Still, the scene is lit by the "continuous blinking" of the television for "two radar days," and Ginsberg finds himself "confused shock-fingertipt [sic] on the rented typewriter" trying to write the poem (*Collected* 333-34). Lawrence Ferlinghetti's "Assassination Raga" was actually written on the occasion of Robert Kennedy's death, but more recently Ferlinghetti's "Americus I" asserts the epochal nature of the JFK assassination by featuring the event as the climactic moment of this first installment of a long poem meant to tell the history of America. Gregory Corso's "Lines Written Nov. 22-23—In Discord—" is clearly influenced by Walt Whitman's two great poems on the assassination of President Lincoln, "Oh Captain! My Captain!" and "When Lilacs Last in the Dooryard Bloom'd." Rhymes Corso, in tough talk that saves the passage from cliché, "When a Captain dies / The ship doesn't sink / And though the crew weeps the loss / The stars in the skies / are still boss" (Corso 141).These poems are not only epitaphs for the slain president but also epitaphs, in a way, for the writers themselves and for the times they lived in.

Like much about America before the assassination, "Beatnik" and "Beat" began to take on a quaintness and innocence of an antebellum past. By 1966, when J. Edgar Hoover explained to Congress why only "clean-cut" men and no "beatniks" could serve in the FBI (Torricelli and Carroll 265), the term *beatnik* was hopelessly dated. By 1967, following the Human Be-In in San Francisco, the release of *Sgt. Pepper's Lonely Hearts Club Band* (1967), and President Johnson's announcement of a draft lottery in March of 1967, "hippie" as an epithet had retired "beatnik" for good. It's tempting to wonder that if Kennedy been killed in 1967 would the right have gone looking for someone who fit the description of a hippie, just as it had done in 1963 when it seemed intent on transforming Oswald into a beatnik. Today, the pictures of a crew-cut Oswald are so familiar that no one would confuse Oswald with a beatnik. The historical context of that moment and the predominant image of the counterculture then current have lost much of their currency. After Kennedy's death, Americans needed more politics, more protest,
harder drugs, louder music, more of everything. Did beatniks kill John F. Kennedy? Of course not. In fact, one can conclude the opposite more readily: The death of John F. Kennedy effectively killed the beatniks.

Acknowledgement: My thanks to Tony Trigilio, Beat scholar and JFK assassination expert, for his critique of multiple drafts of this essay.

Notes

[1] The entire speech ("President Hoover on TV! (1960)") can be viewed at ≤ http://www.youtube.com/watch?v=hFtIpL2t6N0&feature>. A partial transcript of the speech, printed in the July 26, 1960, issue of the *Lawrence Journal-World* ("Who Needs to Win", 4) is available at <http://news.google.com/newspapers?nid=H3xT48m3F74C&dat=19600726&printsec=frontpage&hl=en>.

[2] It is a common mistake in Beat studies to assign the "communist beatniks and eggheads" quotation to FBI Director J. Edgar Hoover rather than to this speech delivered by Herbert Hoover. As far as I can tell, the mistake originates in Ted Morgan's biography of William S. Burroughs, but it may go back further. Morgan does not cite a source for the J. Edgar Hoover quotation.

[3] One of the earliest and best such responses is Richard Hofstadter's *Anti-Intellectualism in American Life* (1964).

[4] Before *Beatnik* was coined, Allen Ginsberg saw *Sputnik* in a positive light, having read that the name—*Sputnik Zemli*—meant "travelling companion of the world." He wrote to his father Louis that a communist country has "succeeded in improving material living conditions." Sputnik was launched the day after Judge Clayton Horn ruled "Howl" was not obscene, October 4, 1957.

[5] Kerouac's 1959 essay "The Origins of the Beat Generation" documents his 1948 coinage of the phrase with John Clellon Holmes (1979, 362). His early writings published in *Atop an Underwood* reveal that Kerouac did go through a brief Marxist period. See, for example, "The Birth of a Socialist."

[6] Shrake, a friend of Texas beat-associated writers Billy Brammer, Larry McMurtry, and Grover Lewis (the "Texas Beats," as Steven Davis calls them in *Texas Literary Outlaws*), was also the longtime companion of Texas governor Ann Richards. When Richards was governor, he was referred to as "Mr. Governor." In addition to his many novels and screenplays, Shrake wrote a play about Jack Ruby. Ruby's headlining stripper at the Carousel Club, Jada, is "Jingo" in *Strange Peaches*.

[7] Warren Commission Hearings, Volume XV, page 407. Testimony of one of Jack Ruby's entertainers, Nancy Powell. Web. 25 Jan. 2013.

[8] Although the term *beatnik* shows up numerous times in the Warren Commission Report, the term *beat*, as in "Beat Generation," does not. Investigators and those interviewed are thus only aware of the stereotype of the beatnik but not of the specific literary origins of the term nor its meaning.

[9] "The Lopez Report": House Select Committee on Assassinations Report on the Kennedy Assassination, Appendix 13, p. 206. Web. 25 Jan. 2013.
[10] Warren Commission Exhibit 2909, p. 2. Web. 25 Jan. 2013.
[11] City of New Orleans Assistant District Attorney Andrew Sciambra memo regarding his interview with Perry Raymond Russo at the Mercy Hospital in New Orleans on February 27, 1967. Web. 25 Jan. 2013.
[12] Warren Commission Exhibit 2460, p. 5. Web. 25 Jan. 2013.
[13] Warren Commission Hearings, Volume 8, p. 434. Web. 25 Jan. 2013.
[14] The Cellar homepage, which includes period photos, can be accessed online.
[15] Warren Commission Report, Volume 5, p. 460. Web. 25 Jan. 2013.
[16] Warren Commission Report, Volume 5, p. 459. Web. 25 Jan. 2013.
[17] See Mariani, Anthony, "Cellar Star Bongo Joe Remembered," which quotes an account given by *Texas Monthly* writer Joe Nick Patoski.
[18] Warren Commission Exhibit 1025, p. 804. Web. 25 Jan. 2013. Kennedy had previously told the Secret Service agents guarding him to tolerate the behavior of people who approached his motorcade: he thought they simply wanted to shake his hand.

Works Cited

Note: The Warren Commission Report is a primary source for this article. It can be accessed at various sites on the web, the most useful of which is the *History Matters* website

Amburn, Ellis. *Subterranean Kerouac*. New York: St Martin's Press, 1998. Print.
Anderson, Eric. "My Beat Journal." *The Rolling Stone Book of the Beats*, Ed. Holly George-Warren. New York: Hyperion, 1990. Print.
Baraka, Amiri. "Cuba Libre." In *The LeRoi Jones/Amiri Baraka Reader,* Ed. William Harris. New York: Basic, 1999, 125-161. Print.
Bockris, Victor. *With William Burroughs: A Report from the Bunker*. New York: Seaver, 1981. Print.
Bolden, Abraham. *The Echo from Dealy Plaza*. New York: Harmony, 2008. Print.
Corso, Gregory. *Mindfield: New and Selected Poems*. New York: Thunder's Mouth, 1989. Print.
Courtwright, Chris. "Oswald in Aliceland? A Tale of Two Days; A Tale of Two Oswalds." Presented to JFK Lancer's November in Dallas Conference on November 21, 1997. Web. 25 Jan. 2013.
Crouse, Jacque and Jim Beal. "Downtown Fixture Bongo Joe Dies." *San Antonio Express News*, December 21, 1999, p. 1. Web. 25 Jan. 2013.
Davis, Steven L. *Texas Literary Outlaws*. Dallas: Texas Christian UP, 2004. Print.

Ferlinghetti, Lawrence. *Americus I*. New York: New Directions, 2005. Print.

---. *The Secret Meaning of Things*. New York: New Directions, 1969. Print.

"Fort Worth Beatniks Back on Bongo Drums." Victoria Advocate, August 23, 1961. Web. 25 Jan. 2013. Print.

Ginsberg, Allen. *Collected Poems 1947-1949*. New York: Harper Collins, 2006. Print.

---. *Family Business: Selected Letters Between a Father and a Son*. Ed. Michael Shumacher. Bloomsbury, 2001. Print.

---. *"Howl" and Other Poems*. San Francisco: City Lights, 1956. Print.

---. *Journals, Early Fifties, Early Sixties*. Ed. Gordon Ball. New York: Grove, 1994. Print.

"Fort Worth Beatniks Back on Bongo Drums." *Victoria Advocate*, August 23, 1961. Web. 25 Jan. 2013. Print.

Hemmer, Kurt. Dir. and Writer. *As We Cover the Streets: Janine Pommy Vega*. 2003. DVD.

Hersh, Seymour M. *The Dark Side of Camelot*. New York: Little Brown, 1997. Print.

Hilty, James W. *Robert Kennedy: Brother Protector*. Temple UP, 2000. Print.

Jacobs, George and William Stadiem. "Sinatra and the Dark Side of Camelot." *Playboy*, June 2003, 91 (forward). Print.

Kashner, Sam. "A Clash of Camelots," *Vanity Fair* Oct. 2009. Web. 25 Jan. 2013. Print.

Kennedy, John F., Party Nomination Acceptance Speech, Commodore Hotel, New York, Sept. 14, 1960. Web. 25 Jan. 2013.

Kerouac, Jack. *Atop an Underwood*. Ed. Paul Marion. New York: Viking, 1999. Print.

---. *Good Blonde and Others*. San Francisco: City Lights, 1994. Print.

---."The Origins of the Beat Generation." In *The Viking Critical Library* On the Road. Ed. Scott Donaldson. New York: Viking Penguin, 1979.

---. *Selected Letters 1957-1969*. Ed. Ann Charters. New York: Viking, 1999. Print.

Leight, Michele. "Jacqueline Kennedy: The White House Years." Web. 25 Jan. 2013.

Maher, Jr., Paul. *Kerouac: The Definitive Biography*. New York: Taylor Trade, 2004. Print.

Mariani, Anthony, "Cellar Star Bongo Joe Remembered." Posted February 2010 by *The Fort Worth Weekly*. Web. 25 Jan. 2013.

Melanson, Philip. *The Secret Service: The Hidden History of an Enigmatic Agency*. New York: Carroll and Graf, 2003. Print.

McNally, Dennis. *Desolate Angel: Jack Kerouac, The Beat Generation and America*. New York: Mcgraw-Hill, 1979. Print.

Miles, Barry. *Ginsberg: a Biography*. New York: Simon and Schuster, 1989. Print.

Morgan, Bill. *I Celebrate Myself: The Somewhat Private Life of Allen Ginsberg*. New York: Viking, 2006. Print.

O'Neil, Paul. "The Only Rebellion Around." Reprinted in Ann Charters. Ed. *Beat Down to Your Soul*. New York: Penguin, 2001. 424-39. Print.

Piereson, James. *Camelot and the Cultural Revolution: How the Assassination of JFK Shattered American Liberalism*. New York: Encounter, 2007. Print.

Podhoretz, Norman. "The Know-Nothing Bohemians." In *Beat Down to Your Soul*. Ed. Ann Charters. New York: Penguin. 2001. 479-93. Print.

"Politics: Beat in the Hip of Texas." *Life*, Mar. 6, 1960, 48. Print.

Posner, Gerald. *Case Closed* (2nd ed.). New York: Doubleday/Anchor, 2003. Print.

Rand, Ayn. "JFK—High Class Beatnik?" *Human Events*, Sept. 1, 1960. Web. Jan. 25, 2013.

Sanders, Ed. *Fug You: An Informal History of the Peace Eye Bookstore, the Fuck You Press, the FUGS, and Counterculture in the Lower East Side*. New York: De Capo Press, 2011. Print.

---. *Tales of Beatnik Glory*, 2nd ed. New York: Thunder's Mouth, 2004. Print.

Schieffer, Bob. *This Just In: What I Couldn't Tell You on TV*. New York: Berkeley, 2004. Print.

Schumacher, Michael. *Dharma Lion: A Biography of Allen Ginsberg*. New York: St. Martin's, 1994. Print.

Talbot, David. *Brothers: The Hidden History of the Kennedy Years*. New York: Simon and Schuster, 2007. Print.

Teichen, Todd. *The Cubalogues: Beat Writers in Revolutionary Havana*. Gainesville: UP of Florida, 2010. Print.

Torricelli, Robert and Andrew Carroll, eds. *In Our Own Words: Extraordinary Speeches of the American Century*. New York: Washington Square, 2000. Print.

Wakefield, Dan. "Introduction." *C. Wright Mills: Letters and Autobiographical Writings*. Berkeley: U of California P, 2000. Print.

Waldron, Lamar and Thom Hartmann. *Ultimate Sacrifice: John and Robert Kennedy, the Plan for a Coup in Cuba, and the Murder of JFK*. New York: Carroll and Graf, 2005. Print.

---. *Legacy of Secrecy: The Long Shadow of the JFK Assassination*. Berkeley: Counterpoint, 2008. Print.

REVIEWS

Jack Kerouac: Collected Poems.
Edited by Mariléne Phipps-Kettlewell.
(New York: Library of America, 2012).

"All this creation / Created to fall"

The 2012 publication of Jack Kerouac's *Collected Poems* as a volume in the Library of America is cause for celebration: now a substantial body of poetry by the renowned author of *On the Road* and other novels will finally be widely and easily available. Edited by Mariléne Phipps-Kettlewell, the volume includes the two books of poetry Kerouac published during his lifetime, *Mexico City Blues* and *The Scripture of the Golden Eternity*, along with several collections Kerouac left in manuscript, among them *Book of Blues, Pomes All Sizes, Old Angel Midnight*, and *Book of Haikus*. These are supplemented by posthumous collections edited by others and unpublished poems found in archives. It is a large book, comprising nearly 700 pages of poems, along with what amounts to an experimental collage in place of an introduction, a note on the text, a series of textual notes, and a very helpful and detailed chronology of Kerouac's life.[1] Phipps-Kettlewell's willingness to introduce new poems from archival sources happily differentiates her from most Library of America volumes, which tend to ignore unpublished and uncollected work.

Despite the size of the book, it should be clear that this is in no way a *Complete Collected Poems*. A collected poems gathered by an author often represents the work he or she wants to be remembered by. Its omissions, often silent, reflect a variety of impulses that require later interpretation and analysis. In the case of posthumous collections edited by an admirer or a scholar, the aim may be more impersonal—to establish the poet's core canon, the works readers should have readily available, and the body of work that scholars will most want to study. For instance, when assembling Edwin Rolfe's *Collected Poems*, I omitted the poems he published as a high school student. My aim in part was to win a new audience for a forgotten poet, and the presence of his juvenilia would not have helped to achieve that aim.

The situation with Kerouac's poetry is not altogether different. He is universally known for his fiction, but his poetry has so far attracted only a much smaller, although devoted, audience. In fact, he wrote a great deal of poetry, some of which is compelling and some of which fails. A collected poems – unlike a selected poems – will inescapably include poetry of both sorts, given that the published books and the finished manuscripts dictate much of the contents. It is far from clear, however, that one would even want to select only his best poems, since diversity of tone, form, subject matter, and seriousness are central to Kerouac's aesthetic. In her introduction to *Book of Haikus*, a collection that adds unpublished archival poems as a supplement to Kerouac's manuscript, Regina Weinreich reports that friends said it was "best not to show Kerouac at his worst" and to "throw away the clinkers" but that she has nonetheless "chosen many against their sound counsel" (xxxix). The haiku that is meticulously crafted stands next to the haiku that is casual or flippant. We cannot understand Kerouac if we filter him through an aesthetic foreign to him.

    The challenges presented by the task of editing Kerouac's poetry do not, however, end there. Although he wrote and published in traditional forms, he also revised older forms and invented new ones. In the case of his blues poetry, he used the label conceptually, thematically, and attitudinally, with no reference to the formal tradition of the blues stanza. In fact Kerouac's blues are more obviously jazz-influenced. His haikus, which helped define an alternative English-language haiku practice—a practice that has since thrived in the work of other poets and shaped a new haiku tradition—abandoned the Japanese syllabic and seasonal standard and turned the haiku into a short poem of varied length on any topic. But, in truth, with Kerouac it is not always even clear what counts as a poem. *Some of the Dharma* is full of what amount to one-paragraph prose poems, as are *The Scripture of the Golden Eternity* and *Old Angel Midnight*, though there is no evidence Kerouac identified all of them as such. His work also contains many examples of what is arguably prose lineated as poetry, or constructed as what we might call shaped paragraph stanzas, as with the 54th section of *Old Angel Midnight* (514). His overall sensibility was so conditioned and inspired by writing over a thousand haikus that his novels are often sprinkled with haiku-like moments of observation, as in the following passage from *The Dharma Bums*: "The old tree brooded over me silently, a living thing. I heard a mouse snoring in the garden weeds. The rooftops of Berkeley looked like pitiful living meat sheltering grieving phantoms from the eternality of the heavens which they feared to face" (*Road Novels* 304).

    The Dharma Bums often appeals particularly to readers of Kerouac's haikus, or, for that matter, to students of haiku poetry generally. Early on in the novel (292-94), Ray Smith has a wonderful discussion with Japhy Ryder about the challenges faced in translating T'ang Dynasty poet Han Shan's famous "cold mountain" poem from Chinese to English. Then later, Ray, Japhy, and Morley climb Matterhorn Peak in Yosemite National Park together, trading spontaneously composed haiku and discussing them with one another:

> "Look over there," sang Japhy, "yellow aspens. Just put me in the mind of a haiku… 'Talking about the literary life—the yellow aspens.'" Walking in

this country you could understand the perfect gems of haikus the Oriental poets had written, never getting drunk in the mountains or anything but just going along as fresh as children writing down what they saw without literary devices or fanciness of expression. We made up haikus as we climbed, winding up and up now on the slopes of brush. "Rocks on the side of the cliff," I said, "why don't they tumble down?" "Maybe that's a haiku, maybe not, it might be a little too complicated," said Japhy. "A real haiku's gotta be as simple as porridge and yet make you see the real thing . . . ." (322)

What is at stake here for Kerouac is not just the near-absolute economy of language desirable in haikus, a principle Pound earlier helped codify for imagist poetry, but also a certain fantasy of the possibility of unmediated representation, the possibility that poetry might give us access to the thing itself without language seeming to intervene. That fantasy would haunt him long thereafter, despite the fact that some of his inventive haikus pivot precisely on evidence of mediation, of the difference that human thought, the mind, makes in what we see and how we see. It would haunt him despite his creation of blues meditations that set aside the principle of economy. And it would haunt him despite the recognition, in his Buddhist poetry and prose, that the world we see is the one we make.

Regina Weinreich quotes another passage from *The Dharma Bums* as evidence of the stylistic conjunction of haiku and prose: "The storm went away as swiftly as it came and the late afternoon lake-sparkle blinded me. Late afternoon, my mop drying on the rock. Late afternoon, my bare back cold as I stood above the world in a snowfield digging shovelsful into a pail. Late afternoon, it was I not the void that changed" (*Book of Haikus* xxv). Then she points out that the same passages occur as three-line haiku in one of Kerouac's notebooks (xxv). In "Hidden Visions: Embedded Haiku in Jack Kerouac's *The Dharma Bums*," author Mark Smith goes one step further, breaking out a series of haiku from the prose of *The Dharma Bums*. As early as 1983, Gerald Nicosia finds some prose lines of *Visions of Gerard* to be "like haiku" (501).

Gerald Nicosia points out that the prose lines of *Visions of Gerard* are actually haiku and then quotes a line from a Kerouac letter to New Direction's founding editor James Laughlin: "All my books are as it were poetry sheeted in narrative steel" (501, 545).[2] James T. Jones suggests that Kerouac is a novelist whose "fictional technique led him directly to poetry" (12).

All this is not to say that the editor of a Kerouac *Collected Poems* can meet all these challenges. No one, including Mark Smith, would expect an editor to be midwife to the birth of innumerable poems from Kerouac's prose. But the evidence suggests the relationship between genres in Kerouac's work is unusually interdependent. That is only one reason why we should welcome the fact that the overall scholarly neglect of his poetry is coming to an end. The other reason, as the *Collected Poems* at least in part shows, is that many of his poems are innovative and unforgettable. It is fitting to cite some examples.

Midway through the *Collected Poems* one comes to "Poems of the Buddhas of Old," composed of forty-five rhymed quatrains divided into five numbered groups. Its thematic, constructed as a narrative parable, centers on what—in the Western context—is the central lesson of Buddhism, here offered in Kerouac's appealing vernacular:

> Life is like a dream,
> You only think it's real
> Cause you're born a sucker
> For that kind of deal (446)

While Kerouac's Buddhism is regularly characterized as an extremely specialized interest—and he was only focused intensely on it for a limited number of years, basically 1954-57—in fact, his Buddhist poetry is often accessible, witty, and of pointed interest to anyone willing to think about the illusions that sustain Western culture. There is no lesson more difficult for Americans to learn than that all they believe to be vitally important is actually evanescent and will pass, and that the meanings they think are linked to material reality are actually mental constructs: "only imagination makes the lilacs grow, / turn blue in July—makes the ant hurry-- / the cat conceive of himself as cat" (*Some of the Dharma* 82). That the lilacs "turn blue," that the ant is "hurrying," that the feline species has the name of *cat*, all this is human cultural construction, though our resistance to coming to terms with that recognition could hardly be greater. Kerouac rings changes on just that recognition in scores of poems, no doubt in part because it offered an antidote to his own suffering. However, Kerouac's personal circumstances should not inoculate us from confronting a fundamental cultural blindness.

"Poems of the Buddhas of Old" is a poem from *Some of the Dharma* that made its way into *Pomes All Sizes* and thus into the *Collected Poems*. So is "'Sight is just dust'" (600) reprinted here, as Phipps-Kettlewell rather uninformatively puts it, "in the form in which it appeared in the posthumous selection *Scattered Poems*" (707). That "form" represents less than a third of a triumphant longer poem, "The Perfect Love of Mind Essence," that no one is likely to discover unless they make their way to page 229 of *Some of the Dharma*. If anything, Phipps-Kettlewell discourages curiosity by characterizing that book simply as "an immense assemblage of notes on Buddhism," adding that she has not taken any poems directly from it because it "needs to be read as an organic whole."[3] *Some of the Dharma* is an astonishing achievement in its entirety, but I cannot accept either an aesthetic or a moral requirement that it *must* be read on its own so its poems cannot be anthologized. Certainly it is Kerouac's most radical mixed form and rewards direct experience, but it includes some of his most important poems, without which a Kerouac canon and a Kerouac *Collected Poems* is unacceptably impoverished. In any case, Phipps-Kettlewell includes the sixty haikus from *Some of the Dharma* that Weinreich appends to Kerouac's *Book of Haikus* manuscript, a body of work substantial enough to undercut rather seriously the argument that everything in *Some of the Dharma* must be read in context. Weinreich, by the way, by no means includes all the *Some of the Dharma* poems Kerouac labels as haiku, let alone the many others unlabeled but open to consideration. Phipps-Kettlewell accepts Weinreich's selections from *Some of the Dharma* without adding or subtracting a single poem. Oddly, she does nothing to describe or acknowledge the work Weinreich did other than listing *Book of Haikus* among her sources.

Here is "The Perfect Love of Mind Essence" in its entirety:

Mind Essence loves everything, because it
Knows why everything is—
It loves everything because everything ends—
Mind essence is like a little child,
It makes no discriminations at all,
All is the same and all's in the mind,
And all's to be loved as it stands,
All's to be loved as it falls.
    The Karma is done
    Mind Essence is one—
    The wheel of thought
    Is no more fought—
    Differences of things
    Are imaginary rings—
    The child of delight
    Rests in the night—
    The mind of bliss
    Is pure happiness—

He never dies   He is never hung
Who has no eyes   Who has no tongue—

He never fears   There is no rain
Who has no ears   Outside the brain

He never goes   Unborn,
Who has no nose--   No lamb shorn---

He is never bawdy   No crying
Who has no body--   In essence undying

    Sight is just dust,   →   Mind alone
    Obey it must—   Introduced the bone
          *   *

    Fire just feeds   →   Only mind
    On fiery deeds.   The flame so kind.
          *   *

    Water from the moon   →   Mind is the sea
    Appears very soon.   Made water agree.
          *   *

    Wind in the trees   →   Wind rose deep
    Is a mental breeze.   From empty sleep
          *   *

    Space in the ground   →   Devoid of space
    Was dirt by the pound   Is the mind of grace.
          *   *

Fire retires   And space accepts   Explaining in
When water admires   The green adepts   droves
                                                 To men in
Fire inhibits   And wind responds   groves
What earth admits   To magic wands
                        And men appear   "Not even alive
Fire and water   With Dharma dear   The Elements Five"
Bring earth a daughter (229)

    Many of these rhymed couplets are haiku-like ("Water from the moon / Appears very soon"). Some have a distinctly Blakean character ("The child of delight / Rests in the night"). Others close in on visionary surrealism ("He never dies / Who has no eyes"). And some are closer to proverbs ("Unborn / No lamb shorn") or aphorisms ("Mind alone / Introduced the bone"). Some offer comic adaptations of unlikely diction ("Fire retires / When water admires"), and others are essentially absurdist ("Explaining in droves / To men in groves"). But all in varying ways embody the primary message: "There is no rain / Outside the brain" or "Wind in the trees / Is a mental breeze." We make a world out of names and the mental relationships they facilitate—foolish, loving, phantasmatic, fearful, or seemingly entirely material. We live amongst projections of values that are as fleeting as we ourselves.

The rhymes help make the poem immensely musical, and they perform out loud extremely well. The couplet form that predominates after the opening didactic stanza allows for a mix of repetition and wild, inventive variety. Kerouac himself famously demonstrated the performative virtues of his poetry in the recordings he made in 1959, with selected haikus counterpointed by tenor saxophone and piano interludes by Zoot Sims and Al Cohn, respectively. They have been reissued on CD as *Jack Kerouac: The Complete Collection*, along with readings accompanied by Steve Allen on piano and a helpful essay by Charles Waring. These recordings are an excellent place to start for those unfamiliar with Kerouac's poetry.

Where the uninitiated should probably not start is with Phipps-Kettlewell's authentically bizarre introduction to this book. Titled "Jack Kerouac, in His Own Words," it alternates between run-on compilations of fragments from Kerouac's work, mostly from the poems themselves, and the editor's prose. They are gathered under fourteen topical headings, a device that apparently saved the editor from the necessity of crafting a continuous argument or commentary on the poems. Phipps-Kettlewell's own contributions are often overheated in a way that is strikingly out of sync with the poetry itself: "Jack Kerouac was like a man observing his river, sitting in the rain, letting it soak through his clothes, his skin, his being, his self; a man weighed down, feeling the cold, his tears as opaque as his heart" (xxi); "To be a poet's poet is to hurt. To hurt singularly, to hurt incomprehensibly, to suffer a wound that never heals, a wound not meant to heal because bleeding is the very nature of this wound—it is a divine gift—it is the wound of a savior" (xxix). Except for the opening definition and last two phrases, I could apply this passage to certain Holocaust poets, but is it appropriate for a poet who wrote both burlesques of the haiku form and comic testimony to the incongruity of haiku grounded in a capitalist and consumerist culture? Here are a few examples from his many radically westernized haikus:

Gee last night—
dreamed
Of Harry Truman
(530)

When the moon sinks
down to the power line,
I'll go in
(547)

Crossing the football field,
   Coming home from work
The lonely businessman
        (546)

2 traveling salesmen
   passing each other
On a Western road
        (542)

August moon—oh
   I got a boil
On my thigh
        (533)

Woke up groaning
   with a dream of a priest
Eating chicken necks
        (555)

    These satiric haikus are, to be sure, only one of the major groups of 2-3 line poems in the Kerouac canon. Indeed there about 700 haiku in the *Collected Poems*, and there could well have been more. As Weinreich writes, "Kerouac considered haiku a loose designation, a springboard to dive from, one he could use freely for his own artistic ends" (xxxiii). Yet he also held to a strict discipline in composing haiku on the seasonal model so honored in Japanese haiku tradition. As he put it in "The Origins of Joy in Poetry," the "mental discipline typified by the haiku" involves "the discipline of pointing out things directly, purely, concretely, no abstractions or explanations":

The barn, swimming
   In a sea
Of windblown leaves
        (546)

Swinging on delicate hinges
   the Autumn Leaf
Almost off the stem
        (642)

Leaf dropping straight
   Into the windless midnight:
The dream of change
        (644)

The trees, already
   bent in the windless
Oklahoma plain
        (567)

    The barn, appearing to float on a surface of blowing autumn leaves, recalls the pictorial duality of Pound's haiku-inspired "In a Station of the Metro." The autumn leaf's hinges open a doorway to mutability and seasonal change. And as the leaf drops, it plummets in darkness through both time and space. The bent trees on an Oklahoma plain give all the appearance of being windblown even though they are becalmed. They testify to past winds that have made them what they are, to winds as well that will return.

    Kerouac also writes longer poems and poem sequences. "Berkeley Song in F Major" begins by invoking Whitman, Ginsberg-style, as a classical deity who will crush the institutions of the military-industrial complex:

> Walt Whitman is striding
> Down the mountain of Berkeley
> Where with one step
> He abominates & destroys
> The whole atomic laboratory
> Wherein it becomes a jewel
> In his heel, O Eloheim! (421)

"Sea" (619-38) seeks to be in and of the sea—tossed by waves, washed up on shore, beached, barnacled, drowned, and swimming—while writing about the sea, gathering in references, allusions, sea stories, and cultural references. The poem layers sound and sense together, imitating the sea's noises while registering its meanings: "here we go, kavara ta / plows, shh, / and more, again . . . more waves coming, / every syllable windy" (630). Kerouac also embeds coherent poem sequences within longer improvisational forms. *Mexico City Blues* concludes with a poignant three-part tribute (Choruses 239-241) to jazz musician Charlie Parker.[4] As James T. Jones points out, it also includes an intensely autobiographical sequence (Choruses 87-104).

This *Collected Poems* is not everything one might have wished. Its chief virtue is the editor's decision to adopt a broad view of what counts as poetry across Kerouac's career and thus give the reader a book that admirably establishes the diversity of forms, styles, and voices Kerouac adopted, from carefully crafted and revised haikus to rhymed forms to prose poems to improvisational poems governed by free association. Part of the problem for uninitiated readers is chronology. The best way into Kerouac's poetry is probably to take small steps, beginning with haiku and with poems clearly focused on a single topic, like "Bus East" (377-81), "Skid Row Wine" (437-38), or "A Curse at the Devil" (473-77). But chronology of publication dictates beginning with his sprawling, spontaneous blues sequences. Without some assistance, not all readers will make their way through the roughly 350 pages of *Book of Blues*. That assistance is not forthcoming here.

For *Mexico City Blues*, Kerouac adopted a particular form, a sequence of "Choruses," most limited to a notebook page, that combined a degree of constraint with pretty much complete license about what he might write about on that page. It was an adaptation of the spontaneity he sought in his road novels. Unlike his work with haiku, moreover, he chose not to revise most of the individual choruses, though some of the choruses were constructed from more than one original text and the overall sequence, as Nancy Grace demonstrates, is carefully constructed and does not follow the order in which the choruses were written (173-76). As Grace shows through her research of the pocket notebooks in which he composed the cycle, "155 of the 244 choruses were published exactly as composed" (165).[5] In the process of composition Kerouac trusted inspiration that would bring things to the page that conscious control might well subvert. The resultant anarchism could produce eruptions of carefully composed humor, as in the "49th Chorus," excerpted here:

> They got nothing on me
>   at the university
> Them clever poets
>   of immensity
> With charcoal suits
>   and charcoal hair
> And green armpits
>   and heaven air
> And cheques to balance
>   my account
> In Rome benighted
>   by White Russians
> Without care who puke
>   in windows
> Everywhere. (38)

But it could also provoke a certain sense of tedium. It helps to realize that Kerouac thought of each Chorus as a little jazz improvisation. Knowing that helps prepare the reader for the character of the aesthetic governing more than half of Kerouac's poetry, encouraging one to dwell on individual choruses, rather than forging ahead for continuities that may not exist. All this belonged in a more professional introduction to the *Collected Poems*.

A more conventional introductory essay would certainly have been far more useful for the many library users of the Library of America unfamiliar with Kerouac's poetry. Some collected poems arrive after the poet's work has already entered into mainstream literary culture, and the poems carry with them a long history of evaluation and interpretation. That is not the case here. Readers new to Kerouac's work would be well advised to skip "Jack Kerouac, in His Own Words" and go first to the chronology, which gives a significant amount of biographical detail. But the volume provides no actual introduction to the poetry.

Given Kerouac's incredibly complex posthumous publishing history, with so many of his "books" prepared for publication by others, Phipps-Kettlewell could also have explained how the various collections she incorporated came about, what sources their editors used, what the principles behind their compilation were, rather than simply listing the books themselves and identifying which texts were in them. One might identify those haiku that were composed on a 1960 road trip with Albert

Saijo and Lew Welch, especially those that grew out of little contests to see which poet could treat a given subject best. Donald Allen compiled a record of that journey and published it as *Trip Trap: Haiku on the Road*. An editor might also point out that Ann Charters drew some of the poems in *Scattered Poems* from Kerouac's letters. Sometimes individual poems cry out for more context. Phipps-Kettlewell tells us that "Sea" is taken from *Big Sur*, but does not tell us it comes at the end of the novel and gives no hint of its relation to the rest of the book. Nor is there even a brief account of its unusual experimental style. Readers are left to discover Kerouac's innovations on their own, which is for the most part a perfectly reasonable editorial strategy, but one that needs to be balanced in this case by a few signposts for at least some poems, both unique and representative. That said, it is great to have all these poems together in one place. Can the book enhance the awareness and reception of Kerouac's poetry? I can offer at least personal testimony. If I had had Kerouac's *Collected Poems* available when I was editing *Anthology of Modern American Poetry* for Oxford University Press, Kerouac would have found a place in the book. He will be included in the second edition.

---Cary Nelson, *University of Illinois*

Notes

[1] Although not acknowledged by Phipps-Kettlewell, it should be noted that the chronology is reprinted from Douglas Brinkley's 2007 Library of America edition of *Jack Kerouac: Road Novels 1957-1960*.

[2] For Kerouac, the distinction between prose and verse is artificial; the two are simultaneous forms whose distinctions are not differences. Kerouac's descriptions of and ideas for his art in the early-to-mid-1950s link matters of technique, form and subjectivity, defining a poetics founded on the collapse of generic distinctions between prose and verse. As Kerouac wrote to his friend the novelist John Clellon Holmes in 1955, "all things are different forms that the same holy essence takes," or, as he wrote to the editor Malcolm Cowley that same year, "[t]he requirements for prose and verse are the same, i.e. blow" (Charters, *Letters* 525, 516). In his 1968 *Paris Review* interview, Kerouac proclaimed "[i]n prose you make the paragraph. [But] every paragraph is a poem" (1968, 81). This refusal of generic distinctions, which is expressed throughout his career, demonstrates Kerouac's participation in and development of literary forms that will be later termed "postmodern"; this refusal of generic distinctions indicates Kerouac's pre-postmodernism.

[3] For an extended discussion of the composition history and literary analysis of *Some of the Dharma*, see Nancy Grace's chapter "The Quest—Part II: *Some of the Dharma*" in *Jack Kerouac and the Literary Imagination*.

⁴ Those who, like Kerouac, are familiar with Japanese short poetic form traditions, might consider these examples of the senryu, a short poem dealing seriously or ironically with the human condition.

⁵ In other words, 64 percent were spontaneously composed, while a hefty 36 percent were edited to varying degrees. Regarding the famous Charlie Parker choruses that end the published version, Kerouac's original draft ended with "what became the 221st Chorus, a poem about the African-American blues musician Huddy Ledbetter (1889-1949), known as Leadbelly. This chorus concludes with the lines 'Old Man Mose is Dead / But Deadbelly get ahead / Ha ha ha.' The play on *Leadbelly* as *Deadbelly* and the slightly demonic laugh that closes this chorus suggest that the jazz musician/poet is a tricksterlike figure transmogrified from 'the furtive madman / of old sane times' into a self-serving modern hipster. . ." (Grace 176) – quite different from the eulogized and beatified Charlie Parker that angelically now concludes the cycle.

Works Cited

Berrigan, Ted. 1968. "The Art of Fiction XLI: Jack Kerouac." *Paris Review* 43: 61-105. Print.

Grace, Nancy M. *Jack Kerouac and the Literary Imagination*. New York: Palgrave- Macmillan, 2007. Print.

Jones, James T. *A Map of Mexico City Blues: Jack Kerouac as Poet*. Carbondale: Southern Illinois UP, 1992. Print.

Kerouac, Jack. *Book of Blues*. New York: Viking/Penguin, 1995. Print.

---. *Book of Haikus*. Ed. Regina Weinreich. New York: Penguin, 2003. Print.

--- *Jack Kerouac: The Complete Collection*. 2 CDs. New Malden, Surrey, Great Britain: Chrome Dreams, 2011.

---. *Jack Kerouac: Road Novels 1957-1960*. Ed. Douglas Brinkley. New York: Library of America, 2007. Print.

---. *Mexico City Blues*. New York: Grove, 1990. Print.

---. *Old Angel Midnight*. Ed. Donald Allen. San Francisco: Grey Fox, 1995. Print.

---. "The Origins of Joy in Poetry." 1958. *Good Blonde & Others*. San Fancisco: Grey Fox, 1993. Rpt. in *Scattered Poems*. Comp. Ann Charters. San Francisco: City Lights, 1971. Print.

---. *Pomes All Sizes*. San Francisco: City Lights, 1992. Print.

---. *Scattered Poems*. Comp. Ann Charters. San Francisco: City Lights, 1971. Print.

---. *Scripture of the Golden Eternity*. San Francisco: City Lights, 1988. Print.

---. *Some of the Dharma*. New York: Penguin, 1997. Print.

---. *Visions of Gerard*. New York: Penguin, 1991. Print.

Kerouac, Jack, Albert Saijo, and Lew Welch. *Trip Trap: Haiku on the Road*. 1973. Ed. Donald Allen. San Francisco: City Lights, 1998. Print.
Nelson, Cary. *Anthology of Modern American Poetry*. New York: Oxford UP, 2000. Print.
Nicosia, Gerald. *Memory Babe: A Critical Biography of Jack Kerouac*. New York: Grove, 1983. Print.
Rolfe, Edwin. *Collected Poems*. Cary Nelson and Jefferson Hendricks, eds. Urbana: U of Illinois P, 1993. Print.
Smith, Mark. "Hidden Visions: Embedded Haiku in Jack Kerouac's *The Dharma Bums.*" *Haibun Today: An Online Journal Devoted to Haibun and Tanka Prose*. 4:4 (Dec. 2010). Web. 14 Dec. 2012. First published in *Jack Magazine* 2:3 (2003).

Postliterary America: From Bagel Shop Jazz to Micropoetries.
Maria Damon
(Iowa City, Iowa: University of Iowa Press, 2012)

Maria Damon is well known in the field of Beat studies for creating a more accurate history of the Beat movement by recovering black and female poets. For Damon this project is part of a broader cultural studies, offering a useful perspective on "marginal" writers in modern American poetry, a perspective that the Beats helped to define by embracing marginality as a principle of both poetics and lifestyle. Since the time of the Beats, however, the American literary landscape has lost the center of a fixed canon; margins are everywhere. Apparently this is the condition that Damon intends to designate as *Postliterary America* in the title of her new book. Though pessimistic about the current political condition of America, Damon views the abundant possibilities of the "postliterary" condition in very positive terms, terms that are more commonly associated with "postmodernism." With due allowance for the postmodern valuation of mobility—Damon likes the trope of "the book as portable homeland" (81, 102, 214)—the "postliterary" condition appears as a kind of promised land, to which the Beats were able to point but which they were unable to enter.

Mapping postliterary America has led Damon to expand her attention well beyond the range of her previous book, *The Dark End of the Street: Margins in American Vanguard Poetry*. While four key figures—Bob Kaufman, Jack Spicer, Robert Duncan, and Gertrude Stein—continue to serve as touchstones in the new book, a fifth figure, Robert Lowell, is now dispersed in occasional references to "confessional" writing. In The *Dark End of the Street*, Damon had juxtaposed Lowell's *Life Studies* with poems by teenagers from a South Boston housing project. The new book presents such work under the broad and fluid category of "micropoetries," including memorial practices among various countercultural groups and the products of e-mail listservs such as the briefly controversial Flarf poetry, which mocked poetry journal submission procedures and practices.[1] A new emphasis on the category of performance similarly expands Damon's definition of poetry, as well as enlivening her prose style. Ranging from the performance art of Canadian feminist Kabbalist Adeena Karasick to more popular modes such as Lenny Bruce's nightclub routines, the poetry slams of the Nuyorican Poets' Café, and self-remaking by jazz (Mezz Mezzrow) and pop (Phil Spector) musicians, several of these examples also extend Damon's chronological range. While *The Dark End of the Street* found its center of gravity in the modern period, a new vantage point in postmodernism now provides the historical distance from which Damon looks back at the Beats.

The historical view of *Postliterary America* is articulated most clearly in the book's longest essay, whose complex agenda is reflected in the title, "Loneliness, Lyric, Ethnography: Some Discourses on/of the Divided Self." Although history does not feature explicitly among the terms of this title, both loneliness and self-division are symptoms of a historical condition, in Damon's view: "the subject in modernity is de facto traumatized by alienation and double consciousness" (163). Damon cites Marx, Freud, Du Bois, and Walter Benjamin for supporting theory, but the Beats supply the literary case with which she opens her essay. They stand "on the cusp of what we now consider the postmodern" (160), Damon asserts, and they anticipate postmodernism in their overcoming of the division between life and art. However, their parallel attempt to overcome the internal division of the modern, alienated self is misguided because it depends on a belief in a unified, authentic self—what Beat expressionism seeks to express. This belief holds the Beats back from the postmodern discovery, namely, that the solution to modern alienation is not "to simply undouble double consciousness" (161) but rather to multiply the number of identities performed by any subject, and to embrace the activity of performance itself as an immediate pleasure preferable to the elusive ideal of authenticity. Since Damon argues that these strategies were already familiar to "minoritized subjects such as black and queer people within...dissenting literary communities" (161), like that of the Beats, we might expect to find black and queer Beats enjoying the benefits implied in the postmodern breakthrough. Instead, the writers whom Damon goes on to treat in this essay, Bob Kaufman (black) and John Wieners (queer), experienced "unbearable psychic strain" (162) as their lives "devolved" into addiction and schizophrenia and "their work became increasingly fragmented and undisciplined" (176). Damon concludes that their position as minorities within a minority entailed too many contradictions, not only with the mainstream culture that posed The Problem, but also with an oppositional subculture that posed an untenable solution.

Obviously, Damon's thesis has many implications for Beat studies. As an explanation for what destroyed "the best minds" of the Beat Generation, it places much greater emphasis on internal contradictions within the Beat project—the impossibility of the unified, authentic self—as opposed to external social conditions such as "the commercialization and sterile suburbanization of USA-style late capitalistic postmodernity" (160), as Damon puts it. While this insight can help adjust the emphasis in standard accounts of the Beats, it is not entirely new. After all, in "Howl" Ginsberg had identified the destructive Moloch as "the Mind" as well as a "sphinx of cement and aluminum" (131), and astute readers of Burroughs and Kerouac have not missed the destabilizing and dispersion of self implicit in the performative mode cultivated by these writers. What I find even more challenging in Damon's thesis—to the extent that I cannot entirely agree with it—are the implications she draws for methodology, both of Beat writing itself and of writing about the Beats.

These implications revolve around the two central terms in the title of Damon's central essay, "lyric" and "ethnography." Although the one term belongs to subjective art and the other term to supposedly objective science, Damon views both types of writing as symptomatic of modern alienation or divided consciousness. In the lyric, the self must split from itself in order to become an object to itself, something for the poem to express. In ethnography, the anthropologist performs as the "participant observer," both the writer who observes and the object of the writing, one who experiences a culture's practices from the inside. These modes of writing are so closely related to each other, in Damon's argument, that she treats Kaufman and Wieners not only as lyric poets but also as participant observers (162, 174), documenting the practices of Beat subculture. Despite her critique of its generating ideology, ethnography serves as a key component of Damon's own methodology, derived from cultural studies, as she explains in an essay rather orphically entitled "Kinetic Exultations." When she envisions practitioners of this method "attending meetings of Persons With AIDS support groups" and "going to slams in bars and community centers," she makes it clear that "we'll be attending as participants, not simply as scholars" (116). That is, she is assigning to herself—and to "us"—the role of participant observer that she also assigns to Kaufman and Wieners.

The historical distance of the Beats presents a problem to ethnographic "thick description," the term that Damon borrows from the anthropologist Clifford Geertz (6, 162, 168). We might be able to attend a slam at our local community center, but we will not find a Beat scene at our local coffeehouse, however nostalgic its décor might be. Damon's solution to this problem is to listen in on "Bagel Shop Jazz," a poem by Bob Kaufman alluding to the Co-Existence Bagel Shop in San Francisco, a legendary Beat hangout. Having alluded to this poem in the subtitle of her book, Damon reprints it in full on the occasion of her first major reference (37-38), and returns to it in two subsequent essays. Approaching the poem as an "ethnographic depiction of 'village life'" (178), she assumes that it "purports to document" (57) the subgroups within the village: women ("Mulberry-eyed girls in black stockings"), ethnic white men ("Caesar-jawed, with synagogue eyes"), and African-American men ("Coffee-faced"). Working from this "demography" (38), Damon explores the attraction of Jewish men to African-American culture ("Jazz-Jews, Jive, and Gender"); the exclusion of gay men from Kaufman's census, despite Kaufman's own involvement in a triangular relationship with Jack Spicer and his lover Russell FitzGerald ("Triangulated Desire and Tactical Silences in the Beat Hipscape"); and finally, the "veiling" behind "this apparently innocuous and wistful poem" (178) of the anxiety Kaufman himself would have felt in his double role as participant observer ("Loneliness, Lyric, Ethnography," the essay discussed above). I believe it is entirely legitimate for Damon to treat this poem as a cultural document—which it is, after all—and in doing so she makes further valuable contributions to information about and interpretation of the Beats. However, Damon's assumption that Kaufman intended the poem as a cultural document, in the sense of ethnographic observation, seems too reductive. It closes off the possibility of the poem doing another kind of "cultural work" –the de-aestheticizing criterion proposed by Jane Tompkins and endorsed by Damon (123, 192)—a kind of work that the Beat writers especially valued.

What that work was for the Beats, and how it poses an alternative to ethnography, emerges most clearly in Damon's essay that is, ironically, most explicitly about ethnography. For instance, at one point in "Loneliness, Lyric, Ethnography," characterizing the divided consciousness of ethnic minority writers participating in a cultural minority like the Beats, Damon states, "these minoritized writers' lyric work witnessed and documented both their own psyches and the societies in which they could only partially participate" (162). I have questioned whether Kaufman would have seen himself as "documenting," but I believe he would have affirmed the role of "witnessing," in the ancient sense of prophecy rather than the modern sense of legal testimony. While Damon explores the latter sense provocatively in her account of Lenny Bruce's 1962 obscenity trial, the ancient sense lies continually just below the surface in her repeated attention to Jewish performers (including Bruce) and writers (including Ginsberg). Following Allen Grossman, Damon asserts: "Jewish poets speak directly to God and no other.... the poet is not responsible to any audience but Absence" (219). Although Damon rejects the legend that Kaufman was Jewish (11), through the "synagogue eyes" of "Bagel Shop Jazz" it is possible to see an Absence very different from the exclusion of gay men that Damon sees. Damon herself recognizes more than that in the poem's final line, "Brief, beautiful shadows, burned on walls of night," which she interprets as possibly "veiled reference to the global violence of the atom bomb, neighborhood violence recorded by spray-painted body outlines on city streets, and epic literary violence in its echo of Virgil's commentary on a mural of the Trojan war, *lacrimae rerum sunt*" (178-79). However we account for this violence, inscribed as "writing on the wall," it culminates in the prophetic sense of doom, hardly "innocuous and wistful," that runs throughout this poem. Although the imagery is condensed, it implies the scale of the epic, as Damon concedes here, rather than that of the lyric mode to which the parallel with ethnography confines Damon's argument.

Despite her attempt to critique it, the lyric norm itself confines Damon's perspective, so that when Kaufman's witnessing breaks out fully into the prophetic mode, as in "The Ancient Rain," Damon diagnoses it as a pathological symptom of "how far Kaufman had traveled from the participant observer coolness of the other . . . into a hell realm of prophetic isolation and other-worldliness" (179). Traditionally, the prophet is isolated because nobody listens, but as Damon observes elsewhere in reference to Jewish tradition, the prophet is not addressing anyone, only "Absence." Although "other-worldly," this Absence has a direct bearing on this world, as a measure both of what it has failed to be and what it might become. The Beats addressed this absence as "America." In "The Ancient Rain," specifically, the rain functions to "wash away the ugliness of American historical narratives so that American history may be written again," as Aldon Nielsen has observed (142), in a special journal feature edited by Damon. Lacking such a vision, *Postliterary America* offers a thin account of America, dwelling on what it is rather than how it might be "written again," as the Beats imagined it. However, Damon's explorations of the "postliterary" helpfully advance the ongoing effort to resituate "marginal" writers, including the Beats.

---Terence Diggory, *Skidmore College*

Notes

[1] According to K. Silem Mohammad (aka Kasey), "the initial aesthetics of Flarf. ...can probably be approximated by the following recipe: deliberate shapelessness of content, form, spelling, and thought in general, with liberal borrowing from internet chat-room drivel and spam scripts, often with the intention of achieving a studied blend of the offensive, the sentimental, and the infantile." The phenomenon began when poet Gary Sullivan submitted a bad poem to Poetry.com as a joke of sorts, but was then informed that his poem was accepted. The Flarf phenomenon was created as he shared the poem on other poetry lists, leading to others sharing their "Flarf" works. Sullivan defines "Flarf" as "a quality of intentional or unintentional 'flarfiness.' A kind of corrosive, cute, or cloying awfulness. Wrong. Un-P.C. Out of control. 'Not okay.'" See http://epc.buffalo.edu/authors/bernstein/syllabi/readings/flarf.html.

Works Cited

Damon, Maria. *The Dark End of the Street: Margins in American Vanguard Poetry*. Minneapolis: U of Minnesota P, 1993. Print.
Ginsberg, Allen. "Howl." *Collected Poems 1947-1980*. New York: Harper and Row, 1984. 126-33. Print.
Kaufman, Bob. "The Ancient Rain." *Callaloo* 25.1 (Winter 2002): 128-32. Print.
Nielsen, Aldon Lynn. "'A Hard Rain': Looking to Bob Kaufman." *Callaloo* 25.1 (Winter 2002): 134-45. Print.

Rub Out the Words: The Letters of William S. Burroughs 1959-1974.
Edited by Bill Morgan.
(New York Penguin, 2012)

Rub Out the Words: The Letters of William S. Burroughs 1959-1974, the second volume of Burroughs' letters, edited by Bill Morgan, presents a sharp contrast with the first collection (from 1944 to 1959), edited by Oliver Harris. The earlier letters are almost entirely addressed to one correspondent, Allen Ginsberg, who had been Burroughs' friend and lover and who continued to be a personal and literary lifeline during the fifties. The second volume consists of letters to a wide range of recipients—friends, family, publishers, agents, strangers—and the primary correspondent is Brion Gysin, Burroughs' artistic collaborator during the sixties. (Of the 307 letters published, almost one-third are addressed to Gysin.)[1] In the first volume, the letters to Ginsberg are more intimate, and also more entertaining, in that Burroughs deploys his outrageous "routines" to maintain Ginsberg's interest. The earlier letters also display the struggle to create that resulted in the breakthrough publication of *Naked Lunch* (1958). As Harris remarks in the introduction to his collection, the letters actually tell a story—the story of the writing of *Naked Lunch*, much of which was included in the letters to Ginsberg (xvi). Morgan's selection of representative letters, illustrating the range of correspondents and typical subject matter, does not produce a story, but a rather mosaic portrait. The Burroughs in *Rub Out the Words* is very much the man of letters pursuing his cutup experiments, writing to earn income, and managing his career. In fact, the contrast between the earlier and later Burroughs almost gives the impression of a personality change, perhaps foretold in the last letter to Ginsberg in Harris' collection: "I sometimes feel you have mixed me up with someone else doesn't live here any more" [*sic*](431). The influence of Gysin and the context of a European avant-garde scene replace Burroughs' Beat or hipster social environment of the forties and fifties. It should also be noted that several deaths occurred that contributed to a break from the past. In the late fifties, Burroughs' Tangier lover Kiki died, and also his old friends in the United States and Mexico, Bill Garver and Dave Tercerero. Kells Elvins, Burroughs' friend from childhood, died in 1962; his father died in 1965, and his mother in 1968. At the same time, Ginsberg had formed a lifetime partnership with Peter Orlovsky, and Kerouac was struggling with alcoholism and fame.

The letters in *Rub Out the Words* show that, once *Naked Lunch* was published, Burroughs felt truly launched as a professional writer, and he pursued his career with dedication. Letters often refer to the fact that he is constantly working—on novels, essays, articles, photography, tape experiments, films and film scripts, editing, interviews, or performances, often collaborating with Gysin, Antony Balch, and Ian Sommerville. He is frequently engaged in what we would now call multi-tasking, several times using the refrain "what am I an octopus." As he remarks in a 1964 letter to his parents, "One has to think of writing as any other job. You work at it all day and everyday if you expect to make a living" (156). We also find him urging Gysin to work, writing in one letter, "I hope you are not goofing. Such a thing as too much fun you know." He then lists the work he has just mailed (46). Another letter to Gysin begins, "Looks like I'll have to come on like a top sergeant here. 'We happy people down here' [Tangier] have no time for sex or any form of self-indulgence. Nothing but work and hours of it every day and beating off my creeping opponents with a spare tentacle." The letter continues with instructions on a photo collage technique that would include Gysin's paintings (77). From 1959 on, Burroughs exhibits confidence in the value of his work, which enables him to carry on in spite of the censorship and controversy that greeted *Naked Lunch* and the often skeptical critical response to the cutup artwork that followed. The cutup technique, discovered in 1959 by Gysin, engaged Burroughs for the next decade as the source of his art—as a technique, a theory, a therapy, and a revolution in consciousness. The letters show Burroughs tirelessly pursuing cutup experimentation in prose fiction, photo collage, scrapbooks, audiotape, and film—and just as tirelessly promoting cutups to his correspondents with do-it-yourself instructions. Although cutups were initially employed with text, Burroughs was exploring other media almost from the beginning. The book is yet to be written about Burroughs as a multi-media artist and about the symbiosis between Burroughs and Gysin, through which they collaborated as a "third mind." It is also interesting to note that Burroughs was sometimes functioning independently as a visual artist during this period—drawing, collaging, and scrapbooking, making his late-life career as a painter not so surprising after all.[2] He remarks several times in the letters that he is a good judge of paintings, and he wrote exhibition copy for friends.

 Those familiar with Burroughs' fiction from this period will not be surprised to find him repeatedly proselytizing for the apomorphine cure for addiction, arguing that addiction is a medical rather than a legal problem, and promoting Scientology's E-meter, Reich's orgone box, and Gysin's dream machine. Repeated references to psychedelic drugs and marijuana show a connection between drug-induced altered states of consciousness and the cutup aesthetic. We are also reminded that psychedelic drugs were legal in the early sixties, and that many artists, scientists, and prominent people (such as Henry and Clare Boothe Luce) experimented with these substances.

 Rub Out the Words is revealing about the management of a writing career, relations with publishers, and finances. Burroughs was aware that unpaid publications in avant-garde little magazines and underground newspapers could create an audience, generate publicity, and lead to book contracts and sales, thus his numerous contributions and often regular columns in *My Own Mag, Mayfair, Rat, Los Angeles Free Press, Crawdaddy*, and others. In this way, he carried on the pattern drawn from his experience with *Naked Lunch*: excerpts had first been published in *Black Mountain Review*, *Chicago Review*, and *Big Table*, which then led Olympia Press to publish the book. He preferred smaller publishing houses because they paid more attention to promoting an author's books. He understood the use of pre-publication publicity and the value of negative reviews that produced controversy. On the other hand, when he thought critics seriously misrepresented his views, Burroughs wrote to the *London Times*, the *Times Literary Supplement*, and the *Los Angeles Free Press*. In his letters to his son, William S. Burroughs, Jr., or "Billy" (1947-1981), the author of *Speed* (1970) and *Kentucky Ham* (1973), and to Gysin, who failed to gain much recognition for his novel *The Process* (1969), Burroughs dispenses advice about publishers, agents, advances, publicity, and retaining manuscripts and correspondence which could be sold to libraries. As Morgan notes in his introduction, Burroughs kept carbons or photocopies of his letters and extensive well organized files of his work.

Unfortunately, Burroughs' contract for *Naked Lunch* with Maurice Girodias of Olympia Press was a lesson in what not to do, for Girodias failed to pay all of the royalties due, and, during the early sixties, Burroughs was fairly impoverished—to the point that he once had to sell his tape recorder and could not afford to repair his typewriter. Morgan includes eleven letters from 1960 to 1967 in which Burroughs complains about Girodias' failure to forward his royalties, discusses his attempts to obtain payment, and remarks upon the difficulty of legally revising his contract so that he could receive foreign royalties directly rather than through Girodias. It took years to correct the situation and to begin earning a decent income so that the middle-aged Burroughs was finally able to tell his parents that he could support himself. He also began to send checks to his son and friends in need. In the early seventies, when his latest books —*The Job* (1970) and *The Wild Boys* (1971)— were not selling well, *The Third Mind* (1978) remained unpublished, and proposed films based on *Naked Lunch* or *The Last Words of Dutch Schultz* (1969) failed to materialize, he sold his papers to a private collector and accepted a teaching job at the City College of New York that Ginsberg had arranged. The volume closes with letters about Burroughs' plans to move to New York in 1974. Surprisingly, even though Girodias had caused him such financial distress, Burroughs still had sympathy for the man, stating that "with all his short coming [sic] .... he has done as much as any publisher living for literary freedom" (149-50).[3]

Morgan's selection also shows that Burroughs made an effort to maintain contact with old friends over the years: he continued to correspond with Allen Ginsberg and Paul Bowles, for example, and kept in touch with Kells Elvins until his death, later writing to Elvins' son. Burroughs also conducted a correspondence with his parents, Mortimer and Laura Lee Burroughs, and his son, William S. Burroughs, Jr. Yes, Williams Burroughs did have a family and he cared about them. If there is a story within this collection, it is that of Burroughs' relationship with his son. As William Burroughs, Jr., grew older, Burroughs attempted to take responsibility for his education, contributed financially to his upkeep, and planned to leave his literary estate to "Billy." He stepped in when his son became unhappy at school and when he was arrested for drug offenses as a teenager. After William, Jr. married Karen Perry in 1968, Burroughs often invited him and Perry to come to London to visit. Most importantly, he encouraged his son to write and supported his career. Living at a distance, Burroughs could be proud of his son's books and seemingly successful embarkation into adult life with marriage and publication. In these letters, which were written before his return to the United States in 1974, Burroughs does not, unfortunately, seem to be aware that his son was becoming an alcoholic. Nevertheless, as Burroughs' biographer Ted Morgan reports, when his son suffered liver failure and received a liver transplant in 1976, Burroughs and Perry were with him at the Boulder, Colorado, hospital for the procedure (Morgan 502). He was unable to preserve the new liver and died in 1981 (Morgan 535).

Bill Morgan achieves his goal of bringing together representative letters that convey Burroughs' movements, friendships, family relations, and professional career, selecting the "best" letters on topics that were important to Burroughs (as evidenced by frequency), while avoiding too much repetition (xxxiii). Although he notes that the length of the volume—444 pages total—was constrained by "publishing budgets" (xxxiii), his selection of 307 from approximately 1000 letters is still close to one-third. An experienced archivist and editor, Morgan's research was extensive and thorough, based on numerous library collections and individuals contacted. Morgan chose to employ the same format as Harris' collection (xv), providing a welcome consistency for scholars. The photographs are particularly well-chosen, showing locations and people mentioned in the letters. The index is thorough and helpful. Morgan's selection creates a compelling portrait of Burroughs' relationships, travels, and discipline (even obsession) as a writer, and of an exciting creative period when Burroughs, Gysin, Sommerville, and Balch were part of the early sixties European avant-garde.

The broad scope of these letters, however, does beg for more scholarly apparatus than Morgan has provided. More annotation of the persons, publications, and public appearances mentioned in the letters is needed, especially concerning Burroughs' own activities. Footnotes that identify someone simply as an "author and poet" could use more amplification by mentioning a few titles. And more information about what Burroughs was working on is needed for this intensely productive period. Morgan's stated policy of avoiding too many footnotes or commentary within the collection so as not to "interfere in the narrative" is valid (xxxii-xxxiii); but, in that case, a fuller introduction providing more context would have been desirable—what we get is rather brief at nine pages. The introduction would also be more informative if it included a summary of the artwork produced in this period. The biographical chronology that accompanies the introduction does not provide a complete listing of publications, so a bibliography of works published by Burroughs from 1959 to 1974 would have been a welcome addition. Also, from the perspective of those who seek to study Burroughs' most innovative and influential work, one cannot help but wonder if, in the desire to avoid repetition, Morgan has omitted a number of letters about the practice of cutups that would be of interest to scholars. As the limitations outlined above suggest, this collection may best suit the general reader rather than the specialist. Nevertheless, *Rub Out the Words: The Letters of William S. Burroughs 1959-1974* will be an important resource for critics and biographers, as well as for those who would like to know more about Burroughs, the man and the writer.

---Jennie Skerl, retired, *West Chester University*

Notes

[1] Although Burroughs and Gysin were close collaborators for several years, they were not always living in the same city; hence their frequent correspondence.

[2] Burroughs refrained from pursuing painting until after Gysin's death because he did not want to compete with him as a painter. See Miles, *William Burroughs* 239.

[3] Girodias' Olympia Press published English-language pornography and avant-garde fiction that mainstream publishing houses rejected, including works by Samuel Beckett, J. P. Donleavy, Terry Southern, Henry Miller, and Vladimir Nabokov, as well as Burroughs. Girodias also owned a failing nightclub, Le Grande Séverine, which he subsidized partly from his authors' royalties. Bill Morgan's notes provide the background on Burroughs' contract with Girodias and the nightclub (23, 145). Miles summarizes the situation in *The Beat Hotel*, going so far as to call Girodias a crook (180). Ted Morgan's biography provides more detail about Burroughs' lost royalties and the nightclub, mentioning that several of Girodias' authors had sued him for unpaid royalties (279-80, 348-49). It is the letters in this collection, however, that best convey the financial impact on Burroughs and the long, frustrating struggle to terminate Girodias' control over all royalties for *Naked Lunch*.

Works Cited

Harris, Oliver. Introduction. *The Letters of William S. Burroughs 1945-1959*. Ed. Oliver Harris. New York: Viking, 1993. xv-xl. Print.

Miles, Barry. *The Beat Hotel: Ginsberg, Burroughs, and Corso in Paris, 1957-1963*. New York: Grove, 2000. Print.

Miles, Barry. *William Burroughs: El Hombre Invisible, a Portrait*. New York: Hyperion, 1993. Print.

Morgan, Ted. *Literary Outlaw: the Life and Times of William S. Burroughs*. New York: Henry Holt, 1988. Print.

The Voice Is All: The Lonely Victory of Jack Kerouac
by Joyce Johnson
(New York: Viking, 2012)

Joyce Johnson is a figure long familiar to both specialists and general readers with an interest in the Beat era. Her immediate claim to fame, her romantic involvement with Jack Kerouac from 1957-1958, should not obscure her own considerable merits as a writer. *Minor Characters* (1983), her coming-of-age memoir that describes her relationship with Kerouac, is essential reading for anyone interested in the Beats and their era. Her published correspondence with Kerouac, *Door Wide Open* (2000), weaves together their letters in a poised and reflective narrative, through which Johnson offers her own insights into Kerouac's complicated personality. In fact, these two works are themselves so richly informative that one is justified in wondering why Johnson then felt compelled to add *The Voice Is All* to the already crowded shelf of Kerouac biographies. There have been nineteen full biographies of Kerouac since Ann Charters' first in 1973, *Kerouac: A Biography;* Johnson's *The Voice Is All* is the twentieth Kerouac biography.

In her introduction, Johnson identifies two distinct but related goals. Firstly, she aims to correct the distortions caused by the "Beat" label, which has obscured "another important side of him that has so far been poorly understood—the deeply traditional Jean-Louis Kerouac, who had been raised in a French-speaking, Catholic, Franco-American family in Lowell, Massachusetts" (xvii). Secondly, she seeks to track development of his distinctive style as a product of that upbringing, asserting that "no one was more aware of Kerouac's dualities and contradictions than he was, and it was his genius to find a voice that would contain them when he was only twenty-nine" (xvii). Johnson's study therefore has a clear agenda: to bring to the surface Kerouac's French-Canadian identity while charting the development of his mature voice. The extent to which she manages to connect the two may be taken as a test of the biography's success overall. However, we should also consider matters of scope and methodology. *The Voice Is All* is a substantial work, consisting of 436 pages of text, with the notes and index taking it to almost 500 pages. Do these 500 pages live up to the book jacket's claims that Johnson provides "a revelatory portrayal of Kerouac"?

Two issues stand out immediately. The first is Johnson's decision to end her study in November 1951, when Kerouac developed the sketching technique that became his spontaneous prose method. Her justification for this choice is not altogether satisfactory: "The bleak details of his decline can be found in other books, but to me what is important is Jack's triumph in arriving at the voice that matched his vision" (xx). However, Kerouac's "bleak decline" certainly did not begin in 1952; furthermore, the deployment of his unique voice through such radical works as *Doctor Sax* and *The Subterraneans* in 1952 and 1953 surely needs to be an integral part of demonstrating his "lonely triumph." As it is, we get only a brief glimpse of the still-underappreciated *Visions of Cody* (written 1952; published 1972) before the biography abruptly ends. If Kerouac's "lonely triumph" was indeed a triumph (in my opinion, it certainly was), then we need to see the prose and hear the voice; however, Johnson was prohibited by the Kerouace estate from quoting any Kerouac work, published or unpublished.

The second issue is a matter of research methodology. Referring in very general terms to the various approaches used by previous biographers, Johnson says that her own approach was to rely upon "Jack's own written words as well as the letters, journals, and books of his closest friends, especially Allen Ginsberg, Neal Cassady, and John Clellon Holmes" (xix). Johnson certainly makes excellent use of the archival documents held in the New York Public Library's Berg collection. Shaping this wealth of material into a readable narrative is no small task. But paraphrasing sections of Kerouac's novels as though they represent the exact circumstances, actions, and feelings of his lived experience is an inadequate approach to biography, and one that the field of Kerouac studies has already seen too much of. Johnson herself seems to criticize this approach in her introduction when she describes prior attempts "to show that everything in *On the Road* or his subsequent 'true life' novels was true," and yet she frequently falls back on this method herself throughout. Worse, she draws on texts like *Nobody's Wife* (2000) the deeply disaffected memoir by Kerouac's second wife, Joan Haverty, to represent sarcastically Kerouac's relationship with his mother, treating Haverty's text as objectively reliable when clearly it is not. Johnson is, of course, entitled to use such sources, but they should be contextualized in a more responsible way (385-6).[1]

Equally significant are the sources that Johnson doesn't use. Perhaps her general lack of reference to previous biographies reflects a desire to maintain the purity of her own vision. However, she may also be seeking to skirt the tensions and allegiances within Kerouac scholarship more generally. For any Kerouac biographer, negotiating the complex terrain of his literary estate is a fraught business. Debates about the legality of Gabrielle Kerouac's will have generated antagonisms and factions. When Kerouac died in 1969, he left everything to his mother Gabrielle; when Gabrielle died in 1973, her will bequeathed the entire estate to Stella Sampas, Kerouac's third wife; in a letter to his nephew Paul Blake Jr., only one day before his death, Kerouac wrote that he was planning to divorce her and leave his estate to Paul (Charters, 1995, 480). When Stella died in 1990, her younger brother John Sampas became the executor of the Kerouac estate. In the meantime, Kerouac's daughter Jan had begun legal proceedings against the Sampas family. She herself died in 1996. In 2009, Gabrielle Kerouac's will was declared a forgery by the Florida courts, destabilizing the ownership of the hugely valuable Kerouac estate, and, inevitably, creating tensions about which materials were available for consultation, and in what ways. Johnson clearly has such tensions in mind when she notes that "while full permission to quote from Jack's unpublished papers remains restricted to writers whose projects have been sanctioned by the Kerouac estate, an exciting new era of Kerouac scholarship has opened up" (xx).

Yet even allowing for such ticklish matters, one would expect Johnson to make more use of prior studies than she does. Paul Maher's primary research into Kerouac's French-Canadian identity and the culture and history of Lowell is far more extensive than hers, yet Johnson cites him a grand total of three times in her almost 500-page book.[2] They both make good use of Steve Edington's *Kerouac's Nashua Connection*, but Maher's sources go far beyond Johnson's to include documents at the Quebec National Archives, materials in the Center for Lowell History, Lowell's own newspapers, and numerous small books on Lowell history that Johnson seems to have been unaware of or uninterested in. Johnson even makes a pointed reference in her introduction to the long wait for a "definitive" biography of Kerouac, ignoring the fact that Maher's 2004 study is titled *Kerouac: The Definitive Biography*. Leaving aside how "definitive" Maher's biography actually is, since he did not have permission to quote the unpublished archive (which was not even open to scholars to view until 2007) Johnson's primary purpose is to connect Kerouac's mature literary voice more fully with his ethnicity— thus the limited extent of her research into that ethnicity is a significant issue.

This is not to say that Johnson's treatment of Kerouac's ethnicity lacks interest or value. She has thought deeply about his own perplexed sense of identity, and writes very candidly of her own realization that, looking back, she hardly knew him at all (16-17). Some fascinating threads are woven into her portrayal of French-Canadian culture, such as the likely presence of the 1921 novel *Maria Chapdelaine* in the Lowell community of Kerouac's boyhood. Since there is no concrete evidence that Kerouac knew the book, the connection can only be thought-provoking: the novel's protagonist is named François Paradis. Through careful study of Kerouac's literary oeuvre, from the juvenilia connected in *Atop an Underwood* (1999) to the multiple drafts of *On the Road*, Johnson brings into sharper focus Kerouac's struggle to reconcile his own sense of self with the characters he was creating, and the extent to which his French-Canadian identity was part of this struggle. Particularly interesting is the description of an unpublished fragment *Les Travaux de Michel Bretagne*, which Kerouac wrote in *joual* in early 1951 as he tried to move forward with his "road" novel (388-390). The introduction of such previously unknown material heightens the significance of other, better known instances of Kerouac's linguistic identity crisis, such as his correspondence with Yvonne Le Mâitre, who reviewed *The Town and the City* for the Massachusetts French-Canadian newspaper *Le Travailleur* (372).

But what of the emergence of Kerouac's voice during these formative years? "Voice" is a literary quality rather than biographical component, and hence calls for a degree of literary analysis. Johnson moves in this direction in her discussion of *Les Travaux de Michel Bretagne*, stating that it "contained some of the most eloquent prose he had ever written" (390). Demonstrating this eloquence for a general readership is tricky, of course, since Kerouac was writing in his native *joual*, but Johnson does trace some cross-over between French and English in Kerouac's own translations of certain passages (390). However, to then assert that the "forthrightness" of Michel Bretagne's first person narrative is the basis of Sal Paradise's voice in *On the Road* seems a bit of a stretch.[2] Surely it would be more relevant to consider the narrative voice in *Visions of Cody* (composed 1952; published 1972) in which Johnson sees Kerouac "find[ing] the courage to cast off the artifices of conventional plot-driven fiction and, finally, the American mask that concealed his identity" (xviii). A cursory attempt to do so is made right at the end, when Johnson notes that the French word for dreams, *rêves*, finds its way into the bilingual passages of *Visions of Cody*, and that "[i]n a later section of the book, he would finally dare to write entire passages in joual, set alongside their translations" (425). Unfortunately, we are given no concrete analysis of such passages, an absence facilitated by Johnson's lack of permission to quote Kerouac's texts and archives.

Given the necessity of a more literary treatment of "voice," Johnson's failure to acknowledge Tim Hunt's *Kerouac's Crooked Road: Development of a Fiction* is a rather serious omission. First published in 1981 and then reissued in paperback in 1996, Hunt's book still stands out as an exemplary literary critical study of Kerouac's development from a traditional novelist to a radically innovative stylist. Focusing exclusively on the relationship between *On the Road* and *Visions of Cody*, Hunt covers much of the same ground as Johnson, but without the benefit of the archival material now housed in the New York Public Library. Johnson's only acknowledgment of Hunt comes in a single reference to a letter from Kerouac to John Clellon Holmes, itself available in the *Selected Letters 1940-1956*. Hunt's story of Kerouac's literary development is actually much more exhilarating than Johnson's, because he works extensively with the prose itself. Drawing on Hunt's foundational work would have given Johnson's study more substance; moreover, Hunt's emphasis on Kerouac's bilingualism in his 1996 introduction to the second edition makes Johnson's emphasis somewhat less than "revelatory." Here, Hunt pinpoints precisely the issues Johnson takes on: "[But] Kerouac, it seems, did not experience literacy and the logics of writing and print as something that subsumed the oral but as something that stood to some extent in opposition to it. French was not only sound and gesture but also the language of family, storytelling, and a child's sense of neighborhood community" (Hunt xx). It is also worth pointing out here that Ann Charters' 1991 introduction to the Penguin edition of *On the Road* also goes uncited, despite the fact that she too carefully delineates the drafting process of *On the Road*, though she does so ten years after Hunt's pioneering book does it. Similarly, the biographer Tom Clark also emphasizes Kerouac's bilingualism in his 1984 study much before Hunt did in 1996.[3]

Tim Hunt, reflecting on Kerouac scholarship in 1996, noted that "we have much to learn from the way his French-Canadian upbringing left him suspended between categories—neither a person of color nor a white middle-class American—and unable to resolve either the dissonance between the period's rhetorics of ethnicity and class....or his sense of marginality—his sense that he was finally alien and an outsider" (xxvi). Does Johnson's biography offer the education that Hunt called for? Despite some inadequacies in terms of source material, I feel that it does. Moreover, Johnson's own prose provides a wonderfully readable, and sensitive, narrative of Kerouac's personal quest for creative fulfillment. But does *The Voice Is All* reveal to us Kerouac's "lonely triumph" as an artist? In this regard, Johnson is less successful. Her failure to analyze the books that Kerouac produced immediately after the discovery of his sketching technique is frustrating because it is these works, not his letters and journal entries, that really demonstrate his "lonely victory." Hence, despite the claims made on the book jacket, this is not a "groundbreaking" biography that "significantly deepens our understanding of Kerouac's achievement as a writer." It does, however, help us to understand the identity issues that propelled Kerouac into the postmodern syncretism of novels like *Doctor Sax* and *Visions of Cody*.

---Fiona Paton, *SUNY-New Paltz*

Notes

[1] Editors' Note: This memoir of Haverty's life with and marriage to Kerouac in the early 1950s was not prepared for publication by Haverty herself. Her son David's brother-in-law John Bowers "put all the pages together...like a puzzle, all the fragments of chapters" made from the loose "crumbling paper-clipped pieces" of paper that had been found by her children Jan and David under Haverty's bed after she died in 1990 (Jan Kerouac, "Introduction" vi).

[2] "It was a voice that would seem to his future readers as American as apple pie but it had been born in French" (391).

[3] Editors' Note: See also Tom Clark. 1984. *Jack Kerouac*. New York: Harcourt. Clark was the first biographer to provide sustained study of Kerouac's history as a speaker of *joual* and its impact on his life, identity, and literary production (Clark

3-11, 17, 21). Johnson does cite Clark in her notes, but to our knowledge does not directly quote him (see Johnson 442, n. 41; 443, n.47; 445, n. 79). And even so, Johnson's citations of Clark are not to document Clark's emphasis on Kerouac's first language *joual* but to substantiate other biographical facts. Not even Nicosia in 1983 makes as much of a case for the impact of Kerouac's first language on his self-definition and writing as Clark does. Oddly, Johnson does quote in her text biographers who are much less reliable than Clark, including Nicosia, Amburn, Miles, and Maher. Indeed, Miles' work was much hampered by his clear dislike of the subject of his 1998 biography *Jack Kerouac: King of the Beats*.

Works Cited

Amburn, Ellis. *Subterranean Kerouac: The Hidden Life of Jack Kerouac*. New York: St. Martin's Griffin, 1998. Print.
Charters, Ann. "Introduction." *On the Road* by Jack Kerouac. New York: Penguin, 1991. Print.
---. *Jack Kerouac: Selected Letters 1940-1956*. New York: Viking, 1995. Print.
---. *Jack Kerouac: Selected Letters 1957-1969*. New York: Viking, 1999. Print.
Clark, Tom. *Jack Kerouac*. New York: Harcourt, 1984. Print.
Edington, Steve. *Kerouac's Nashua Connection*. New Hampshire: Transitions, 2000.
Hunt, Tim. *Kerouac's Crooked Road: the Development of a Fiction*. 2nd ed. Berkeley: U California P, 1996. Print.
Johnson, Joyce. *Door Wide Open: A Beat Love Affair in Letters, 1957- 1958*. New York: Viking, 2000. Print.
---. *Minor Characters: A Memoir of a Young Woman of the 1950s in The Beat Orbit of Jack Kerouac*. Boston: Houghton Mifflin, 1983. Reprint 1990. Print.
Kerouac, Jack. *Atop an Underwood*. Ed. Paul Marion. New York: Viking, 1999. Print.
---. *Visions of Cody*. New York: McGraw-Hill, 1972. Print.
Kerouac, Joan Haverty. *Nobody's Wife: The Smart Aleck and the King of the Beats*. Berkeley, CA: Creative Arts. 2000. Print.
Maher, Paul. *Kerouac: the Definitive Biography*. NY: Taylor Trade, 2004. Print.
Miles, Barry. *Jack Kerouac: King of the Beats*. New York: Holt, 1998. Print.
Nicosia, Gerald. *Memory Babe: A Critical Biography of Jack Kerouac*. New York: Grove, 1983. Print.

Review of *The Philosophy of the Beats.*
Edited by Sharin N. Elkholy,
and a survey of the field.
(Lexington, Kentucky: University of Kentucky Press, 2012)

The concept of the collection *The Philosophy of the Beats* is a provocative approach to Beat studies scholarship, one that promises to fill gaps in the criticism and reveal facets of Beat art heretofore unrecognized or insufficiently probed. Many Beat writers read deeply in a vast array of philosophical literature, the result being that their works and their legacy are indebted to and manifest many philosophical traditions, although seldom "systematically" in the philosophical sense of that word. Novelist John Clellon Holmes, for example, in "The Philosophy of the Beat Generation" (1958), leaves little doubt that he certainly thought so – and from his perch in the midst of the formative years of this literary/social movement, he participated in intimate discussions with Jack Kerouac, Allen Ginsberg, and others about those philosophies. His is by no means the final word, but he accurately understood one of the essential definitions of *beat*: as he wrote, "[t]o be beat is to be at the bottom of your personality, looking up; to be existential in the Kierkegaard, rather than the Jean-Paul Sartre sense" (229). For Holmes, the key question driving a Beat philosophy was not "Why are we alive?" or "What is the meaning of life?" but rather "How are we to live?" He concluded that his beat answer to that was most often couched "in personal terms . . . [in] the dark night of the individual soul" (231). Within this context, the pursuit of Beat scholarship integrating literary and traditional philosophical perspectives resonates as a highly appropriate direction for the field to pursue.

However, such an approach is not new, since all explorations of literary texts fundamentally draw upon traditional and contemporary philosophical systems, theories, and constructs. This statement is not a flippant "everything is philosophy" vision of the world, rather a recognition that the very *practices* of literary production and criticism trace their histories back to the pre-Socratics and are still immensely indebted to Socratic, Platonist, and Aristotelian poetics and rhetoric, even while adopting more contemporary perspectives on aesthetics, language, and epistemology. From the earliest reviews of Beat novels to the most recent critical anthologies, writers exploring the Beat movement have used philosophical methods and insights, all implicitly and many explicitly, although their titles sometime elide the connection. For instance, *The Beats: Essays in Criticism* (1981), edited by Lee Bartlett and one of the best collections available on the Beat writers, features at least seven essays that draw upon conventional philosophical theories and thinkers. "Unscrewing the Locks: The Beat Poets" by John Clellon Holmes, specifically addresses the existential character of selected Beat writers, while Thomas S. Merrill's "Allen Ginsberg's *Reality Sandwiches*" is a cogent reading based on existential philosophies. R.G. Peterson, in "A Picture is a Fact: Wittgenstein and *Naked Lunch*," explores William S. Burroughs' allusions to Wittgenstein's *Tractatus Logic-Philosophicus*. The poet William Everson tackles the significance of ancient Greek thought in "Dionysius and the Beat Generation." "Lawrence Ferlinghetti's Fourth Person Singular and the Theory of Relativity" by L.A. Ianni focuses on the epistemological implication of the theory of relativity within Ferlinghetti's dramatic works. The morality of the friendship between Sal Paradise and Dean Moriarty is the topic of George Dardess' essay "The Delicate Dynamics of Friendship: A Reconsideration of Kerouac's *On the Road*" and Gary Snyder's epistemological radicalism is explicated in a deeply philosophically grounded article titled "Clearing the Ground: Gary Snyder and the Modernist Imperative" by Robert Kern.

Likewise, *Daybreak Boys: Essays on Literature of the Beat Generation* (1990) by Gregory Stephenson elucidates a Beat philosophy with "the goal of circumventing or of breaking through rational, logical intelligence, the ego consciousness, to establish contact with the unconscious mind, with the deepest levels of being" (180). Stephenson addresses Kerouac's spontaneous prose, Burroughs' cutup method, Ginsberg's improvised poetics, and others, including Gary Snyder and Michael McClure's use of Amerindian and Asian philosophies and theologies.

Reconstructing the Beats (2004) edited by Jennie Skerl advances, although not intentionally, the philosophical direction of Bartlett and Stephenson's work in several essays, including the philosophy of civil disobedience discussed in "'I Want to Be with My Own Kind': Individual Resistance and Collective Action in the Beat Counterculture" by Clinton R. Starr and the influence of the German philosopher Oswald Spengler on Beat writers in Mexico in Daniel Belgrad's ground-breaking article "The Transnational Counterculture." Then, too, Robert Holton's "'The Sordid Hipsters of America': Beat Culture and the Fold of Heterogeneity" employs philosopher Herbert Marcuse, Fredrick Jameson (the Marxist political theorist, expert on the Frankfurt School), and Pierre Bourdieu (sociologist) to reveal the complexities and significance of the term "bohemian" to Beat culture and writing. In "'All Things are different appearances of the same emptiness': Buddhism and Jack Kerouac's Nature Writings," Deshae E. Lott explores the presence of Buddhist philosophies in Kerouac's literature, and his spontaneous style as Beat aesthetic is philosophically explicated in the essay "Jack Kerouac, Charlie Parker, and the Poetics of Beat Improvisation" by Richard Quinn.

Many other essays and books have taken similar approaches. Buddhist philosophy has been explored in *Ecology and Oriental Philosophy in Beats* by

Brahma Dutta Sharma (2000), Tony Trigilio illuminates Ginsberg's Buddhist philosophy in *Allen Ginsberg's Buddhist Poetics* (2007) and *Strange Prophecies Anew: Rereading Apocalypse in Blake, H.D., and Ginsberg* (2000). The metaphysics of automatic writing (to some extent, a part of Kerouac's philosophy and a practice of the poet Jack Spicer and others) has been addressed in a number of texts acknowledging the various romantic roots of Beat aesthetics. Spontaneous prose as an aesthetic practice is addressed in detail by Regina Weinreich's *The Spontaneous Poetics of Jack Kerouac: A Study of the Fiction* (1987), Tim Hunt's *Kerouac's Crooked Road*, Michael Hrebniak's *Action Writing: Jack Kerouac's Wild Form* (2006), and my *Jack Kerouac and the Literary Imagination* (2007). My work also analyses Kerouac's *Doctor Sax* from the perspective of Plotinus. John Lardas' *The Bop Apocalypse* focuses on Kerouac, Ginsberg, and Burroughs' use of Spengler's *The Decline of the West*, in addition to other linguistic and aesthetic theorists. The French philosopher Michel Foucault provides the critical lens through which Helen McNeil constructed "The archaeology of gender in the Beat Movement" in A. Robert Lee's *The Beat Generation Writers* (Pluto Press 1996). The works of Deleuze and Guatarri, and Judith Butler, and others have been employed in the critical explications of Beat art and life.

In this context, *The Philosophy of the Beats*, edited by Sharin N. Elkholy and published in 2012 as part of the University of Kentucky's Philosophy of Popular Culture series, adds little to the extant scholarship, despite Elkholy's introductory claim that the collection "provide[s] cutting-edge analysis of beat style—literary, personal, and political—by drawing on philosophical theories and framework to recast the themes explored in Beat writings. . . ." (2). In fact, the introduction fails to explain how the collection fits within the growing body of Beat studies and cultural/popular studies literature—and to delineate how philosophical lenses will advance our already substantial understanding of the Beat corpus. Elkholy does not explain why philosophical perspectives such as film/critical race/feminist theories, deconstruction, Descartes, environmentalism, are applied—nor does she distinguish between philosophical treatments of these topics and other disciplinary approaches (e.g., not all feminist theories reflect traditional philosophical methods). More importantly and even more disappointing is the failure of the introduction to evince a solid understanding of the significance of philosophy to Beat writers themselves.

Aside from what's missing, much of the introductory material borders on the banal and often falls into the clichéd and under-researched. For instance, Elkholy quotes Jack Kerouac's famous "mad ones" passage from *On the Road* to present him as the archetypal "high energy" Beat (2), but does nothing else to address other features of his expansive Beat persona, such as lyricism, didacticism, and humility. She quotes several lines from Allen Ginsberg's "Howl" — "I saw the best minds . . . . hysterical naked, ... Who threw their watches off the roof. . . for the next decade," but the lines themselves are not discursively connected to the claim that precedes them: "Obscenity violations further added to the poem's popularity and the notoriety of what would come to be called the Beat Generation"(3).[1] A connection focused on prevailing mid-century U.S. attitudes towards philosophies of morality and the good would have helped to ground such floating passages to the theme of the volume.

In addition, she relies heavily on uninformed claims, such as "[t]he Beats initiated a radical break with the old formalistic forms of expressions, introducing a new relation to power and language, particularly the poetic voicing of personal experience and the articulation of positions of marginality" (3). As with all stereotypes there is some truth, but, again, the field of Beat studies, and many of the Beat writers themselves, repeatedly articulated the conventional and experimental progenitors of their aesthetics practices. Kerouac and Ginsberg's recognition of the classic bardic structures and performances that they sought to revive exemplify such indebtedness.

Elkholy's construction of the volume and the essays themselves reflect these problems. Too many of the essays ignore or are ignorant of the existing research; rely on unsupported generalizations; repeat standard and tired interpretations; present either the literary text or the philosophical tool as highly subordinated to the other or altogether invisible; conflate literary critics, psychoanalysts, and sociologists with philosophers; and eschew extended discussion of complex texts, i.e., illogically using one small part to represent the whole. The Beat Generation is a literary movement and social phenomenon that is both national and global, with levels of complexity – historically, socially, spiritually, and aesthetically – that render it an awkward object to investigate, whether philosophically or from other perspectives, unless one has considerable knowledge of the work already done in literary and cultural criticism. Unfortunately, Elkholy is not a Beat studies scholar and appears to have no background in Beat studies. The ability of the editor to vet the proposals as well as the completed essays—and to assist the authors to revise their work appropriately—stands as central to the success of the project. So too does the ability of the editor to conceptualize an anthology that fits within the existing Beat scholarship and to make key decisions about the appropriate philosophical approaches to the topic(s). While her expertise as a philosopher prepares her to deal with certain aspects of this project, it apparently did not prepare her to evaluate critical literature in the field of English studies and its subfield Beat studies.

This lack of professional expertise jarringly reveals itself in all facets of the volume. First, Elkholy divides the essays into four sections loosely focused on subculture, the self, experimentation, and ethics, but the sections do not emerge as mutually exclusive categories, nor does the introduction provide any explanation for why these topics were chosen and what others could have been but were rejected.

The sections themselves say very little about traditional philosophy *per se*, and many of the essays could easily reside in more than one of the sections: e.g., Jane Falk's essay on Joanne Kyger and Descartes, as well as Ed D'Angelo's essay on anarchism, could be part of the "Creating a subculture" section, just as logically as "Selfhood and Experimentation" and "Ethics and Affinities," respectively. The volume would have been more coherent with a brief introduction to each section, as did Richard Ellman and Charles Feidelson in their classic anthology *The Modern Tradition*, or at the very least Elkholy could have employed her introduction to clearly explicate the divisions.

Key philosophical topics are also missing. Existentialism appears but notably absent is the major existential influence on both Kerouac and Ginsberg (and other Beat writers), Fyodor Dostoyevsky, often called the "founder" of existentialism. To my knowledge, only two published essays exist that address his connection to the Beats: one, by Maria Blotsyen and one by Jesse Menefee. The novels of Camus and Gide also influenced many Beats, and these existential connections to the Beats have not yet been investigated in depth. Gide's concept of the "gratuitous act" played a central role in Joyce (Glassman) Johnson's novel *Come and Join the Dance* (1962), the first Beat novel written by a woman. Gide also influenced Norman Mailer, whose controversial essay "The White Negro" remains an important primary explication of a Beat philosophy. An essay on that essay would be immensely valuable, both as a way of addressing philosophies of authenticity but also of race, gender, self, and language in hipster and Beat subcultures of the 1950s.

The importance of German Romanticism on Beat production is another area that deserves serious exploration, since it plays a primary role in Kerouac, Ginsberg, and Corso's writing. Elkholy herself has scholarly expertise in the field of German Romanticism, which she might have brought to bear, particularly through an analysis of Kerouac's novel *Doctor Sax: Faust, Part III*. Other philosophical areas that do not appear include Christian philosophical theology, metaphysics, rhetoric, and the philosophy of care in the context of Beat practice. With respect to the last one, an essay on motherhood, applying the theories of philosophers such as Sarah Ruddick and Nell Noddings could produce a pioneering feminist reading of selected Beat texts.

Despite Elkholy's claim that the collection is "cutting edge," only four of the seventeen essays approach that mark: David Sterritt's "Wholly Communion: Poetry, Philosophy, and Spontaneous Bop Cinema," addresses a little-known experimental film titled *Wholly Communion* made by Peter Whitehead in the late Beat period (1965), using the aesthetics of Mikhail Bakhtin and the schizoanalysis of Gilles Deleuze and Felix Guiattari to explore the context and composition history of the film as Beat production, convincingly demonstrating the rhizomatic and dialogic structuring of the film that resists monologic discourse while reaffirming rational and logical construction. Jane Falk's "Joanne Kyger 'Descartes and the Splendor Of': Bridging Dualisms through Collaboration and Experimentation" presents what many readers might expect to be the dominating paradigm of the volume: a discussion of an author's explicit use of a classical philosophical text (which the volume is not). While some of her analytic comments remain superficial, she skillfully sets the historical scene for the discussion of Kyger's use of the new medium of television to respond to Rene Descartes' *Discourse on Method.* This section is followed by a detailed and clear comparison of Descartes and Kyger's texts, illustrating how Kyger used burgeoning technology to manipulate language, sound, and image to undermine Descartes' concepts of masculinity and body-mind dualism. Falk's essay is extremely well researched and meticulously documented.

In "From Self-Alienation to Posthumanism: The Transmigration of the Burroughsian Subject," Sean Michael Bolton studies alienation in Burroughs' fiction by applying theories of Jacques Derrida, Jacques Lacan and N. Katherine Hayles. Neither Lacan nor Hayles are trained philosophers: Lacan, of course, is a French psychoanalyst and psychiatrist, while Hayles is a U.S. literary critic with a doctorate in English. Despite this problem in terms of the volume's titular focus, Bolton smoothly wields his theoretical tools to build a compelling argument, based on close reading, that Burroughs' characterizations rely upon fragmentation and alienation in a posthuman universe in which the self is in constant flux with its environment (75), paradoxically acting to regain both selfhood and autonomy. Through his blending of analytic multidisciplinary tools, Bolton comes very close to constructing an interdisciplinary approach to answer complex questions about late twentieth-century relationships between living material forms and technology.

An historically based essay rather than literary analysis, Ed D'Angelo's "Anarchism and the Beats" constitutes a valuable historical overview of an often misunderstood political philosophy associated with Beat writers, many of whom are often incorrectly labeled anarchists. He identifies various kinds of anarchism, connecting them to Beat and Beat-associated writers, such as Diane di Prima, Tuli Kupferberg, and Kenneth Rexroth, and taking the discussion up to Ginsberg's 1955 reading of "Howl." The essay offers a sturdy vision of how anarchism and the labor movements of the early twentieth century have been effectively erased from U.S. history.

While these essays deserve our attention, several others do not even belong in the volume, again demonstrating Elkholy's lack of expertise. A. Robert Lee's overview of Beat ethnicities and multicultural character (granted, an important topic in Beat studies) does little to apply theories of Edward Said, Jacques Lacan, Michel Foucault, Homi Bhabha, Anthony Appiah, and other cultural critics whom Lee, a truly outstanding scholar, uses to establish the critical foundation for the essay. The inclusion of the essay on Kierkegaard and Bukowski by Andreas Seland is also highly questionable, since Bukowski was never really part of the Beat coterie, and his poetics do not reflect Beat literary experimentation.

Many of the remaining essays are under-researched and underdeveloped, all too often merely repeating commonly held understandings about core Beat writers and texts—failing to clarify, or simplify as appropriate, both key Beat and philosophical concepts. The only other essay in the volume to address directly gender, Roseanne Giannini Quinn's "Laugh of the Revolutionary," for example, which uses the feminist philosophy of Helene Cixous to discuss di Prima's *Memoirs of a Beatnik* (1969) and *Loba* (1978), wastes the opportunity it promises: the essay emerges as a superficial and unwieldy hybrid, including personal anecdotes about di Prima, literary analysis, and political diatribe. Quinn appears ignorant of the more recent scholarship on di Prima, including Anthony Libby's "Diane di Prima: 'Nothing is Lost: It Shines In Our Eyes," a penetrating study of di Prima's writing within feminist and other contexts. While Libby's essay never mentions Cixous, it says much more about di Prima and writing the body than does Quinn's essay, which also overlooks two foundational literary studies on women Beat writers.

Similarly, Christopher Adamo's "Beat U-topos or Taking Utopia on the Road" suggests an innovative reading of *On the Road* and other Beat road tales, but the brief discussion of political liberalism via John Stuart Mill and Thomas More's *Utopia* is given short shrift. The subsequent application to *On the Road* focuses only on the Mississippi Gene scenes in the novel, ignoring all else in the wake of standard statements about Kerouac's use of the hobo trope, including Frederick Feied's *No Pie in the Sky: The Hobo as American Cultural Hero in the Works of Jack London, John Dos Passos and Jack Kerouac* (1964). Eric Mortenson's analysis of the correlation between Kerouac and Ginsberg's styles and their drug use deploys Deleuze and Guatarri's notion of "hecceity," or the opening up of a new sense of time and the molecular for the drug user (167). This issue is interesting in and of itself, but Mortenson's effort to explain how a reader experiences drug use through the drug-induced style remains unconvincing: he quotes what he calls passages illustrative of either marijuana or amphetamine use but does not provide the grammatical or musical analyses necessary to show how the styles achieve a particular bodily vision or effect. His discussion of Ginsberg's style is also underdeveloped compared to that of Kerouac.

Existentialist philosophies are lumped together as a single entity in Tom Pynn's essay on Bob Kaufman and Ann Charters' essay on John Clellon Holmes.[2] Perhaps most egregious is Jones Irwin's "William Burroughs as Philosopher: From Beat Morality to Third Worldism to Continental Theory," which confuses the critics Jennie Skerl and Daniel Belgrad, attributing to Skerl direct quotations from Belgrad's essay "The Transnational Counterculture: Beat-Mexican Intersections" published in Skerl's *Reconstructing the Beats*. This error undermines faith in both essay and the volume's editor.

These problems, especially in a field with such a rich history and equally rich potential, stem to some degree from the complexity of the topic itself, as I have already noted—but to a much greater degree from Elkholy's lack of background in Beat studies and from sloppiness in the intellectual hypothesis of the volume. Then, too, there is the fact that the concept upon which the collection is based is fundamentally an interdisciplinary topic that demands from authors and editor a solid background in the two (or more) disciplines that are being conjoined and an equally strong sense of what truly constitutes interdisciplinary work. The field of interdisciplinary studies has long defined such work as that "which critically draw[s] upon two or more disciplines and which lead[s] to an *integration* of disciplinary insights" (Newell and Green 24, emphasis mine). This process involves careful use and analysis of assumptions and methods and aims to produce a whole that is greater than the parts. Its focus on synthesis distinguishes it from multidisciplinary work, which uses different disciplinary perspectives but brings them together in isolation and does not critique methods and assumptions, as well as from cross-disciplinary work, which assumes a dominant-subordinate disciplinary form in which the practice of one discipline is the subject of another. In effect, this is just what literary critics have done for decades: borrow theoretical tools from other disciplines and read the literature through those lenses. The resulting work privileges one perspective over the other or slights both—and in either case falls far short of addressing problem-centered rather than disciplined-centered questions. This is exactly the weakness of *The Philosophy of the Beats*: a collection of literary essays that references only a smidgen of philosophical principles but does very little real philosophical work and produces little that is recognizable as a synthesis of ideas and methods.

Beat studies needs a thoughtful book on the Beats and philosophy, one that will illustrate the fundamental interdisciplinary nature of Beat life and art and, in so doing, rejuvenate the scholarship. This means that scholars need first to ask big questions, such as about the historical under-valuation of Beat literature, the nature of Beat literature, the condemnation of Beat literature as dangerous and iconoclastic, and the mechanisms that perpetuate the continued fascination with Beat art and life. Structuring a volume to address specific philosophical questions or to foreground distinct philosophical and critical perspectives can lead to the development of an interdisciplinary methodology to answer such questions. One could, for instance, highlight key philosophically based Beat questions and issues, including codes of ethics (e.g., the inviolably of comradeship, the respect for confidences, and an almost mystical regard for courage), the individual vs. the collective, absolutism vs. relativism, the relationship between the individual and society, the good as supernatural or transcendent vs. the good as natural, the nature of human freedom, hedonism, and the pursuit of power. Another approach is the one mirrored in Falk's essay on Joanne Kyger: to feature the particular philosophers who had a direct influence on Beat writers, such as Spengler, Dostoyevsky, Thomas Aquinas, the Scottish empiricists, and Descartes. A variation is to read the literature through particular philosophical areas, both historically and topically: the Beats and metaphysics; epistemology; ethics; aesthetics; political philosophy; and ancient Asian, Mesoamerican, or 18th- and 19th-century European philosophy. All of these can be integrated with literary critical methods, as well as methods and theories from sociology, political science, psychology, and other fields, even if only in a close reading of texts. When unions such as these take place, scholars are engaging the sphere of interdisciplinary research.

Unfortunately, Beat studies has yet to take seriously this kind of project. To do so means working along the margins, in the interstices of knowledge, to ask expansive questions that cannot be answered through our standard methods and procedures, to be both philosopher and literary critic (in cases such as *The Philosophy of the Beats*), to write philosophically and literarily, to articulate why one lens is not enough and to strive for synthesis in the process of problem solving. This book of the future will look and read radically differently from Elkholy's collection, but the "cutting edge" of Beat studies from an interdisciplinary philosophical approach will lead us directly into Holmes' "dark night of the individual soul" and will, ultimately, reveal and explain just as much about human behavior and human history as about Beat literature itself.

---Nancy M. Grace, *The College of Wooster, Ohio*

Notes

[1] Elkholy also makes small but significant errors. For instance, she does not provide the exact name and date of the 6 Gallery Reading, which she incorrectly presents as "Six" and October 1955, instead of October 7, 1955; she also presents "beatnik" as a cognate of "beat" without identifying "beatnik" as a mainstream pejorative—all of the correct information is very easily accessible for a trained researcher.

[2] See Ann Charters' *Brother-Souls: John Clellon Holmes, Jack Kerouac, and the Beat Generation*. Jackson, Mississsippi: UP Mississippi, 2010. Print.

Works Cited

Bartlett, Lee. Ed. *The Beats: Essays in Criticism*. Jefferson, North Carolina: McFarland, 1981. Print.

Belgrad, Daniel. "The Transnational Counterculture: Beat-Mexican Intersections." In Skerl, Jennie. *Reconstructing the Beats*. New York: Palgrave-Macmillan, 2004. 27-40. Print.

Bloshteyn, Maria. "Dostoevsky and the Beat Generation." *Canadian Review of Comparative Literature*. September 2001: 218-242. Print.

Dharma, Brahma Dutta. *Ecology and Oriental Philosophy in the Beats*. New Dehli: Anmol, 2000. Print.

Ellman, Richard and Charles Feidelson, eds. *The Modern Tradition: Backgrounds of Modern Literature*. New York: Oxford UP, 1965. Print.

Glassman, Joyce (Johnson). *Come and Join the Dance*. New York: Atheneum, 1962. Print.

Feied, Frederick. *No Pie in the Sky: The Hobo as American Cultural Hero in the Works of Jack London, John Dos Passos and Jack Kerouac*. New York: Citadel, 1964. Print.

Grace, Nancy. *Jack Kerouac and the Literary Imagination*. New York: Palgrave-Macmillan, 2007. Print.

Holmes, John Clellon. "The Philosophy of the Beat Generation." *Beat Down to Your Soul*. Ed. Ann Charters. New York: Penguin, 2001. 228-38. Print.

Hrebniak, Michael. *Action Writing: Jack Kerouac's Wild Form*. Carbondale, Illinois: Southern Illinois UP, 2006. Print.

Hunt, Tim. *Kerouac's Crooked Road: The Development of a Fiction*. Berkeley, California: U of California P, 1996. Print.

Lee, A. Robert. Ed. *The Beat Generation Writers*. London: Pluto Press, 1996. Print.

Libby, Anthony. "Diane di Prima: 'Nothing Is Lost: It Shines In Our Eyes.'" In Johnson and Grace, *Girls Who Wore Black: Women Writing the Beat Generation*. New Brunswick, New Jersey. Rutgers UP 2002. Print.

Mailer, Norman. "The White Negro." *Advertisements for Myself*. New York: Putnam's-Berkeley Medallion, 1966. 311-31. Print.

Menefee, Jesse. "Dostoevsky and the Diamond Sutra: Jack Kerouac's Karamazov Religion." *Texas Studies in Literature and Language*. Winter 2011: 53:4. Print.

Newell, William H. and William J. Green. "Defining and Teaching Interdisciplinary Studies." Special Section: *Interdisciplinary Studies in Improving College and University Teaching* 30:1 (Winter 1982): 23-30. Print.

Skerl, Jennie. *Reconstructing the Beats*. New York: Palgrave-Macmillan, 2004. Print.

Stephenson, Gregory. *Daybreak Boys: Essays on Literature of the Beat Generation*. Carbondale, Illinois: Southern Illinois UP, 1990. Print.

Trigilio, Tony. *Allen Ginsberg's Buddhist Poetics*. Carbondale, Illinois: Southern Illinois UP, 2007. Print.

---. *Strange Prophecies Anew: Rereading Apocalypse in Blake, H.D., and Ginsberg*. Madison, New Jersey: Fairleigh Dickinson UP, 2000. Print.

Weinreich, Regina. *The Spontaneous Poetics of Jack Kerouac: A Study of the Fiction*. Carbondale, Illinois: Southern Illinois UP, 1987. Print.

The Beat Review Index

With the advent of the *Journal of Beat Studies*, the executive board of the Beat Studies Association decided to end the publication of *The Beat Review*, the last issue of which was edited by Fiona Paton and published in December 2012. The reviews below are available on the BSA website as are all previous issues of *The Beat Review*. We thank all of our reviewers for their commitment to promoting Beat literature and scholarship.

The Beat Review is available online at http://www.beatstudies.org/reviews/default.html.

Abbott, Keith. *Downstream from Trout Fishing in America* (revised). Reviewed by John Whalen-Bridge (Volume 4, Issue 3).

Baker, Deborah. *A Blue Hand: The Beats in India*. Reviewed by Keith Abbott (Volume 2, Issue 4).

Baker, Phil. *William S. Burroughs*. Reviewed by Katharine Streip (Volume 4, Issue 3).

Ball, Gordon. *Films by Gordon Ball* (DVD video). Reviewed by Kurt Hemmer (Volume 5, Issue 1).

Ball, Gordon. *East Hill Farm: Seasons with Allen Ginsberg*. Reviewed by Marc Olmsted (Volume 6, Issue 1).

Buhle, Paul, Ed. *The Beats: A Graphic History*. Text by Harvey Pekar, et al. Art by Ed Piskor et al. Reviewed by Matt Theado (Volume 3, Issue 2).

Burroughs, William S., and Jack Kerouac. *And the Hippos Were Boiled in Their Tanks*. Reviewed by Fiona Paton (Volume 3, Issue 1).

Burroughs, William S. *Everything Lost: The Latin American Notebook of William S. Burroughs*. Geoffrey D. Smith and John M. Bennett, eds. Oliver Harris, Volume Ed. Reviewed by Jennie Skerl (Volume 2, Number 4).

Cassady, Neal. *Collected Letters: 1944-1967*. Reviewed by Jonah Raskin (Volume 2, Issue 1).

Charters, Ann, and Samuel Charters. *Brother-Souls: John Clellon Holmes, Jack Kerouac, and the Beat Generation*. Reviewed by Matt Theado (Volume 4, Issue 4).

Cohen, Mark, Ed. *Missing a Beat: The Rants and Regrets of Seymour Krim.* Reviewed by Craig Svonkin (Volume 5, Issue 3).

Cohn, Jim. *Sutras & Bardos: Essays & Interviews on Allen Ginsberg, the Kerouac School, Anne Waldman, The Postbeat Poets & the New Demotics.* Reviewed by Jonah Raskin (Volume 5, Issue 3).

Conners, Peter. *White Hand Society: The Psychedelic Partnership of Timothy Leary & Allen Ginsberg.* Reviewed by Marc Olmsted (Volume 5, Issue 1).

Diano, Giada, and Elisa Polimeni, eds. *Lawrence Ferlinghetti (60 Years of Painting).* Reviewed by William Lawlor (Volume 4, Issue 3).

Diggory, Terence. *Encyclopedia of The New York School of Poets.* Reviewed by Tim Hunt (Volume 4, Issue 1).

Ebenkamp, Paul, Ed. *The Etiquette of Freedom: Gary Snyder, Jim Harrison, and The Practice of the Wild.* Reviewed by Tom Pynn (Volume 5, Issue 1).

Edington, Stephen. *The Beat Face of God: the Beat Generation Writers as Spirit Guides.* Reviewed by Matt Theado (Volume 2, Issue 3).

Edington, Stephen. *Kerouac's Nashua Connection.* Reviewed by Matt Theado (Volume 2, Issue 3).

Epstein, Rob, and Jeffrey Friedman, dir. *Howl.* Reviewed by Kurt Hemmer (Volume 4, Issue 4).

Farrar, Jay, and Benjamin Gibbard. *One Fast Move or I'm Gone: Music from Kerouac's Big Sur.* CD. Reviewed by Tom Pynn (Volume 4, Issue 1).

Ferlinghetti, Lawrence. *A Coney Island of the Mind: Special 50th Anniversary Edition.* Reviewed by Tom Pynn (Volume 3, Issue 1).

Ferlinghetti, Lawrence. *Poetry as Insurgent Art.* Reviewed by Tom Pynn (Volume 3, Issue 1).

Geiger, John. *Nothing is True, Everything is Permitted: The Life of Brion Gysin.* Reviewed by Jennie Skerl (Volume 4, Issue 4).

Gewirtz, Isaac. *Beatific Soul: Jack Kerouac on the Road.* Reviewed by Ann Charters (Volume 2, Issue 1).

Gewirtz, Isaac. *Kerouac at Bat: Fantasy Sports and the King of the Beats*. Reviewed by Penny Vlagopoulos (Volume 4, Issue 3).

Ginsberg, Allen. *The Letters of Allen Ginsberg*. Ed. Bill Morgan. Reviewed by Jonah Raskin (Volume 2, Issue 4).

Ginsberg, Allen, and Gary Snyder. *The Selected Letters of Allen Ginsberg and Gary Snyder*. Ed. Bill Morgan. Reviewed by Jonah Raskin (Volume 3, Issue 1).

Grace, Nancy M. *Jack Kerouac and the Literary Imagination*. Reviewed by Fiona Paton (Volume 2, Issue 2).

Gray, Tim. *Gary Snyder and the Pacific Rim*. Reviewed by Keith Abbott (Volume 1, Issue 2).

Harris, Latif, and Neeli Cherkovski, eds. *Beatitude Golden Anniversary 1959-2009*. Reviewed by Chad Weidner (Volume 4, Issue 4).

Harris, Oliver, and Ian Macfadyen, eds. *Naked Lunch @ 50: Anniversary Essays*. Reviewed by Katharine Streip (Volume 3, Issue 2).

Harris, Oliver, Ed. *Queer (25th Anniversary Edition)* by William S. Burroughs. Reviewed by Ryan Ehmke (Volume 5, Issue 3).

Hemmer, Kurt, and Tom Knoff. *Wow!—Ted Joans Lives!*; *Rebel Roar: The Sound of Michael McClure*; *As We Cover the Streets: Janine Pommy Vega* (DVD videos). Reviewed by Terence Diggory (Volume 5, Issue 1).

Hoffman, John. *Journey to the End*. Reviewed by Brian Jackson (Volume 2, Issue 2).

Holladay, Hilary, and Robert Holton. *What's Your Road, Man? Critical Essays on Jack Kerouac's* On the Road. Reviewed by Nancy M. Grace (Volume 3, Issue 2).

Hrebeniak, Michael. *Action Writing: Jack Kerouac's Wild Form*. Reviewed by Fiona Paton (Volume 1, Issue 2).

Hunt, Tim. *Kerouac's Crooked Road: The Development of a Fiction* (revised). Reviewed by Jonah Raskin (Volume 4, Issue 3).

Johnson, Rob. *The Lost Years of William S. Burroughs*. Reviewed by Jennie Skerl (Volume 1, Issue 1).

Jones, Hettie. *Doing 70*. Reviewed by Tony Trigilio (Volume 4, Issue 4).

Katz, Eliot. *Love, War, Fire, Wind: Looking Out from North America's Skull*. Drawings by William T. Ayton. Reviewed by Tony Trigilio (Volume 3, Issue 2).

Kerouac, Jack. *Book of Sketches*. Reviewed by Dave Moore (Volume 2, Issue 1).

Kerouac, Jack. *On the Road: The Scroll*. Reviewed by Matt Theado (Volume 1, Issue 2).

Kerouac, Jack. *Wake Up: A Life of the Buddha*. Reviewed by Jonah Raskin (Volume 2, Issue 4).

Kerouac, Jack, and Allen Ginsberg. *Jack Kerouac and Allen Ginsberg: The Letters*. Bill Morgan and David Stanford, eds Reviewed by Jonah Raskin (Volume 4, Issue 2).

Kerouac-Parker, Edie. *You'll Be Okay: My Life with Jack Kerouac*. Reviewed by Nancy M. Grace (Volume 1, Issue 2).

Kyger, Joanne. *About Now: The Collected Poems of Joanne Kyger*. Reviewed by Jonah Raskin (Volume 1, Issue 2).

Lamantia, Philip. *Tau*. Reviewed by Brian Jackson (Volume 2, Issue 2).

Lee, A. Robert. *Modern American Counter Writing: Beats, Outriders, Ethnics*. Reviewed by Jennie Skerl (Volume 4, Issue 2).

Leland, John. *Why Kerouac Matters: The Lessons of On the Road (They're Not What You Think)*. Reviewed by Tim Hunt (Volume 3, Issue 1).

Lenrow, Elbert, and Katherine H. Burkman, eds. *Kerouac Ascending: Memorabilia of the Decade of* On the Road. Reviewed by Tim Hunt (Volume 6, Issue 3).

Leyser, Yony. *William S. Burroughs: A Man Within* (DVD). Reviewed by Kurt Hemmer (Volume 6, Issue 1).

Marksbury, Tom, Ed. *I Just Hitched In from the Coast: the Ed McClanahan Reader*. Reviewed by Nancy M. Grace (Volume 6, Issue 3).

McClure, Michael. *Mysterioso and Other Poems*. Reviewed by Tom Pynn (Volume 4, Issue 2).

McClure, Michael. *Of Indigo and Saffron: New and Selected Poems*. Ed. Leslie Scalapino. Reviewed by Tom Pynn (Volume 5, Issue 2).

Miller, Henry. *Sextet*. Reviewed by Tom Pynn (Volume 4, Issue 4).

Mills, Katie. *The Road Story and the Rebel: Moving Through Film, Fiction, and Television*. Reviewed by Jennie Skerl (Volume 3, Issue 1).

Morgan, Bill. *Beat Atlas: A State by State Guide to the Beat Generation in America*. Reviewed by Jimmy Fazzino (Volume 5, Issue 2).

Morgan, Bill. *I Celebrate Myself: The Somewhat Private Life of Allen Ginsberg*. Reviewed by Tony Trigilio (Volume 2, Issue 3).

Morgan, Bill. *The Typewriter is Holy: The Complete, Uncensored History of the Beat Generation*. Reviewed by Tom Pynn (Volume 4, Issue 3).

Mortenson, Erik. *Capturing the Beat Moment: Cultural Politics and the Poetics of Presence*. Reviewed by Phil Dickinson (Volume 5, Issue 1).

Nicosia, Gerald, Ed. *Jan Kerouac: A Life in Memory*. Reviewed by Marc Olmsted (Volume 3, Issue 2).

Nicosia, Gerald, and Anne Marie Santos. *One and Only: The Untold Story of* On the Road *and of Lu Anne Henderson, the Woman Who Started Jack and Neal on Their Journey*. Reviewed by Nancy M. Grace (Volume 6, Issue 1).

Nock-Hee Park, Josephine. *Apparitions of Asia: Modernist Form and Asian American Poetics*. Reviewed by Jason G. Arthur (Volume 2, Issue 3).

Sandison, David, and Graham Vickers. *Neal Cassady—The Fast Life of a Beat Hero*. Reviewed by Steve Edington (Volume 2, Issue 2).

Smith, Patti. *Woolgathering*. Reviewed by Tom Pynn (Volume 6, Issue 1).

Snyder, Gary. *Back on the Fire*. Reviewed by Tom Pynn (Volume 3, Issue 2).

Snyder, Gary. *Passage Through India: An Expanded and Illustrated Edition*. Reviewed by Tom Pynn (Volume 3, Issue 2).

Stevens, Michael. *The Road to Interzone: Reading William S. Burroughs Reading*. Reviewed by Kurt Hemmer (Volume 3, Issue 3).

Tietchen, Todd F. *The Cubalogues: Beat Writers in Revolutionary Havana*. Reviewed by Phil Dickinson (Volume 4, Issue 4).

Trigilio, Tony. *Allen Ginsberg's Buddhist Poetics*. Reviewed by Tom Pynn (Volume 2, Issue 3).

Von Vogt, Elizabeth. *681 Lexington Avenue: A Beat Education in New York City, 1947-1954*. Reviewed by Amy Friedman (Volume 2, Issue 3).

Waldman, Anne. *In the Room of Never Grieve: New and Selected Poems, 1985-2003*. Reviewed by Todd Nathan Thorpe (Volume 3, Issue 3).

Waldman, Anne. *The Iovis Trilogy*. Reviewed by Linda Russo (Volume 6, Issue 3).

Waldman, Anne. *Manatee/Humanity*. Reviewed by Todd Nathan Thorpe (Volume 3, Issue 3).

Waldman, Anne. *Outrider*. Reviewed by Jane Falk (Volume 2, Issue 2).

Weaver, Helen. *The Awakener: A Memoir of Kerouac and the Fifties*. Reviewed by Jonah Raskin (Volume 3, Issue 2).

Weddle, Jeff. *Bohemian New Orleans: The Story of the Outsider and Loujon Press*. Reviewed by Nancy M. Grace (Volume 5, Issue 1).

Welch, Lew. *Ring of Bones: Collected Poems*. Reviewed by Keith Abbot (Volume 6, Issue 3).

Whalen-Bridge, John, and Gary Storhoff, eds. *The Emergence of Buddhist American Literature*. Reviewed by Tony Trigilio (Volume 3, Issue 3).

Whalen, Philip. *The Collected Poems of Philip Whalen*. Reviewed by Keith Abbott (Volume 2, Issue 1).

Wilson, Rob. *Be Always Converting, Be Always Converted: An American Poetics*. Reviewed by Matt Theado (Volume 5, Issue 2).

Wilson, Rob. *Beat Attitudes: On the Roads to Beatitude for Post-Beat Writers, Dharma Bums, and Cultural Activists*. Reviewed by Matt Theado (Volume 5, Issue 2).

Worden, Curt, dir. *One Fast Move or I'm Gone: Kerouac's Big Sur*. Reviewed by Tom Pynn (Volume 4, Issue 1).

Call for Proposals for the *Journal of Beat Studies* #3: Cambridge-Boston and the Rise of Beat Poetics

Incubation in the informal literary communities of Cambridge and Boston instilled rising Beat writing with local versions of Black Mountain and nascent New York School poetics. The Poets' Theater at Harvard University and Boston's Beacon Hill were pivotal locales in early Beat writing allowing surprising mutual influences and collaborations before the emergent literary schools and their associated poetics were solidified. Many Beat writers confronted dynamics of the movement's archetypal dilemma of status inclusion that was especially acute in the insider-outsider exclusivity of Cambridge-Boston. This area of study will be the focus of the third issue of the *Journal of Beat Studies*.

Essay proposals can address the following:
- Individual writers such as John Wieners, Charles Olson, V.R. ("Bunny") Lang, and Robert Creeley
- Gregory Corso's poetry and drama
- The influence of Allen Ginsberg or Jack Kerouac on emerging Beat poets in Cambridge-Boston
- The Poets' Theatre
- Poetry Readings at the Charles Street Meeting House
- Poet Isabella Gardner's Beat Connections

Please consult style guidelines published in this issue and posted on the Beat Studies Association web site: http://www.beatstudies.org/jbs/index.html.

Essays should be sent no later than August 1, 2013, and proposals no later than June 1, 2013, to Ronna C. Johnson (ronna.johnson@tufts.edu) and Nancy M. Grace (Ngrace@wooster.edu) simultaneously.

Call for Proposals or Essays for the *Journal of Beat Studies* : Beat Artists, Literature, and Language Writing

Seeking proposals or essays of productive discussions of the multiple relations and interrelations, overlaps and departures, influences and legacies effected between these disparate literary movements of the postwar, postmodern rise. Consider questions of Beat writers, Language poets, and the virtues and limitations of assimilation into the academy; or questions of cooptation each movement faces in the 21st-century academy. Discussions may take inspiration from a past body of scholarly work on the Language movement that has sought to claim an authenticity for poets who are skeptical about such claims and that has sought to place the rejection of closure that is so important to Language poetry within the broader map of postwar poetries (including the Beats) that increasingly embraced a poetics of indeterminacy and the politics of poetic form. How do Beat literature and writers fit experimental demands of Language writing and writers?

Topics might investigate:
- Shared precursors between the Beat and Language movements (Stein, Zukofsky, Pound, et al.)
- The influence of individual Beat poems ("Wichita Vortex Sutra," among others) or techniques (the cutup, among others) on the Language movement
- Beat literature and individual writers of the Language movement (Ron Silliman, Leslie Scalapino, Barrett Watten, Michael Davidson, among others)
- Self and language: Beat writing and the dispersed subjectivity of Language poetry
- Language poetry's experiments with autobiography (texts such as Hejinian's "My Life," Howe's "My Emily Dickinson," and the collective autobiography "The Grand Piano," among others)
- Major presses and journals of the Language movement
- Spiritual poetics and the materiality of language
- The line in Beat poetry and Language poetry
- Experiments with syntax in Beat poetry and Language poetry
- Beats, Language poets, and the politics of poetic form
- Beat writing and Post-Language poetries

Please consult style guidelines published in this issue and posted on the Beat Studies Association web site: http://www.beatstudies.org/jbs/index.html.

Essays should be sent no later than August 1, 2013, and proposals no later than June 1, 2013, to Ronna C. Johnson (ronna.johnson@tufts.edu) and Nancy M. Grace (Ngrace@wooster.edu) simultaneously.

Notes on Contributors

Terence Diggory is professor emeritus of English at Skidmore College in Saratoga Springs, New York. His many publications on art and literature include *Encyclopedia of the New York School Poets* (Facts on File, 2009), *The Scene of My Selves: New Work on New York School Poets*, co-edited with Stephen Paul Miller (Orono: National Poetry Foundation, 2001), *William Carlos Williams and the Ethics of Painting* (Princeton UP, 1991), and *Yeats & American Poetry: The Tradition of the Self* (Princeton UP, 1983).

Nancy M. Grace is the Virginia Myers Professor of English at The College of Wooster in Wooster, Ohio. She is the author of *Jack Kerouac and the Literary Imagination* (Palgrave-Macmillan, 2007), co-editor of *Girls Who Wore Black: Women Writing the Beat Generation* (Rutgers UP, 2002), co-editor and co-author of *Breaking the Rule of Cool: Reading and Writing Beat Women Writers* (UP Mississippi, 2004), and co-editor of *The Transnational Beat Generation* (Palgrave-Macmillan, 2012). She is a founding member of The Beat Studies Association and co-editor of the *Journal of Beat Studies*.

Rob Johnson teaches courses on the Beat Generation at The University of Texas–Pan American, located near the Mexican border in Edinburg, Texas. He is the author of *The Lost Years of William S. Burroughs: Beats in South Texas* (Texas A&M UP, 2006) and co-editor of *"The Beatest State in the Union": Texas and the Beat Generation of Writers* (Lamar UP, forthcoming). He is a major contributor to the *Encyclopedia of Beat Literature* (Facts on File, 2007). His essay on Burroughs' life in east Texas is included in *Naked Lunch at 50: Anniversary Essays* (Southern Illinois UP, 2009).

Cary Nelson is Professor of English and Jubilee Professor of Liberal Arts and Sciences at the University of Illinois at Urbana-Champaign. Among his more than 25 authored or edited books are *Repression and Recovery: Modern American Poetry and the Politics of Cultural Memory, 1910-1945* and the *Anthology of Modern American Poetry*, published by Oxford University Press. He hopes to include Kerouac's poetry in a new edition—if permission is granted. He completed six years as president of the American Association of University Professors in 2012.

Fiona Paton is an Associate Professor of English at The State University of New York at New Paltz, where she teaches a wide range of graduate and undergraduate classes, including courses on the Beats and Jack Kerouac. Her scholarship focuses primarily on Kerouac, but she has recently begun working on the Scottish Beat writer Alexander Trocchi. Her most recent publication is "Cain's Book and the Mark of Exile: Alexander Trocchi as Transnational Beat" in

The Transnational Beat Generation (Palgrave-Macmillan, 2013). She is the book review editor for the *Journal of Beat Studies*.

Davis Schneiderman is chair of the English Department at Lake Forest College, where he teaches William S. Burroughs and Bryon Gysin; he is also director of Lake Forest College Press/&NOW Books. He is the co-editor of *Retaking the Universe: Williams S. Burroughs in the Age of Globalization* (Pluto, 2004) and *The Exquisite Corpse: Chance and Collaboration in Surrealism's Parlor Game* (U of Nebraska P, 2009). His creative work has appeared in numerous publications including *Fiction International, The Chicago Tribune, The Iowa Review*, and *TriQuarterly*, and he is a blogger for *The Huffington Post*.

Jennie Skerl was associate dean of the College of Arts and Sciences at West Chester University in West Chester, Pennsylvania. She is the author of *William S. Burroughs* (Twayne, 1986), co-editor of *William S. Burroughs at the Front: Critical Reception, 1959-1989* (Southern Illinois UP, 1991), the author of *A Tawdry Place of Salvation: The Art of Jane Bowles* (Southern Illinois UP, 1997), editor of *Reconstructing the Beats* (Palgrave-Macmillan, 2004), and co-editor of *The Transnational Beat Generation* (Palgrave-Macmillan, 2012). Skerl edited the Winter 2000 special issue of *College Literature on Teaching Beat Literature* and contributed to *Naked Lunch @ 50* edited by Oliver Harris and Ian Macfadyen (Southern Illinois UP, 2009).

Tony Trigilio is a Professor of English at Columbia College-Chicago. His books include *Allen Ginsberg's Buddhist Poetics* (Southern Illinois UP, 2012) and *"Strange Prophecies Anew": Rereading Apocalypse in Blake, H.D., and Ginsberg* (Fairleigh Dickinson UP, 2000). He is the author of five volumes of poetry, the most recent of which is *White Noise* (Apostrophe Books, 2013).

Anne Waldman is the author most recently of the long allegorical poem *Gossamurmur* (Penguin Poets, 2013) and the feminist epic *The Iovis Trilogy: Colors in the Mechanism of Concealment* (Coffee House, 2011) which won the PEN America Literary Award for Poetry in 2012. She co-founded The Jack Kerouac School of Disembodied Poetics at Naropa University in 1974 and continues to direct its Summer Writing Program. She is also the editor of numerous anthologies including *The Beat Book* , and co-editor of *Civil Disobediences: Poetics and Politics in* (Action and Beats) *at Naropa*. She is the winner of the Shelley Memorial Award and is a Chancellor of the Academy of American Poets.

John Whalen-Bridge is an Associate Professor of English at the National University of Singapore. Author of *Political Fiction and the American Self* (U of Illinois P, 1998), he is co-editor with Gary Storhoff of the SUNY series "Buddhism and American Culture." This series includes *Emergence of Buddhist American Literature* (2009), *American Buddhism as a Way of Life* (2010), and *Writing as Enlightenment* (2010). He is co-editor of *Embodied Knowledge: Traditional Asian Martial Arts in a Transnational World* (SUNY, 2011), and he edited *Norman Mailer's Later Fictions* (Palgrave, 2010). His article "Multiple Modernities and the Tibetan Diaspora" has appeared in *South Asian Diaspora*, and he is completing a study of Engaged Buddhism and countercultural writing in postwar America, focusing on Gary Snyder, Charles Johnson, and Maxine Hong Kingston.

Essay Abstracts

"On a Confrontation at a Buddhist Seminary": Naropa, Guru Devotion, and a Poetics of Resistance by Tony Trigilio

Radical individualism, autonomy, candor, and populism are crucial to Naropa University's experimental tradition and to its influence on Beat Generation literature. Yet Naropa's influence on Beat poetics draws from two contradictory categories of understanding: the neo-Romanticist urgency of the unfettered imagination and, in contrast, the obedience and containment required by guru devotion, one of the core doctrinal principles of Vajrayana Buddhism, the mode of Buddhism that was taught and practiced by Naropa's founder, Chögyam Trungpa Rinpoche, whose students included Allen Ginsberg and Anne Waldman, co-founders of the Jack Kerouac School of Disembodied Poetics. This essay historicizes the tension between theory and practice in Naropa's influence on Beat poetics as a way of understanding the complex forces that both enable and vex Beat oppositional writing. It examines how guru devotion contributed to the infamous Snowmass scandal of the mid-to-late-1970s, perhaps the touchstone example of the complicated relationship between the liberatory and spiritual impulses of Beat writing. Looking at representative poems from Ginsberg's later career, this essay explores how Snowmass dramatizes the gap between Beat oppositional poetics and the spiritual urgency that authorized this same poetics.

Trungpa, Naropa, and the Outrider Road: An Interview with Anne Waldman by John Whalen-Bridge

In this interview, the majority of which took place in 2009, John Whalen-Bridge and Anne Waldman discuss Naropa's "Poetry Wars," the relationship between Buddhism and poetics at Naropa University, and the development of the Jack Kerouac School of Disembodied Poetics. The interview addresses Waldman's relationship with Naropa's founder Chögyam Trungpa Rinpoche, her own Buddhist practices, and her thoughts about the future of Buddhism in the United States. The interview was updated in November and December 2012.

Did Beatniks Kill John F. Kennedy? by Rob Johnson

At the time of the John F. Kennedy assassination, the term *beatnik* served as a general label for members of the American youth counterculture and was associated with communists, anti-segregationists, and general juvenile delinquency. Kennedy's death on November 22, 1963, and its immediate aftermath inspired two main suspect profiles: he was either killed by a pro-communist (a label often associated with "beatniks") or by a right-wing anti-communist and pro-segregationist. A search of the Warren Commission Report and associated documents reveals that the term *beatnik* is a key one in the Commission's attempt to create a "Lone Gunman" motivated by his communist sympathies. The political aspects of this profiling of the assassin are viewed through Texas "Beat" writer Bud Shrake's 1972 novel *Strange Peaches*, set in Dallas and Fort Worth at the time of the assassination. The dramatic center of the essay explores The Cellar, a Fort Worth "beatnik" nightclub where Secret Service agents drank and partied the night before the assassination. The essay concludes with a discussion of the reaction of Beat writers to the assassination, including William S. Burroughs, Jack Kerouac, Allen Ginsberg, and Gregory Corso.

The Miraculous and Mucilaginous Paste Pot: Extra-illustration and Plagiary in the Burroughs Legacy by Davis Schneiderman

This essay charts the connections between an early user-based textual strategy known as extra-illustration and the cutups practice of William S. Burroughs. Extra-illustration dates from the late eighteenth century through the early twentieth century, and this essay offers the work of John Mansir Wing of the Newberry Library in Chicago as a specific exemplar whose practice aligns with that of Burroughs. The second section of the essay explores Burroughs' small-press works and archival typescripts, centered on the repeated use of text taken from the September 17, 1899 front page of the *New York Times*. This section draws upon significant archival research as a method of exploring cut-up practices in terms of an expanded tradition of user-text interaction that pre-dates the Modernist literary moment.

American Literary History

Recent Americanist scholarship has generated some of the most forceful responses to questions about literary history and theory. Yet too many of the most provocative essays have been scattered among a wide variety of narrowly focused publications. Covering the study of US literature from its origins through the present, *American Literary History* provides a much-needed forum for the various, often competing voices of contemporary literary inquiry.

Visit **www.alh.oxfordjournals.org** to:

- **Browse** tables of contents and abstracts
- **Sign up** for table of contents email alerts
- **Read** a free sample issue

And more!

www.alh.oxfordjournals.org

OXFORD
UNIVERSITY PRESS

Tulsa Studies in Women's Literature
Publishing scholarship on women's writing for 30 years

SUBMIT

Guidelines at
www.utulsa.edu/tswl

College **Literature**

a journal of critical literary studies

Graham MacPhee, Editor

West Chester University
201 E. Rosedale Avenue
West Chester, PA 19383
Tel: 610.436.2901
collit@wcupa.edu

College Literature publishes innovative scholarship from across the various periods and fields that comprise the changing discipline of literary studies. The journal aims to scrutinize the theoretical parameters and assumptions underlying contemporary critical practice, and to examine the political and institutional limits that define the discipline.

http://www.wcupa.edu/_academics/sch_cas.lit/

MELUS

Multi-Ethnic Literature of the United States

PUBLISHED QUARTERLY, *MELUS* features articles, interviews, and reviews reflecting the multi-ethnic scope of American literature. Lively, informative, and thought-provoking, *MELUS* is a valuable resource for teachers and students interested in African American, Hispanic, Asian and Pacific American, Native American, and ethnically specific Euro-American works, their authors, and their cultural contexts.

INSTITUTIONS, colleges, universities, and libraries can subscribe to the journal for $120.00 per year for US institutions; the non-US institutional rate is $140.00. Checks payable to *MELUS* may be sent to the Editorial Office at *MELUS*, Department of English, U-4025, 215 Glenbrook Road, University of Connecticut, Storrs, CT 06269-4025. Institutions may also subscribe through PayPal at www.melus.org.

INDIVIDUAL SUBSCRIBERS become members of The Society for the Study of the Multi-Ethnic Literature of the United States. To subscribe, send a check payable to *MELUS* to Professor Georgina Dodge, Membership Chair, University of Iowa, 111 Jessup Hall, Iowa City, IA 52242 (georgina-dodge@uiowa.edu). Regular US membership is $50.00 per year; students and retirees, $30.00; regular non-US membership is $70.00; non-US students and retirees, $50.00. You may also subscribe through PayPal at www.melus.org.

For more information about submitting essays, ordering back issues, and placing advertisements, see www.melus.org or e-mail us at:
melus@uconn.edu

Policy

The *Journal of Beat Studies* invites articles on the works of Beat movement writers and their colleagues, especially New York School, Black Mountain School, and San Francisco Renaissance writers, as well as those connected to these movements, in the United States and globally. The *Journal* intends to represent the breadth and eclecticism of critical approaches to Beat Generation writers, and welcomes new perspectives and contexts of inquiry.

Articles that are deemed appropriate are sent for review anonymously to a member of the Editorial Board and at least one other reader. Manuscripts should not be under consideration elsewhere, and we do not publish previously published work. It is strongly advised that those submitting work to *JBS* be familiar with the journal's content. Among criteria on which evaluation of submissions depends are whether an article demonstrates recognition of and thorough familiarity with scholarship already published in the field, whether the article is written clearly and effectively, and whether it makes a genuine contribution to Beat studies.

Preparation of Copy

1. Articles are typically between 25 and 30 pages, and do not exceed 9000 words, including notes and works cited. Inquiries about significantly shorter or longer submissions should be sent to the editors.

2. A separate page should include the article's title, author's name, address, telephone & fax numbers, and e-mail address. The author's name and identifying references should not appear on the manuscript to preserve anonymity for our readers.

3. All submissions must include an abstract of no more than 250 words.

4. The manuscript should be in Times New Roman 12, double-spaced, and should adhere to the most recent MLA style.

5. Submissions may be sent by email as word documents ("doc" only, not "docx") to Ronna C. Johnson (ronna.johnson@tufts.edu) and Nancy M. Grace (ngrace@wooster.edu) simultaneously. Mailed submissions may be sent to Nancy M. Grace, Department of English, 400 E. University Street, The College of Wooster, Wooster, Ohio 44691. For mailed submissions, please send three copies of the article and abstract.

6. Submissions may also be sent via the online submission form at http://www.beatstudies.org/jbs/submission_guidelines.html.

7. Authors of accepted manuscripts are responsible for any necessary permissions fees and for securing any necessary permissions.

8. All editorial, review, and advertising inquiries should be addressed to ronna.johnson@tufts.edu and ngrace@wooster.edu.

9. Inquiries concerning orders should be addressed to PaceUP@pace.edu.

www.ingramcontent.com/pod-product-compliance
Lightning Source LLC
Chambersburg PA
CBHW061450300426
44114CB00014B/1920